"Prosperity is not an accident. We turned New Jersey around with good policies and the hard work of its many residents. This book speaks to the importance of every individual in producing the Great Prosperity that Kadlec is convinced can be ours."

THE HONORABLE CHRISTINE TODD WHITMAN
New Jersey

"Readers should pay heed to Kadlec's targeting of positive changes in economic policy as the key to our prosperity. His claim that the Dow can reach 100,000 by 2020 if economic policy stays on track should spur the readers to read the book."

WAYNE D. ANGEL
Sr. Managing Director & Chief Economist
Bear, Stearns & Co., Inc.

"Kadlec delivers what he promises: a useful guidebook to the Road to Dow 100,000—what will get us there, what could go wrong, and concrete investment strategies to take advantage of the Great Prosperity that lies ahead. Financial advisers and investors who are looking for more than a simplistic prediction of the future to help them build and manage their wealth will get a high return on their investment in this book."

LARRY KUDLOW
Chief Economist
American Skandia

DOW 100,000
Fact or Fiction

CHARLES W. KADLEC
Foreword by Ralph J. Acampora

NEW YORK INSTITUTE OF FINANCE

NEW YORK • TORONTO • SYDNEY • TOKYO • SINGAPORE

Library of Congress Cataloging-in-Publication Data

Kadlec, Charles W.
    Dow 100,000 fact or fiction / by Charles W. Kadlec.
        p. cm.
    Includes bibliographical references and index.
    ISBN 0-7352-0137-4 (cloth)
        1. Investments—United States. I. Title. II. Title: Dow one
    hundred thousand fact or fiction.
    HG4910.K26   1999
    332.63'222'0973—dc21   99-34489
                                                                CIP

© 1999 by Charles W. Kadlec

All rights reserved. No part of this book may be reproduced in any form
or by any means, without permission in writing from the publisher.

Printed in the United States of America

10 9 8 7 6 5 4 3 2 1

ISBN 0-7352-0137-4   ISBN 0-13-087204-0 (Seligman)

ATTENTION: CORPORATIONS AND SCHOOLS

Prentice Hall books are available at quantity discounts with bulk purchase for educational, business, or sales promotional use. For information, please write to: Prentice
Hall Special Sales, 240 Frisch Court, Paramus, New Jersey 07652. Please supply: title of
book, ISBN, quantity, how the book will be used, date needed.

 NEW YORK INSTITUTE OF FINANCE
An Imprint of Prentice Hall Press
Paramus, NJ 07652

On the World Wide Web at http://www.phdirect.com

To my parents, Walter and Irene,
To my wife, Joyce
and our two sons,
Benjamin and Jason.

ACKNOWLEDGMENTS

———•———

THIS BOOK, LIKE SO MUCH ELSE IN OUR LIVES, REFLECTS THE WORK AND ADVICE OF many people who have contributed directly and indirectly to its creation. Four individuals, in particular, deserve special thanks and appreciation. Arthur B. Laffer, who was my professor when I was a student at the University of Chicago Graduate School of Business, taught me classical economics, which forms the foundation of the book. I later joined his economic consulting firm, Laffer Associates. Fernando Flores, the CEO of Business Design Associates, a management consulting firm, taught me philosophy and contributed to my ability to see and appreciate the underlying human dimension that so frequently is lost in the conversations and writings of economists. In many respects, this book benefits from the innovations each of these men has brought to their respective fields.

In addition, many of the ideas and formulations that make up this book were developed in a series of discussions and conversations with Russell Redenbaugh that span the last twenty years. Russell is the former chief investment officer of a leading money management firm and currently is a private investor and board member of several technology firms, and a Commissioner on the U.S. Commission for Civil Rights. In particular, the notion that money is a human invention for the coordination of action, and the role of trust in producing a stable value for money are based on ground-breaking research done by Russell and Fernando Flores and on unpublished papers which they shared with me. Steve Hodgdon, the President of Seligman Advisors, Inc., helped me shape and position Seligman Time Horizon Matrix^{sm} as a strategy for building wealth, and contributed directly to the design and creation of Seligman Harvester^{sm}, our strategy for managing risk for those who must look to a pool of assets to provide income over extended periods of time.

I owe many others my personal thanks. Wayne Angell, Larry Kudlow, Alan Reynolds, and Jude Wanniski, through their writings and conversations with me, have contributed to whatever insights I have had on the economy and economic policy. Jack Kemp, Steve Forbes, and Governor Christine Todd Whitman gave me the opportunities to participate in the nexus between economics and politics. Robert Bartley and his colleagues on the Editorial Page of *The Wall Street Journal* have provided me and all of their other readers an extraordinarily rich source of facts, ideas, and perspectives, not only in their editorials, but also through the articles they publish by a variety of contributors on all of the key issues of our time. I have always considered it an honor to have articles I have written appear on that page. My thanks also go to Lawrence Mone and his colleagues at the Manhattan Institute for the many luncheons they have organized around the publication of a variety of books, each of which has deepened my appreciation for the historical moment in which we live. The bibliography acknowledges many of these authors as well as others whom I have never met, but who have contributed to my thinking and the contents of this book.

I appreciate the support and confidence of the management committee and my fellow managing directors and colleagues at J. & W. Seligman & Co. Incorporated. The development of my ideas also has benefited from the many conversations and questions I have had with Seligman's sales force and the thousands of financial advisers whom I have had the privilege of meeting during the past five years. It is hard to imagine how I could have written this book without the experience of working with them to produce strategies and solutions for their clients, individuals with specific financial goals and unique financial circumstances.

This book would not have been possible without the efforts and guidance of my agent, Julian Bach, and my editor, Ellen Schneid Coleman. Julian saw in only the briefest outline of the book its full potential, and guided me through the rigorous process of creating a proposal that would sell the book to a publisher. Ellen provided me the encouragement and direction that allowed me to find my voice, if you will, in speaking directly to the reader. To each of them, I also express my personal thanks and appreciation.

The final manuscript also benefits in innumerable ways from the work of numerous individuals including research assistants, Mike Aquilar, Emily Calcagno, Nick Hughes, and Mark Parsons; Rebecca Shroyer, who assisted me in the design of many of the Figures and Tables, graphics creator Ian Lebowitz, and my secretary Crystal Dawn Smith. Barry Richardson helped by reviewing the manuscript and making other contributions to the successful completion of this book. My good friend, Arnold Slavet, assisted me with his thoughtful and perceptive comments and suggestions whenever I asked for them.

My final thanks go to my wife, Joyce, whose unswerving love, support, and willingness to give up more than one Saturday night and virtually every Sunday and evening to this endeavor provided the peaceful environment that made completing this book within some tight deadlines possible. I will forever appreciate her commitment to me during these past months. I love her deeply, and dedicate this book to her, my parents who made my life possible, and to our sons to whom we inevitably will leave the future.

Each of these individuals has in his or her own way made this book better than it otherwise would have been.

TABLE OF CONTENTS

Part I   The Signposts

Part II   The Map

PART III   The Road Ahead

FOREWORD

WHEN I PREDICTED IN JUNE 1995 THAT THE DOW WOULD REACH 7000 IN THE first quarter of 1998, many people scoffed. The Dow at that time was trading in the 4500 area and most experts feared the Dow was already too high. I turned out to be wrong, of course. The Dow hit 7000 on February 13, 1997—a full year ahead of my predicted date. Our incredible bull market has fooled everyone time and time again.

Rather than respecting the persistent strength of this market, the gloom-and-doom pundits came out in full force in early 1997. The bull market had gone on for too long to continue. The Dow never posts big gains three years in a row. A major correction was coming in 1997, they warned, surely a bear year if there ever was going to be one. Technicians and fundamental analysts alike were predicting negative results. I began talking in terms of Dow 10,000. The experts again laughed.

Now, as the laughter fades, we've passed 10,000. Predictions have been made for Dow 20,000 . . . Dow 30,000 . . . Dow 50,000. Once again, the critics are having a field day. "How can anyone in their right mind be talking numbers like this?" they snicker. Not to be intimidated, here comes Chuck Kadlec, daring to raise the possibility of the Dow reaching the unimaginable—100,000 by 2020! I, for one, am not laughing. I hope he's right. While I've only gone so far as to project the Dow out to 18,500 in 2006, I'll certainly listen to any reasonable scenario, especially when it reflects my own raging bull philosophy. This book makes a solid argument in favor of Kadlec's prediction. And, as I say, I've been known to underestimate this market's performance.

Chuck's careful fundamental analysis of the current economic, political, and sociological situation both here in the United States and abroad has brought him to his 100,000 forecast. As a technician, I have used a different approach, comparing this bull market to bull markets of the past, but I have arrived at the same overall conclusion. The market is going up and it will be going up for a long time. We are seeing a secular trending bull market, probably the greatest bull market in history.

Of course, there will be corrections along the way. There always are. Declines during bull markets can be rapid and very painful. The higher the Dow goes, the scarier those declines will be. A 10% correction when the Dow is at 2000 is pretty frightening. When the Dow is over 10,000, a 10% correction is downright bone chilling. But in each case, it is still 10%. These corrections are normal and shouldn't shake your confidence in the overall market trend. Investing history is replete with sad stories of people who panicked out when the market dropped down (*selling low*), then bought back in as the market reached new heights (*buying high*).

During a 1971 conversation with the venerable Ken Ward, longtime technical analyst for Hayden Stone & Company, I asked, "What was the most difficult period on Wall Street for a practicing technician?" He responded: "You would think it was the 1929 Crash, but it wasn't. The most trying time for a practicing technician was the market between the low in 1962 and the high in early 1966." But the stock market went up in those years, I pointed out. "Yes. It went up and up and up!" he exclaimed. "It rolled over all the bears and even the bulls—the market never looked back. It forged ahead despite being extremely overbought and needing a normal correction. The biggest mistake we all made was that we sold the good-looking stocks too early. It was a time of vicious rotation, but, more important, a time to really believe that we had a positive long-term trend." I share this story with you because I believe that we are in a similar situation today.

Chuck Kadlec presents his case well for the Dow reaching 100,000 by 2020. Equally important, he provides you with practical advice: Guidelines to help you recognize that the bull market is indeed on track, warning signs that might reveal changes in direction along the road, and proven investment strategies for taking full advantage of this market.

His message is clear: Believe in the long-term trend. Get into this wild and wonderful bull market and ride it as far as it goes. Stay invested for the long term. Do not be shaken by violent declines. In fact, use these declines to buy in to, not drop out of, stocks that you like. This bull market is here to stay for a good long time.

Good luck! I hope to see you along the road to Dow 100,000.

Ralph Acampora
Prudential Securities

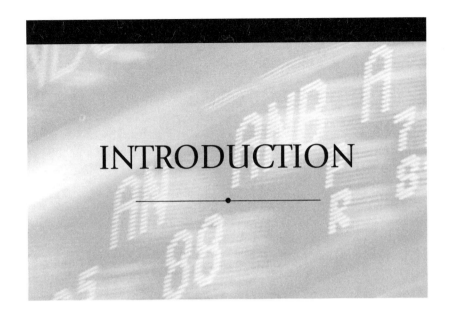

INTRODUCTION

THIS BOOK BEGAN AS A PRESENTATION THAT I CREATED IN THE FALL OF 1994. I HAD just moved from being a portfolio manager of institutional growth accounts at J & W Seligman & Co. Incorporated, to assume my present role as chief investment strategist for Seligman Advisors, Inc., the marketing company for Seligman's group of mutual funds. I don't know how many of you remember 1994, but it was a very difficult year for investors. Interest rates had shot up, and the price of bonds had gone down, making 1994 the worst bond market in U.S. history. The S&P 500 was up a little over 3 percent. The Dow Jones Industrials Average was up a little more than 2 percent, closing the year at 3834. Some 90 percent of mutual funds that year had negative total returns.

The mood of our clients—brokers, financial planners, and financial advisers—was gloomy. Individual investors were nervous. The political situation was unsettled: The Republicans had just won both the House and the Senate for the first time since 1952. The economy was growing, but it was the slowest recovery from a recession in the post-World War II era. There was doubt in the air about where the economy and the stock market were headed.

In thinking about how I could make a contribution to our clients, and to their clients, the individual investor, I was struck by the almost exclusive focus on the short-term among pundits, economists, and all of the talking heads on television. Simply making sense out of the daily flow of economic and financial data, itself, seemed overwhelming. One week, I would read that interest rates had gone up that day because the dollar was strong; the next, the same author would write, quoting another group of experts, that interest rates had gone up that day, but this time because the dollar was weak. Reducing the budget deficit was supposed to produce lower interest rates, yet, interest rates had gone up that year even though the deficit had been cut by nearly $100 billion over the prior two years. Financial markets would gyrate based on the latest unemployment report, or on speculation about whether the Federal Reserve would raise or lower interest rates at its next meeting. Everywhere, people were trying to decide whether the market's next move would be higher or lower, whether it was time to buy or to sell today, to be in or out of the market, to increase or reduce their allocation to stocks, bonds, or cash.

What was missing was a context, a framework within which to interpret the daily dose of data that could make some sense out of what was going on in the world. During the first half of the 1980s, I had worked closely with one of the leading economists in the world and one of the founders of supply-side economics, Arthur Laffer. As the director of research for his firm, I had been a consultant to large institutional investors that manage some of the nation's largest pension plans. Time and again, our focus on tax, monetary, and trade policies had given us the edge in anticipating the strong economic performance of the 1980s and the overall direction of equity prices and interest rates.

I had joined Seligman in December 1985. As a strategist in its equity-research department, then as director of equity research, and finally as a portfolio manager in my own right, I was able to speak with and follow the best economists and strategists on Wall Street. During this time, I became absolutely convinced that no one, *no one* can consistently predict where the stock market or interest rates are going over the short term.

I had also heard too many stories of individuals who, out of fear, had sold most or all of their stocks or bonds near the market's low, missing almost completely the ensuing recovery. Some of them, always waiting for the next pullback, would miss most of the next several years of extraordinary advances in the stock market. Think of the cost: realizing all of the losses and then missing all of the subsequent gains that would have been theirs if only they had had a prudent strategy to maintain their investments.

The key to building wealth over time or to managing your investments during retirement is to implement a prudent, long-term strategy that you are able to follow through the day-to-day volatility and uncertainty that is part and parcel of investing in equity markets. Yet, when it comes to investing in financial markets, the availability of instant information and everyday pricing creates an almost irresistible pressure to invest tactically. We strive to pick *the* hot mutual fund or stock that we hope will double over the next year. We become transfixed by the short term and lose sight of our longer-term goals. We react out of fear and greed. Too often, this leads individuals to chase yesterday's winners, only to be disappointed when they fail to replicate their last year's results. We never seem to get around to pulling together a longer-term strategy that is so important to actually realizing our financial goals.

Let me put this in more practical terms. If you and I approached investing in a house the same way many individuals approach investing in the stock market, few of us would ever own our home. Think of it. You know the month after you buy a house it would be unlikely to sell for what you paid plus the commissions to the real-estate brokers and the money you spent fixing up the house and garden the way you like it. Think of how crazy you would feel if you checked the price of your house (assuming it were available) every day in the local newspaper. Buying a house is a strategic investment. We do it with borrowed money and a mortgage, not for the returns it will provide over the next month or year, but over the next five to ten years. It is only because we can imagine owning the house over this period of time that we are able to make what, for most Americans, is the biggest single investment of their lifetimes.

The same is true for investing in the stock market. Only by imagining owning stocks or bonds over the next five or ten years can we create an investment strategy. Yet, there was and is a dearth of assistance in helping us to see what is likely to happen to the stock market over periods longer than a year.

So, in my new role as a strategist, I decided that the real opportunity to add value, to increase the capacity of financial advisers to contribute to the success of their clients, was to provide a strategic view of where the economy and stock market were headed. I knew that my audiences would be expecting me to focus, like everyone else, on short-term calls on the economy and financial markets. But I was committed to developing a view of the economy and financial markets so powerful that it would extend over five or ten years or even longer. I knew that if we could just get the general direction of equity prices and interest rates right, that would dramatically simplify the task of building a strategy to build wealth over time. It would also offer the possibility of reducing the anxiety, fear, and stress that many of us feel with every dip of the market. That would reduce the risk of individuals selling when prices were low, only to buy back in when prices were high.

In formulating that presentation, I identified five historical forces that, together with tax, monetary, and trade policies, have and are continuing to shape the future of the economy and the direction of financial markets. Recognizing these historical forces allows us to make sense out of the moment in history in which we live. Just as important, understanding these forces increases our capacity to make good investment decisions in the face of an unknown future, because the act of investing confronts us with the fact that we do not know the future. As a consequence, until we can make sense out of the present and build a coherent narrative about the future it is almost impossible to develop an investment strategy to reach our financial goals.

To counter audiences' natural anticipation that I would be focused on where the markets would be going in the next several months, I began to play a little joke. Near the beginning of the presentation, I would ask the audience how many would like me to tell them where the stock market would be at the end of the year. Usually, between half and three-quarters of them would raise their hands. Then I would ask: "How many of you would believe me if I told you?" Everyone would laugh.

So I proposed a different question. A bigger question, but one, ironically, that we had a better chance of answering. The Dow had closed the year 1994 just under 4000. So, the question that I proposed was this: Are we headed to 10,000 on the Dow? (At the time, this sounded like a heroic question.) Or, was the record rise in interest rates in 1994 signaling the end of the bull market? Was 1994 the equivalent of 1965, when the bull market of the 1960s ended? Did we have before us 10 to 15 years of below-average economic or financial-market performance?

If we could answer that question, then we would have the opportunity to put together a plan for their clients, investors in our mutual funds, that could build wealth and otherwise reach their financial goals. At the time, I told my audiences that, given the historical forces that were in play, I was sure that the Dow was headed to 10,000 over the next 10 years. As it turns out, we got there even faster than I anticipated.

Let me now ask you the same question I have been asking audiences for the past five years: Would you like me to tell you in this book where the stock market will be at the end of next year? Of course, you would. But if that is all this book did, would you believe it? Would it be worth your time to read it?

Let's take on the bigger question. It's one that we face today, with the market's advances earlier this year to Dow 10,000 and then, a month later, to 11,000. These events produced a euphoria that led some to predict 40,000 or even 50,000 on the Dow while others pointed to the sky-high valuations of many stocks and talked about a bubble economy and the inevitable crash that lies ahead. How high can the Dow go? What is a reasonable expectation? How long will it take?

Just as important, What could go wrong? What forces might end the bull market and dictate a totally different investment strategy?

During the past 17 years, the Dow has posted a 10-fold increase, but in the prior 17 years, it didn't go up at all. What was the difference? Are we close to the equivalent of 1965, looking out on an extended period of below-average economic and financial performance? Or can we expect another 10-fold increase in the Dow in the years ahead?

In short, Dow 100,000: fact or fiction?

Given the historical forces that are shaping the future, my answer is that the bull market will continue. We are headed to Dow 100,000. How soon? In a little over 20 years. Is it a sure thing? No. We do not know the future for sure, and there are dangers that lie ahead that could end the bull market, but the odds have seldom, if ever, been as good for long-term investors in equities as they are today. It is therefore reasonable to assume that we can surmount the obstacles that lie ahead and reach Dow 100,000 by the year 2020.

The primary purpose of this book is to help you to anticipate this future and to design investment strategies that are coherent and in tune with your financial goals and what lies ahead. In Part 3, we offer two distinct strategies: one for those of you who are accumulating or building your wealth and a second for those of you who are in a position to look to a pool of assets as a source of income over time. This would include those of you who are approaching or are in retirement or have a fiduciary role in regard to a foundation or trust.

Use this book as a map of the road to 100,000 on the Dow. Read it to increase your ability to make sense out of the present and better anticipate the future. This book is not a pollyannaish view that says we know the future, but a guide that will help you navigate through some of the uncertain times that are sure to lie ahead, and help you keep your bearings when facing unexpected turns in the road. We will be exploring the historical forces that will propel the U.S. and international equity markets to historic highs, identifying the false traps that could lead you astray and providing you with a strategic approach to investing that will help you reach your financial goals.

Just as important, we will identify those signs that warn of an end to the good times, an end to rising equity prices, the policies that would spell the need to create a different investment strategy. Knowing the dangers that may lie ahead increases our ability to execute a long-term strategy in the face of the uncertain future. *From my experience of speaking with and advising thousands of financial advisers, I am sure that the key to consistently building wealth over time is to stick to an investment process that is coherent and is founded on a strategic view of where the world is headed.*

My second purpose in writing this book is to share with you the joy and excitement, compassion, and wonder that I have experienced and felt in seeing how human beings have created the future that we now study as history and how each of us today, in our own ways, is creating the future that will be ours in the years ahead. As human beings, we seldom get it right the first time, but have an incredible resilience to learn from our mistakes, both big and small. More often than not, we find our way to a better future for our children. We live at a remarkable moment in history. We have before us the opportunity to create a Great Prosperity in which we can achieve financial independence. It will not be given to us by government, but by the actions and investments that you and I and others choose to make or not make in the years ahead. Not least among these actions will be the government policies and private institutions that we choose to support or oppose as we respond to the opportunities and vagaries of life that lie ahead.

I invite you to read this book as an active participant in the design of your investment strategy and as an active creator of the future. My goal is to increase your capacity to be successful in both endeavors. By so doing, this book will make its own contribution to reaching Dow 100,000 by the year 2020.

CHAPTER ONE

SETTING THE COURSE:
THE GREAT PROSPERITY

THE FUTURE IS NEVER KNOWN WITH CERTAINTY. YET, THERE ARE MOMENTS IN history when powerful forces are so aligned that they allow us to anticipate with unusual confidence the shape of the future and the direction of financial markets. Now is one of those moments. This book is about that future and how to develop investment strategies that will allow you to take advantage of the remarkable financial-market performance that lies ahead.

Sometimes, such as at the end of the 1960s, historical forces are warning of trouble ahead. The deepening involvement of the United States in a distant war, increasing pressures for protection against foreign competition, the initial cracks in the international monetary system, and the prospect of significantly higher tax rates all suggested an era of stagnation and below-average economic and financial-market performance. What followed was the Great Inflation of the 1970s.

But now, historical forces are aligned to produce a Great Prosperity—*at least two decades of above-average economic growth with price stability*. This will be a period of enormous business opportunities, rising living standards, and a historic expansion in world commerce. Businesses and corporations will prosper by finding new and better ways to satisfy consumers. Real incomes will rise on a wave of productivity improvements brought by technological advances. Radical reductions in the cost of communication will produce a global marketplace, if not a global village. The spread of freedom will bring with it extraordinary increases in prosperity in the developing world. Equity markets around the world should move higher, with the Dow Jones Industrials Average crossing 35,000 by the end of the next decade and reaching 100,000 in the year 2020.

Reaching 100,000 on the Dow by the year 2020 probably seems unrealistic, perhaps even fanciful. One reason is our habit of measuring advances in the Dow in points instead of percentage terms. Figure 1–1 shows how we think about the market, with every 1,000-point advance in the Dow moving the line in the chart up by the same amount.

However, a 100-point move today, with the market above 10,000, is only one-tenth as important as it was when the Dow was at 1000. One way to keep things in perspective is to plot the Dow using a log scale. Now, a 10-percent increase in the Dow, which was 100 points back in 1980 and 1,000 points today, moves the line up by the same amount (Figure 1–2).

A second reason why Dow 100,000 may seem like fiction is our short-term orientation in thinking about our investment strategies. We are so taken by the debate over whether the Dow will be up or down by the end of the week, to say nothing of the end of the year, that we lose perspective and cannot see the power of compounding.

To help answer the question, "Dow 100,000: Fact or Fiction?" think of this. To reach Dow 100,000 by the year 2020 requires a 10-fold increase in the Dow in a little less than 21 years. We know that is possible. *We have just lived through an equivalent 10-fold increase in the Dow in just 17 years.* A 10-fold increase over the next 21 years implies an 11.1-percent annual advance, with the Dow doubling on average about every 7 years, crossing 20,000 in the year 2005, 40,000 in the year 2012, 80,000 in 2018, and making its final 25-percent move in the next two years to reach 100,000 by year-end 2020 (Figure 1–3). As we shall see, such a rate of advance is achievable in the years ahead.

Today's Risk

The biggest risk to investors today is failing to realize that projecting the trends of the seventies and eighties gives you a misleading sense of the future. In the early 1970s, those who ignored the implications of the

FIGURE 1–1 Dow Jones Industrials, 1950–1999* (Point Scale)

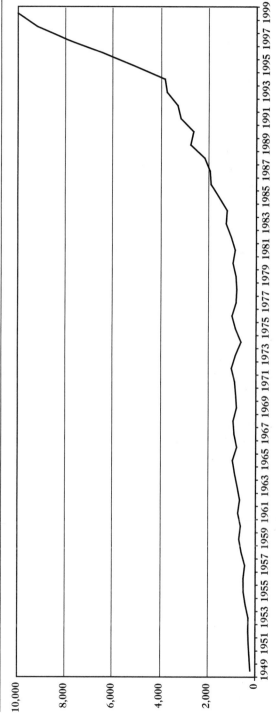

*March 29, 1999.

Note: An investor cannot invest directly in an unmanaged index, such as the Dow Jones Industrial Average. Past performance is no indication of future results.

Source: Dow Jones

FIGURE 1–2 Dow Jones Industrials 1950–1999* (Log Scale)

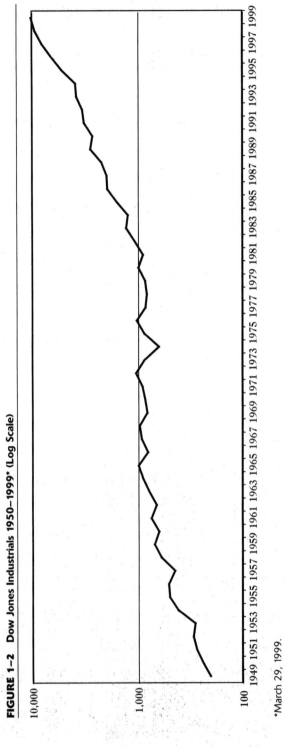

*March 29, 1999.

Note: An investor cannot invest directly in an unmanaged index, such as the Dow Jones Industrial Average. Past performance is no indication of future results.

Source: Dow Jones

4

FIGURE 1–3 Dow 100,000: Fact or Fiction?

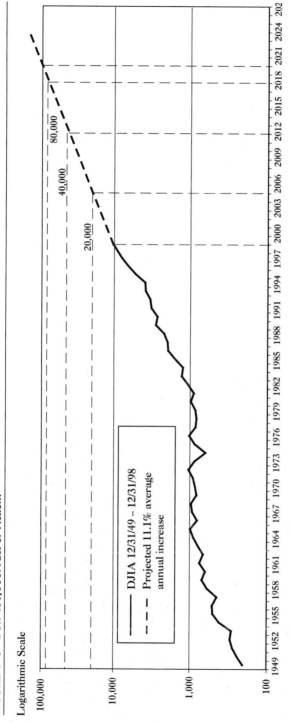

*March 29, 1999.

Note: An investor cannot invest directly in an unmanaged index, such as the Dow Jones Industrial Average. Past performance is no indication of future results.

Source: Dow Jones

devaluation of the dollar, the destruction of the international monetary system, and the reversal in U.S. free-trade policy saw the real value of their stocks and bonds fall by more than half in 1973 and 1974. They were the worst two years for the stock market in inflation-adjusted terms with the exception only of 1930 and 1931.

Similarly, those who failed to anticipate the implications of the turn in policy toward lower tax rates and lower inflation that began in the early 1980s saw their income from short-term bank certificates of deposit or Treasury bills plummet by more than two-thirds as interest rates fell. Others who speculated in real estate and oil, because for more than 10 years such investments had been sure winners, saw the value of their investments stagnate and then fall even as the stock market moved to historic highs. Fortunes were made and lost, companies, farms, and banks collapsed even as investments in new technology companies produced fabulous returns.

Failure to anticipate the Great Prosperity carries its own risks. Those who today are fretting that the market is too high, or too volatile, or who are trying to predict where the market will be over the next quarter or year are missing the forest for the trees. If you have not asked—and answered—the question, "Dow 100,000: Fact or Fiction?" you are speeding into the future but with little idea where you or your financial security are headed. One consequence may be the tranquility of not knowing; another, the swings from euphoria to fear that come from knowing you don't know. If you have not put in place a strategic plan to reach your investment goals, you risk missing some of the greatest investment and business opportunities of all time. You may forgo an extraordinary increase in personal wealth that will be realized by those who correctly anticipate the implications of the Great Prosperity for their businesses and their investments.

The Key: A Strategic Approach

Taking a strategic approach can keep you from making the mistakes of many commentators, some of whom acknowledge that we are in a new era, but who still remain transfixed by short-term developments. For example, in April 1998, *The Economist* newsmagazine published a cover story on "America's bubble economy"![1] Even though broad measures of inflation show price stability, the editors worried about the steep rise in stock prices and the likely inflation that was to follow. They recommended that the Federal Reserve attack this symptom of prosperity with a deflationary monetary policy, missing completely that this was the error committed by the Japanese in the early 1990s. Less than six months later, the Federal Reserve lowered interest rates to fend off deflationary forces emanating from the Asian currency crisis.

As we go to press, there are increasing worries about the risks of a severe economic disruption including a possible recession caused by computer breakdowns due to potential software problems in the year 2000.[2] There, no doubt, will be some disruptions caused by the Y2K millennium bug, but even if they cause a short-run contraction in the economy, they will not end the Great Prosperity. Instead, we will exit the year 2000 with a technologically modern infrastructure while business in the United States and around the world will be free to redirect the billions in resources that in the last two years have been spent to repair the Y2K bug.

The most noteworthy example of the cost of failing to understand the historical moment in which we live are the pronouncements and prognostications of Federal Reserve Chairman Alan Greenspan. On December 5, 1996, Mr. Greenspan worried aloud about the high price of the stock market, warning against "irrational exuberance."[3] The Dow Jones Industrial Average that day had closed at 6437. Over the next 15 months, the DJIA advanced more than 40 percent to over 9000. For his part, Mr. Greenspan in his February 1998 Humphrey Hawkins testimony before Congress spoke of the "exemplary performance" of the economy, but worried that we may run out of workers.[4]

These commentators are all missing the most important variable. We are at the beginning of a new era, a moment of discontinuity in which projecting the trends of the past eras misleads about the future. Let me give you one important example. Today, economists and pundits are debating whether inflation may be headed higher, or whether we are in danger of slipping into a deflation, such as the one that occurred in the 1930s.

What they don't see is that the truth lies in the middle. *We have entered a period of price stability.* Price stability does not mean precisely zero inflation. Nor does it mean that some prices won't be going up while other prices are going down. By price stability, I mean that broad measures of the price level over a 12-month period are within a band of plus or minus 2 percent. Historically, during such periods, the United States has experienced above-average growth and above-average equity-market returns.

7

Toward Dow 100,000

Anticipating the direction of the economy and financial markets over the next 10 or 20 years requires taking a step back from the press of everyday business and the immediacy of today's headlines. The sheer volume of information that is transmitted daily and the urgency with which it is presented in our daily papers and 24-hour business television stations teaches us to focus on the road immediately ahead. But as all of us who have ever learned to drive a car know, to be effective, we must lift our eyes and extend our vision to read the road signs and anticipate the flow of traffic and the general direction of the highway.

To raise our vision to the future, deepen our understanding of the economy, and increase our capacity to take advantage of the opportunities that lie ahead, let's begin from a vantage point high above the Earth. From here, we can observe a phenomenal amount of interaction among human beings. Conversations, data, television signals are sent to satellites and beamed to other points all over the globe. Airlines fly nonstop between virtually all of the major cities of the world: New York, London, Tokyo, Los Angeles, Sydney, Beijing, Buenos Aires, and every city in between. Zooming in closer to Earth, we see trains hauling cargo across the United States and trucks and cars speeding on the interstate highway system. Rising out of the Earth are cities with their buildings reaching as high as 100 stories into the sky and millions of people living and working and commuting and eating and going to the theater and restaurants and sporting events.

In labeling this incredible cacophony of activity the "economy," we too often strip it of its blood and sinew, its vitality, ambition, its success and failure. In short, its humanness. We forget that humans, more than any other animal, are not self-sufficient. Instead, we live in communities of cooperative action in which we trade with other human beings. These mutually beneficial exchanges—work for money, money for food, shelter, entertainment, and the like—constitute the foundation of what is called the economy.

Trade, Economic Growth, and the Stock Market

Creating and increasing our capacity to trade with other human beings is central to how we live our lives. For just a moment, imagine what life would be like without the ability to trade.

- What individual acting alone would have the time or resources or talent to build an airplane, far less operate an entire airline?
- Who would build telephone systems that span the globe?
- Who would have the time to get the food to our supermarkets, or even work the cash registers to check out and bag our groceries?

Without trade, what we know as the economy would collapse into a primitive state of self-sufficiency in which each of us would spend virtually all of our time in providing food and shelter for ourselves and our families.

All over the world, human beings from many different cultures have organized their societies to permit and facilitate trade among themselves and their neighbors. All who read this book enter into trades to take care of themselves and their families, first and foremost to provide for and sustain their lives—food and shelter. As our productive capacity increases beyond sustenance, then the variety and number of concerns that we can address increase exponentially. They include every manner of what makes up our daily lives, from the pursuit of material wealth, to matters of spirituality and contributions to the religious organizations of our choice, to voluntary work in our communities, to taking care of the poor and less fortunate among us. We go to school, increase our skills, and work late into the night in an effort to increase our capacity to enter into more fruitful exchanges, thereby increasing the fortunes of those we trade with at the same time we enrich our own lives. We change jobs, plan our careers, and raise our families. We save to put our children through college and invest to provide for ourselves when we retire from full-time work. And all of this, ALL OF THIS, rests on our capacity to enter into an ever-expanding variety of trades with other human beings.

The foundation of what is called "the economy" is trade among human beings. Businesses are formed to harness and focus the collective efforts of large numbers of people to provide goods and services to their customers. Employees are compensated with wages, which they use to purchase the goods and services provided by other human beings, from the local grocer and shopkeeper to organizations that bring complex systems and capital to our individual disposal, such as airlines and phone companies.

Economists call an increase in trade economic growth. It shows up as more retail sales, more employment, more construction and production of everything from factories and computers to the cars we drive and the gasoline that powers them. The sum of all the resulting purchases including changes in inventories and adjustments for international trade is called the nation's Gross Domestic Product.

On the other side of the ledger is the sum total of personal, business, and corporate income. *Thus, an expanding economy implies rising incomes and increasing corporate profits.* Portfolio managers and investors track the increase in corporate profits as one of the key variables in deciding how much they are willing to pay for a company's stock. Generally speaking, the higher current and anticipated future profits are, the more investors are willing to pay for a company. Stock prices rise, and stock indexes, such as the Dow Jones Industrials Average, go to new highs.

Charting the road to Dow 100,000 requires us to identify those government policies and economic forces that will increase our ability to trade with other people. The more we and others trade with one another, the more we produce economic growth. Higher economic growth produces increased incomes, more consumption and investment, and higher corporate profits. In the end, higher corporate profits today, and the anticipation of even higher corporate profits in the future, is what drives the stock market higher.

Strategists, then, speak of expanding economies and rising corporate profits in terms of advances in equity markets. *The road to 100,000 on the Dow will be built on a foundation of a historic expansion in trade among human beings, which will be recorded as an expanding economy and rising corporate profits.*

The Road Signs Ahead

Identifying the few key road signs that point the direction of the economy and financial markets can simplify our task just as lifting our eyes when driving a car makes driving so much easier—and safer. The first step, then, in drawing our map of the road to 100,000 on the Dow is to identify those key variables that can make it easier or more difficult for us to trade or do business with other human beings, not only within our communities and country, but around the world.

To no one's surprise, an examination of roads already traveled show that government policies play a vital role in expanding or contracting the space within which trade can take place. The key government policies that we must anticipate are

10

- Changes in tax rates
- Monetary stability
- Efforts to liberalize or restrict trade, either domestically or internationally

We will address each of these critical road signs in Part One.

The Key Historical Forces

Next, we need to identify those historical or secular forces that are interacting with these variables and thereby shaping the direction of the economy and financial markets in the years that lie ahead.

The end of the Cold War and the desires of the baby boomers to accumulate the savings they need for retirement are two extraordinarily powerful secular forces that point to lower taxes and continued price stability. As we shall see, lower tax rates and price stability make it easier for human beings to trade with one another. They are always part of the foundation upon which Great Prosperities are built.

The third historical force, *advances in technology*, is contributing to our prosperity directly through productivity increases, many of which are not measured. How do you calculate the value of a mobile cellular phone to everyone who uses one during the business day, whether in the car, on a train, or even 35,000 feet above the Earth on a coast-to-coast-flight. The technological revolution is also radically reducing the cost of communication. The Internet has been called an "information highway." But now, we are just beginning to use it as a commercial thoroughfare that is bringing the world to our doorstep and taking the products we offer to the rest of the world.

As powerful as these forces are, they are being complemented by the fourth historical force, *the spread of freedom* from Asia to Latin America to Eastern Europe and the continent of Africa. Increased freedom is unshackling the creative energies of individuals to take care of their families and communities and finding new ways to provide goods and services to customers down the street and around the world. *Freedom is the most powerful social organization ever discovered by human beings for the creation of prosperity.*

Competition among governments is the fifth and final historical force that is shaping the future. Governments are being forced to compete for the location of economic activity by providing the right mix of social programs, legal rights, and economic freedom. Competition is good because it

11

fosters policies that work and forces institutions to discard what doesn't work. The one sector of the world economy that has been relatively immune from competition is governments. But now, the "good ideas" of legislators and bureaucrats are starting to face the test of the marketplace. In a world of instant communication and electronic commerce, policies that significantly reduce the ability to trade domestically or internationally will quickly lead to economic contractions and higher unemployment, setting in motion a search for a better mix of policies.

The Risks Ahead

No map of the road ahead would be complete without a list of potential danger signs. There are always risks—we know that there are no sure things. The road to 100,000 on the Dow will not be straight: The Great Prosperity does not rule out short-term economic shocks or stock-market corrections of 10 percent or more. During the post-World War II prosperity, for example, the Dow Jones Industrials advanced at an average annual rate of 10.4 percent from the end of 1949 through 1965. However, during those 16 years, the Dow fell by more than 10 percent seven times, and by more than 15 percent twice (Figure 1–4).

Then, as now, there will be doubters and naysayers all along the way. They will encourage you to sell your stocks when markets are down, only to miss out on the subsequent rises to new highs. Distinguishing between such short-term shocks and era-threatening changes—between "Fact and Fiction"—is therefore essential in preparing for and building wealth during the Great Prosperity.

Historians and economists are of only limited assistance in understanding what brings prosperous eras to an end. Most of the reasons given seem ad hoc and less than satisfying. The Great Depression, for example, is blamed on the prosperity of the 1920s and the stock-market crash of 1929. In East Asia, the crash of 1997 and the end of 20 years of extraordinary growth and increased living standards was blamed on "Crony Capitalism," a system in which bureaucrats, big business, and leading families allocated capital and managed their economies. The only problem with this theory is that, for the prior 10 years, it was this same system that had been credited with these same countries' extraordinary economic performance.

For the map of the road ahead, I have identified five historical events that are potentially powerful enough to destroy the Great Prosperity and keep us from reaching Dow 100,000.

FIGURE 1–4 Stock-Market Corrections During the Post-World War II Prosperity (Dow Jones Industrial Average 1950–1965)

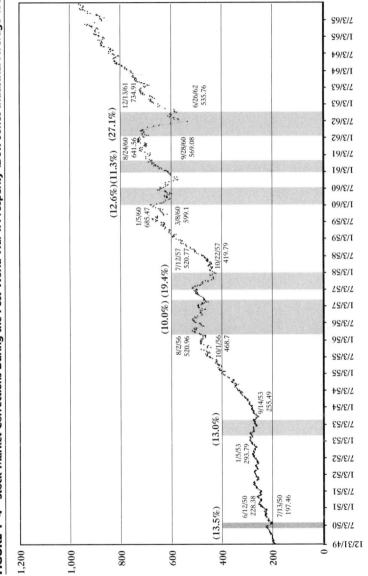

Source: Dow Jones

A war in which one or both sides used a weapon of mass destruction would disrupt world trade and threaten a new global emergency, attended by further government intrusions in the private sector, regulation of trade, and loss of freedom.

A terrorist attack using germ warfare, especially if it occurred in the United States, would create a new "state of emergency." The populist impulse unleashed by the end of the Cold War would be undercut by those who would seek to respond to this emergency by expanding government's role in our everyday lives.

Our fear of China, and a misbegotten effort to protect ourselves from this growing economic power with trade restrictions, is the third potential force. Starting a trade war with China, now the third-largest economy in the world, would threaten the world's trading system and capital markets. At a minimum, a trade war with China would cause a sharp economic contraction in the United States. *We can reproduce the 1930s. All we have to do is replicate the policy errors.* The Smoot–Hawley tariffs were the trigger to a series of events that produced the Great Depression. They included the destruction of the international trading system, the disruption of international capital flows, an increase in the top personal income-tax rate from 24 percent in 1929 to 63 percent in 1932, and the deflationary collapse of the U.S. banking system.

An international currency crisis that destabilized the dollar, the Euro, and the Japanese yen could destroy price stability throughout the world. The currency crisis of 1998 showed the pernicious effects of devaluations. Currency instability destroys the usefulness of money as the foundation of commercial agreements. It scrambles the meaning of prices, the language of business. Capital markets cease to function, interest rates soar, financial intermediaries go bankrupt, credit disappears, and economic activity collapses. In October 1987, the United States Treasury Secretary threatened Germany with a devaluation of the dollar, and the following Monday, the Dow Jones Industrials fell 23 percent. Until an international monetary system that can assure currency stability is restored, we must remain guarded in our confidence in the longer-term outlook.

The financing of Medicare raises the specter of massive tax increases that would end the era of growth, threaten price stability, and condemn the American people to an intergenerational fight over the distribution of a shrinking economic pie. Medicare is far more than a financial question. Ultimately, we will be faced with the question: How do we ration medical care provided at public expense? This is a profound ethical question. How we answer this question will be the legacy of the baby boomers, for good or for ill, because it will do much to shape the world that we leave behind.

It would be foolish to assume that the Great Prosperity is guaranteed, that it will last forever, that economic policies have nothing to do with the outcome. Prosperity, once achieved, has to be nurtured and protected. Its enemies include wars, both good and bad. They also include greed and envy, human drives so powerful and pernicious that God reserved one of the Ten Commandments to warn us against them.

Believing in a certain future also takes away your power, not only to change strategies if the environment changes, but, just as important, to be a participant in the design of the future that will be ours. When the currency crisis erupted in Asia, most corporate managers waited to change strategies, believing press reports that devaluation would somehow increase the competitiveness of Southeast Asian economies. By the time they recognized the devastating consequences, it was late. Some of them paid with their jobs.[5]

Moreover, each of us has a say in that future through the businesses we build and the innovations we bring to the marketplace. In addition, the future is formed by the direction and substance of public policies, which themselves are shaped by the policies we support, the politicians we elect, the organizations we give to, and the values we teach our children. Those who care about the future can have an important say over its design.

But to focus only on the risks, on the potential negatives, to focus only on the threats, and to fail to see the sweep of history, creates a different kind of risk. *The two biggest risks facing individuals today are first, taking a short-term view and missing the long-term opportunities, and second, being lulled into complacency, believing that the future is certain and therefore investing without the benefit of a strategy.*

The Prosperity Ahead

Historians may quibble about when the Great Prosperity began. I pick the year 1998 when, for the first time since the 1960s, the economy

15

recorded its third consecutive year of 3 percent-plus growth, and the year-over-year change in the Consumer Price Index was below 2 percent. The beginning of the Great Prosperity was heralded by record advances in the stock market, even as economists and pundits fretted that above-average growth would lead to higher inflation. It was challenged in 1998 by global currency turmoil and the first stock-market correction since 1990. Today, it is reasserting itself as we look forward into the first decade of the twenty-first century.

Doubts that a period of above-average growth and low unemployment can continue without sending inflation higher are prevalent and pervasive. These doubts are rooted in our experience of the Great Inflation of the 1970s and the prolonged period of disinflation that commenced in 1982. During the subsequent 14 years, inflation was gradually brought down from the double-digit highs of 1980 and 1981, to under 2 percent. During this period, unemployment gradually fell, even as U.S. businesses downsized and rightsized and made historic investments in technology to regain their former preeminent competitive positions in the global economy.

Our skepticism about a Great Prosperity also has been conditioned by the experience of the last 100 years, a century of wars—both hot and cold. These wars were but the last chapter of an epic struggle in which freedom in the form of democratic capitalism has triumphed over authoritarian governments in all their forms.

But the skeptics and cynics alike are ignoring the historical forces that now hold sway over the U.S. political system and economy. As a result, they are unable to see the investment opportunities that lie ahead. The United States in particular, and Western Europe, Japan, and eventually most of the rest of the world, have just begun an extended period of above-average growth with price stability.

Growth with price stability is normal in the United States. What is abnormal is the Great Depression and deflation of the 1930s, and the Great Inflation and stagnation of the 1970s. The Great Prosperity, in an important way, is a return to a normalcy that we have nearly forgotten.

During the 40 years prior to World War I, for example, economic growth in the United States averaged near 4 percent, while inflation remained well below 1 percent. And in the post-World War II prosperity, economic growth averaged 4.3 percent, unemployment averaged 4.7 percent, and inflation averaged just 1.6 percent.

16

Now, after one of the bloodiest centuries in history, with two world wars and a 45-year cold war brought to a close, the preconditions are in place for an extended era of peace and prosperity. Previous eras of prosperity have lasted 10 or 20 years. The Great Prosperity should last at least as long, if not longer.

We are just beginning to get a sense of the potential of the Great Prosperity. Federal budget deficits—which only six years ago were estimated to be $200 billion as far as the eye could see—have given way to surpluses so vast that the politicians cannot spend all of the money. The Federal government ran a $70 billion surplus in the fiscal year ending September 1998, and $100-billion-a-year surpluses are in the offing. The Federal surplus is now estimated to be nearly $2.7 trillion over the next decade. Sustained peace and burgeoning governmental surpluses provide the American people enormous resources and flexibility in meeting the challenges that lie ahead.

The Risk of Market Timing

Those of you who are trying to avoid risk by taking a tactical, short-term approach to investing in your business or the stock market are facing an even greater risk of being left behind in one of the great expansions and bull markets in history. Although everyone wants to know where the market will be over the next quarter or year, and most pundits spend their time and effort in trying to answer this question, our experience tells us that no one can consistently forecast the direction of the market over such short time frames. In fact, over the short run, the movement of financial markets is dominated by unexpected events that make attempts to time markets, to move money in and out of the stock market, counterproductive.

For example,

- If you had invested in the S&P 500 at the end of 1981 and had reinvested all of your dividends, you would have seen your investment grow by 21 percent a year through 1998.
- But, if you had missed the best 10 days out of those entire 17 years, your return would have fallen to 16 percent a year.
- Missing the best 20 days would have reduced your average annual return to 13 percent.

- Incredibly, missing the best 30 days out of those 17 years, which includes nearly 4,400 trading days, would have cut your return to only 9 percent a year (Figure 1–5).

To put that in dollars and cents, a $10,000 investment in the S&P 500 held for those entire 16 years would have grown to $255,836, but if you had missed the best 30 days, at the end of 16 years, your $10,000 investment would have grown to only $45,488. The difference: an astounding $210,348.

We will be asking—and answering—a question that is bigger and, as a practical matter, more important than guessing where the market will be over the next year. It is also a question that we have a better chance of answering: What are the major political and economic forces that are shaping the direction of the economy and financial markets, not over the next year, but over the next 10 to 20 years? What are the risks that could end the Great Prosperity? The answers to these questions make a compelling case that the road ahead will be a period of an extraordinary increase in prosperity that will carry the Dow to 30,000 before the end

FIGURE 1–5 The Penalty for Missing the Market, 1982–1998

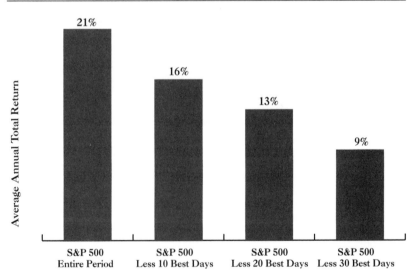

Note: An investor cannot invest directly in an unmanaged index, such as the S&P 500. Past performance is no indication of future results.

Source: International Strategy and Investments, New York City; Factset; Compustat

of the next decade and to 100,000 by the year 2020. This is also a moment in history when taking a strategic approach to investing is coherent with the world in which we live. In Part Three of this book you will find strategies that will help you take advantage of the opportunities that are before us today.

But first, let's turn to those key variables, changes that can dramatically expand or contract the amount of trade or economic activity that occurs among all of us human beings. Once they are clear, we can then examine how the five historical forces are interacting with them to shape the direction of the economy and the financial markets in the years ahead.

NOTES

1. "America's bubble economy," *The Economist*, April 18, 1998.

2. Edward Yardeni, "Y2K—An Alarmist View," *The Wall Street Journal*, May 4, 1998.

3. Alan Greenspan, Remarks at the Annual Dinner and Francis Boyer Lecture of The American Enterprise Institute for Public Policy Research, December 5, 1996.

4. Alan Greenspan, Monetary Policy Testimony and Report to Congress, February 24, 1998.

5. Hal Lancaster, "Stock Market Slide Gives Headhunters An Opportune Wedge," *The Wall Street Journal*, September 29, 1998, p. B1.

PART I

THE SIGNPOSTS

Success in building a business or executing an investment strategy takes more than a vision. It also takes courage, conviction, and a certain amount of wisdom. The purpose of the next three chapters is to increase the power of your conviction, enhance your wisdom, and, in that way, produce the steadfast and sometimes bold actions that are essential to successful investing.

The road to 100,000 on the Dow will not be straight and narrow. It will be full of curves and pitfalls that will conspire to push you off course—away from your investment strategy, leaving you vulnerable to the emotions of fear and greed. Suddenly, your investment horizons will shrink; the road ahead will collapse into a series of daily surprises. The power of the commentators that appear daily on television will rise. Their conflicting messages will become confusing. You and your hard-earned money will be subject to whatever is the investment craze of the moment. Your conviction will evaporate into a search for the secret formula that guarantees success, or that long-shot bet you hope will produce the financial security you seek. If you let it, your future would rest on the proverbial luck of the draw.

The next three chapters are designed to reduce your risk of having such an accident. We are going to look at the three key "signposts" that will continually help us answer the question—fact or fiction—and guide us toward 100,000 on the Dow. I promise you that we will not be using formulas, or math, or other jargon and devices used by economists to obscure, and sometimes confuse, and often explain away their policy errors.

During my first year as Seligman Advisors' Strategist, I was invited to give a presentation on "The Practical Applications of Economics" at the annual meeting of a national organization of financial planners. I had anticipated that this group would be skeptical, that they would doubt they could learn anything *practical* by listening to anyone talk about economics. To my pleasant surprise, the ballroom was filled with more than 200 people.

So, as I began my presentation, I told the audience that I was somewhat apprehensive about the topic that I had been assigned—demonstrating some actual practical applications of economics. I saw some smiles.

I decided to ask the audience how many of them had ever listened to a debate among economists and, after it was over, had felt that they had a better understanding of what the economy was all about, or the true implications of economic policy?

No hands went up.

So, I then asked them if they had ever seen a "practical economist."

Again, no hands went up, but there was some nervous laughter.

Faced with these responses, I told the audience that I could think of only two possible reasons why all of them were in the room listening to me. First, there was the possibility that hope springs eternal. Second, that they had really come to see, live at the front of the room, an oxymoron.

The crowd burst into laughter. We were off to an exciting 90 minutes in which we looked at how changes in tax and monetary policy were absolutely critical in anticipating the direction of the economy and financial markets. After the presentation, I was gratified to have many individuals in the audience tell me how much they appreciated the way I had demystified these policy variables.

Some readers may want to take it just on my word that lower tax rates, stable prices, and increasing international trade are positive for the economy and the stock market, and can then either move directly to Part Two, where we explore the historic forces that are shaping our future, or take a look at the figures on pages 34, 36, 51, 54, 83, and 84 that summarize these relationships before moving on.

For those who want to increase their ability to interpret the future that lies ahead, see fully the power of the historical forces that are shaping that future, and understand what may threaten the prosperity that lies ahead, I recommend you read first why these three economic variables are the key signs on the road to Dow 100,000. The practical benefit will be an increase in your conviction, which I believe is essential to designing, beginning, and then successfully implementing a long-term investment strategy to seek your investment goals.

SIGNPOST #1:
THE DIRECTION
OF TAX RATES

The power to tax is the power to destroy.
JOHN MARSHALL (MCCULLOCH V. MARYLAND)

THERE ARE A THOUSAND DIFFERENT ECONOMIC VARIABLES THAT ARE REPORTED by the Federal government that can be used to monitor the economy on a day-to-day basis. Everything from housing starts to industrial production to auto sales to personal income to the unemployment rate is covered in the evening news and in our daily newspapers.

Each of these variables is important in its own right. However, attempting to anticipate the direction of the economy over the next ten to twenty years, as opposed to the next three to six months, by tracking 1,000 different variables is like trying to understand a forest by examining each of the trees or by trying to see an oil painting by examining each of the strokes of the brush.

Our task demands a different approach. To answer the question, fact or fiction, and to map the road to 100,000 on the Dow, we need to identify a few key variables that increase or decrease our ability to enter into exchanges or trade with other people. In today's modern world, those exchanges or trade can occur with individuals down the street, across the country, or halfway around the world.

Taxes, or to put it more exactly, changes in tax rates, is the first of these key variables.

Tax Policy and Prosperity

There are few policy changes as fraught with risk and opportunity for our businesses and our careers as changes in the tax code. The roaring twenties and the go-go sixties were times of declining tax rates. For the most part, so has the last 17 years which produced a 10-fold increase in the Dow. By contrast, the prior 17 years in which the Dow failed to advance and the depression of the 1930s generally coincided with rising tax rates.

In the grand sweep of history, taxes have also played a vital role. The fall of the Roman Empire and the creation of feudalism can be traced, in part, to the extraordinary efforts by the emperor, Diocletian, to enforce an oppressive tax system on landowners and artisans. In order to reduce tax avoidance by aristocrats deserting their land and artisans deserting their trades, he decreed that those citizens who worked the soil were bound to the soil, and that those who worked in one shop or guild could not leave to join another without government consent. This decree was later confirmed in 332 by a law of Emperor Constantine. Less than 100 years later, the Vandals sacked Rome, and the Dark Ages were upon all of Europe.[1]

Nearly a thousand years later, the nobility of Britain exacted from King John the Magna Carta, a charter that limited the powers of the king, especially the power to tax the nobility *without their consent*. Two hundred years later, the Renaissance was in full swing. And, 400 years later, the tiny island nation of Britain would dominate the entire world economy.

American history began as a common people sought a new land free from religious persecution and oppressive taxation. One hundred years later, "No taxation without representation" became a rallying cry for the colonists seeking their independence from Great Britain. Two hundred years later, the United States is the dominant economic and military power in the world.

While politicians like to claim publicly that taxes matter little to the performance of the overall economy, when it comes to writing a tax bill, they know that every line, every stipulation, can alter the well-being of a few wealthy contributors or the global competitiveness of entire industries.

Why Taxes Are Important

The political, economic, and financial market effects of changes in tax rates are far more profound than many political leaders, most economists, and virtually all pundits are willing to admit. To see why, let's begin again with the question: What is the economy? What constitutes economic activity? What does all that jargon economists toss about called the macro economy, or aggregate demand, or aggregate supply, or national income, or gross domestic product mean, anyway?

First, the economic activity that is *measured* by government does not include anything that occurs within your family, your church, or in other voluntary organizations. What is counted are income-producing exchanges that take place in the marketplace. Baby-sitting clubs among young mothers are not part of measured economic activity. Paying a day-care school to watch your children is.

Economic activity occurs every time there is an exchange in the marketplace. It originates with our capacity and desire as humans to trade with one another. Every time we go to work, or go to a grocery store, or take a plane, or drive a car, we are engaged in myriad explicit and implicit exchanges with people all over the country and the world. Buying a car employs autoworkers and parts suppliers; purchasing groceries is an exchange with farmers, food processors, truck drivers, individuals who build refrigerator units, owners of the grocery store, the checkout clerks, marketing executives, packaging designers, producers of TV commercials, and on and on.

Thus, all economic activity engages us not only as individuals, seeking our own advantage, but also as people who must seek to satisfy another individual. *At its foundation, economic activity is based on our ability and willingness to compete and cooperate with other human beings in entering into exchanges or trade in the marketplace.* Producing satisfied customers and thereby gaining the income to demand satisfaction in exchange for our hard-earned money is what makes the economy go round. More exchanges or trade are recorded as an increase in economic activity, or what economists call Gross Domestic Product (GDP). We experience it as an increase in output, employment, profits, and income.

Tax rates are important because they interfere with our ability to enter into exchanges with other individuals. This is so important, so fundamental, but so often overlooked by economists, politicians, and pundits that I am going to say it again: *Changes in tax rates are important because they alter the space or opportunities to trade with other human beings.*

You can think of domestic income and sales taxes as the equivalent of tariffs on domestic economic activity. Let me ask you a simple question:

> If you raise the tariffs on the trade between two countries,
> what happens to the volume of trade?

That's right, it goes down. That is why tariffs are known as barriers to trade. In the same way, sales taxes, corporate income taxes, capital-gains taxes, and other taxes are barriers to domestic trade or commerce.

Sales taxes, for example, raise the prices of goods at a store just as a tariff raises the prices of goods we purchase from foreign suppliers. By making the goods more expensive, a sales tax decreases demand. With less demand, producers tend to cut their prices and reduce their output. Fewer sales take place. There is less trade. Less production. Fewer jobs. Less profit. Lower stock prices.

In the same way, personal income tax rates increase the price employers must pay relative to the wages that employees receive. That decreases the demand for and the supply of people willing to work. As tax rates rise, the opportunities for employment fall. There are fewer jobs, less employment. Less trade takes place. Need I repeat it? Less profit. Lower stock prices.

Of course, it also matters how the money collected through taxes is spent. If the tax is relatively low, and the money is used to provide a legal system, or build bridges, or otherwise reduce barriers to trade, economic activity may expand. However, if the money is used to pay people not to work, or not to plant crops, or to subsidize companies or businesses or workers that are unable to produce satisfied customers at the price they are charging, then, unambiguously, the total amount of economic activity declines.

In general, an increase in tax rates *reduces* our possibilities to trade with other human beings. Less trade means less economic growth or even a contraction in economic activity. That's what economists call a recession or, in a few cases, a full-blown depression. An economic contraction means lower incomes, less consumption and investment, lower corporate profits, and lower stock markets.

But even more insidious, higher tax rates divide us and separate us from our fellow human beings. Let me give you an example of how this works. Let's say you are hiring a contractor to do some work on your house. In bidding the job, he wants to receive $10,000. How much more do you think he has to charge?

First, he has to add an extra $600 to pay the sales tax. Next, he has to charge an additional $3,888 to cover his income tax (at a 28-percent rate). That brings his total bill up to $14,488.

28

But the story does not end there. Let's assume that you are successful, are having a good year, and therefore are in the highest personal income tax bracket of 39.6 percent. To net the $14,488 to pay the contractor, you have to earn $23,987.

That's right. With today's tax system, you have to earn more than twice as much as your contractor will receive to get your house remodeled. And this calculation does not even include payroll taxes.

The next time you hear a politician or a friend argue about tax fairness, ask yourself if the current situation is fair to either you *or your contractor*. High tax rates reduce our possibilities to trade with other human beings. They make us more of a hermit, and therefore less of a human being. Tax policy goes to the core of what it means to be human. No wonder debates over tax policy are so emotionally intense. No wonder history is full of revolts over tax policy—some political, some bloody. No wonder empires, from Roman to modern times, have risen and fallen in part because of the magnitude of their tax burdens and the manner in which they imposed them upon their citizens.

Reductions in tax rates have the opposite effect. They reduce the barriers to domestic commerce, just as a reduction in tariffs reduces the barriers to international trade. Lower tax rates increase the possibilities to trade with other human beings. They make us less of a hermit and increase our contact with others because they make it easier to discover opportunities for trades that produce an increase in mutual satisfaction. As tax rates are reduced, more trade takes place. More trade means more economic growth, higher incomes, more consumption, production, and employment, and higher corporate profits. And higher corporate profits imply higher stock prices.

We would therefore expect to find increases in tax rates to be associated with slower growth in the U.S. economy and poor financial-market performance, and would expect reductions in tax rates to be associated with faster growth and better financial-market performance.

Let's take a look and see.

Tax Policy, the Economy, and the Dow

To chart the direction of tax rates, we used the top personal income-tax rate in the United States. Although this is a crude measure of tax policy, it is an indicator of the direction of tax rates. The top tax rate has varied widely since its inception in 1913, beginning at a low of 8 percent in 1913 and rising to a high of 90 percent during and after World War II (Figure 2–1). Remember our goal here is not to measure or explain every short-term wiggle in the economy or the stock market, but rather to get right the direction of the economy and financial markets over the longer term.

We begin our analysis in 1926, the first year of the S&P 500. By 1926, the Roaring Twenties were well under way, and the Dow Jones Industrials Average, which closed 1925 at 157, had more than doubled during the prior five years. The top personal-income tax rate had been cut to 56 percent in 1922 from their wartime levels of 73 percent on taxable incomes over $1 million. The top tax rate was cut again in 1924 to 46 percent, and then to 25 percent in 1925, with a final reduction to 24 percent in 1929.

During the four years ending in 1929, the economy expanded at a 3.2 percent annual rate. The Dow Jones Industrials *more than doubled again*, reaching a high of 381 on September 3, 1929. Even after the severe correction that coincided with the progress of the Smoot–Hawley tariffs in the infamous stock-market crash of October 1929 (see Chapter 4), the Dow ended the year and the decade at 248.

By contrast, the Great Depression was a period of rising tax rates. In an effort to balance the budget, the top tax rate was increased to 25 percent in 1930, and then to 63 percent in 1932. Between 1929 and the end of 1935, the economy contracted at a 2.1 percent annual rate. The top tax rate was raised again in 1936, this time to 79 percent on incomes over a virtually unreachable $5 million a year. Between 1935 and the end of the decade, the economy bounced back from its depression lows, advancing at a 5.5 percent annual rate. Nonetheless, for the decade as a whole, total output increased 9.6 percent, for an annual rate of less than 1 percent per a year. No wonder they call it the Great Depression.

As tax rates went up, the Dow Industrials went down. After 10 years of rising tax rates, the Dow closed the decade of the thirties at 150. Although that was well above its lows of 1932, the Dow at the end of 1939 was still less than half of its peak in 1929, and no higher than it had been in 1926, 13 years before.

Tax rates remained high during World War II, but this does not tell us much about the relationship between economic activity and tax rates. During war, the entire point of economic activity changes from entering into exchanges to provide mutual satisfaction to defending the country. Taxes become the manner in which a society funnels all available resources into this central effort. Young men go to war and risk their lives, not to provide satisfied customers, but to protect their way of life

FIGURE 2–1 The Top Personal Federal Income-Tax Rate 1913–1999

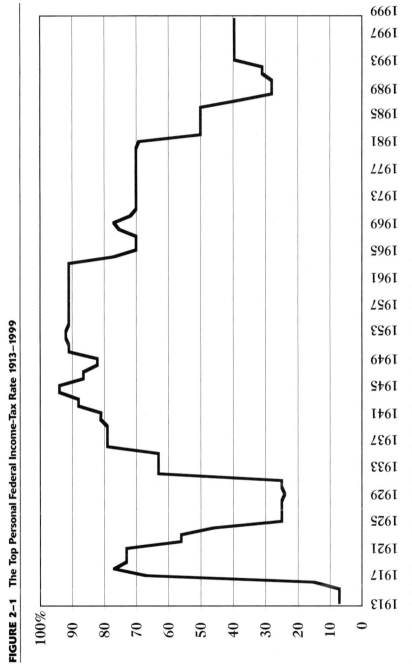

Source: Joseph A. Pechman, *Federal Tax Policy*. The Brookings Institution, 1987; Price Waterhouse

and families from a hostile enemy. Those who are making the tanks and growing the food to supply the troops are donating much of their time and energy to the war effort by turning over most of their income to the government, which uses the money to purchase the guns and supplies needed to fight the war.

The relationship between tax rates and economic growth was also distorted by the end of the war. For example, the top tax rate was reduced modestly in 1946 and again in 1948, but the demobilization of troops and the immediate reduction in defense spending produced a statistical contraction in measured economic activity. For this reason, we pick up the relationship again in 1950, the beginning of a decade with most of the postwar adjustment out of the way. At the close in 1949, the Dow Industrials stood at 200.

Tax rates were again increased in the early 1950s, in part to finance the Korean Conflict. Thanks in part to a sharp increase in military spending, the economy advanced at a 6.7 percent annual rate. The Bretton Woods Monetary system was also bringing a stable price environment to the industrialized world. This system provided a global monetary system based on gold that went into effect in 1947. Under this system, the United States guaranteed the dollar's value as being worth one thirty-fifth of an ounce of gold ($35 to the ounce). Other nations then guaranteed the value of their currencies by exchanging them at a fixed rate into the dollar. (We will have more say about the importance of price stability in the next chapter.) The result was a stable, global monetary system and an increase in world trade.

The rebuilding of Europe and Japan were augmenting U.S. economic growth as well. And, in spite of the fact that the top tax rate continued to inch higher, the Dow by the end of 1952 had soared to 292.

Perhaps the 1950–1952 period should have been eliminated from the analysis. Doing so would have strengthened the reported relationship between taxes and economic growth and the stock market, but it also could have raised questions about whether or not the data were being manipulated to make my point. Once again, we are looking for broad relationships, not precise statistical formulations.

Tax rates remained unchanged from 1953 through 1963 as the United States maintained its armed forces to counter the Soviet military threat in Europe and the strategic threat against American cities. During these 10 years, the economy expanded near its long-term average annual rate of 3 percent. The Dow finally went to new highs in 1954, 25 years after the stock-market crash of 1929. It declined during the recessions of 1957 and 1960 and again in 1962. In spite of those corrections, the Dow had reached 763 by the end of 1963.

The Kennedy tax cuts, which began in 1964, took the top tax rate down in two steps to 70 percent in 1965 from 91 percent. Growth accelerated to 5.3 percent, and the sixties became known as the "go-go" decade. The Dow soared, trading above 1000 for the first time on February 6, 1966, but closed that day just below the 1000 mark. The next day, Lyndon Johnson would call for a tax increase to finance an escalation in the Vietnam War. The Dow ended the year below 800. Not until November 1982, nearly 17 years later, would the Dow break back above 1000 to stay.

Tax rates did go back up before the end of the decade to finance the Vietnam War and a significant expansion in domestic social spending. Once again the economy slowed, though the Vietnam buildup kept growth at an above-average 3.9 percent. The Dow remained in a trading range between 800 and 950.

The repeal of the Johnson surtax in 1971 and 1972 led to an acceleration in economic growth and better stock-market performance. Economic growth in 1972 increased to 5.5 percent, the best year for the economy since 1966. And the Dow closed above 1000 for the first time on November 14 of that year.

Rising monetary instability and increased trade restrictions, however, were bringing the good times to an end. Growth remained positive, but retreated to slightly below its long-run average of 3 percent. During the remainder of the 1970s, the top tax rate was left unchanged. Individuals, however, were being pushed into higher tax brackets as their wages rose to keep even with inflation. Domestic trade became more difficult. Unemployment remained stubbornly high. And stock prices remained in a trading range. The Dow Industrials would have to await the tax-rate reductions that began in 1982 before it would move decisively above the 1000 mark.

The dramatic reduction in tax rates during the 1980s is once again associated with increased domestic trade, increased employment, and increased output. Economic growth accelerated to an above-average 3.4 percent a year, and a positive environment for equity markets. The Dow doubled, rising above 2000 in 1987, and then almost tripled, rising to nearly 3000 by the end of 1989.

By contrast, the Bush and Clinton tax increases are associated with a period of slower growth. For the four years ending in 1994, the economy

33

grew at a paltry 1.9 percent a year. Over that period, the Dow advanced at half of the rate of the 1980s, climbing slowly to 3834 at the end of 1994.

A period of stable tax rates began at the end of 1994 as the Republicans took control of the Congress. Once again, economic growth accelerated to a 3.3 percent average annual rate and stock-market performance improved. During the next four years the Dow would more than double, closing at 9181 at year-end 1998, and above 10,000 on March 29, 1999, a ten-fold increase in 17 years.

Who says the direction of tax rates aren't important?

Over this entire period of time—from 1926 through 1998 (not including the 1940s)—the economy, as measured by the Gross Domestic Product, grew at an average annual rate of 3 percent in real, or inflation-adjusted terms. That's pretty good, especially when you consider that it includes the decade of the 1930s. For all its imprecision, over the entire 62 years, the following pattern is evident (Figure 2–2):

FIGURE 2–2   Tax Rates vs. Economic Growth 1926–1998*

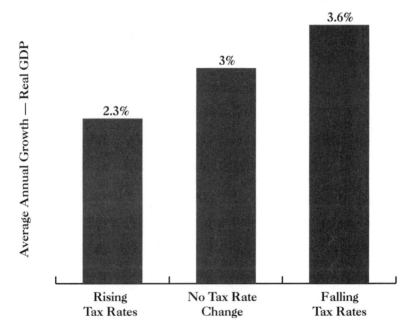

*Excludes 1940–1949 because of distortions caused by World War II. Average annual growth for entire period (excluding the 1940s) was 3.0%.

Source: Joseph A. Pechman, *Federal Tax Policy*. The Brookings Institution, 1987; National Income and Product Accounts; Price Waterhouse

- During periods of rising tax rates, the economy grew at a below-average annual rate of 2.3 percent a year.
- During periods when tax rates weren't changed, the economy grew an average of 3 percent per year—right on the average.
- During periods when tax rates were falling, the economy grew at an above-average 3.6 percent per year.

The point here is not the precision of these numbers, but rather the direction. Historically, as tax rates have risen, generally, less domestic trade has occurred and the economy has tended to slow. Conversely, as tax rates have fallen, generally more domestic trade has occurred and the economy has grown faster.

This overview is also supported by studies that examine tax rates and growth among the 50 states. In general, states that are increasing taxes relative to the average experience slower growth in income, employment, and population, while those states that reduce their tax burden relative to the rest of the nation experience above-average growth.[2] Moreover, states that levy a lower, flat income-tax rate tend to grow more rapidly than those that raise the same amount of money but use graduated income-tax rates.[3] Other studies show the same general relationship between tax burdens and economic growth among countries. Those countries with the lowest tax burdens and flattest tax rates in general have higher average growth, while those countries with higher tax burdens and more progressive tax-rate systems in general experience slower growth rates.[4]

The same pattern is evident between tax rates and the Dow as well as between tax rates and the broader S&P 500 stock index, which, as its name implies, is made up of a diversified group of 500 companies. To measure the implications of taxes on investment results, we are going to use the *total return* for the S&P 500, which includes price appreciation and assumes the reinvestment of dividends. This approach is similar to investing in a mutual fund and reinvesting all capital gains and dividends.

Once again, we go back to 1926 and omit the 1940s. From 1926 through the end of 1998, the S&P 500 produced an average annual total return of 11.5 percent. However, the total return of the S&P 500 was

- 6.1 percent during periods of rising tax rates
- 12.5 percent during periods of no change in tax rates
- 16.0 percent during periods of tax-rate reductions (Figure 2–3)

35

FIGURE 2–3 Tax Rates vs. The Stock Market 1926–1998*

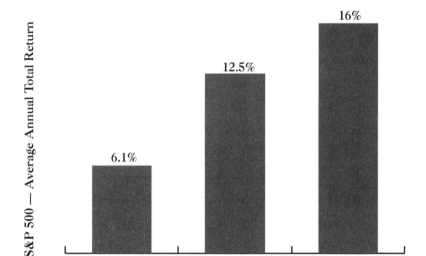

*S&P 500 Total Return; excludes 1940–1949 because of distortions caused by World War II. Average Annual Total Return for entire period (excluding the 1940s) was 11.5%.

Source: Compustat; Facset; Joseph A. Pechman, *Federal Tax Policy*. The Brookings Institution, 1987; Price Waterhouse

Taxes are not the only thing that matters to the economy and our quality of life. But the direction of tax rates is "Signpost #1" to the prospects for the economy in general, our businesses in particular, and our financial well-being. Periods of rising tax rates are associated with below-average stock-market performance, periods of no tax changes with near-average performance, and periods of tax-rate reductions with well above-average stock-market returns.

To answer the question, fact or fiction, to anticipate the direction of the economy and the stock market, we always need to be tracking the debate over tax policy. As we shall see, the prospects for lower tax rates are good, both in the United States and around the world. They are a key signpost on the road to Dow 100,000.

Dangerous Curves

The current tax debate, not only in the United States, but also in Europe, Japan, and elsewhere in the world, is therefore vital to our outlook. It deserves your attention, and your participation. In following the tax debate, look out for the following political devices that are used to keep tax rates high. Think of them as curves in the road to Dow 100,000, which can increase the risk to the value of your investments, especially if they are used to fend off real tax-rate relief.

Tax credits are not tax rate reductions. Tax credits are used to reduce the tax bill of politically favored groups. For example, the kiddie-tax credit reduces the tax bill of many middle-class families up to $500 per child.

At best, tax credits provide only superficial relief for the negative consequences of high tax rates. Why do I say superficial? Because they leave in place the tax barriers to commerce and do nothing to ameliorate the divisive force of high tax rates on domestic commerce. Whether or not you get a kiddie-tax credit does nothing to reduce the barriers between what you have to earn to pay the contractor to remodel your house and what he receives.

Moreover, generally limiting these credits to incomes below $100,000 penalizes America's high-cost urban areas, where incomes and the cost of living are both higher. Finally, they set off a scramble by special-interest groups to qualify for this new form of government largess. Tax credits, whether to individuals or corporations, are just another way politicians attempt to buy their popularity by taking from one group of taxpayers and giving the money to another.

The tuition-tax credit, for example, is given to those who have children in college. Similarly, the kiddie-tax credit is given to married joint filers with incomes below $110,000 and children below the age of 17. Clearly, a portion of the money to fund these credits is being taken from individuals with no children who have lower incomes than those who benefit from the credits. Although you may believe the tuition and kiddie-tax credits are well deserved, they are more akin to a government transfer payment than a tax reduction. To the extent they are used in lieu of tax-rate reductions, they reduce the prospects for economic growth and above-average financial market returns. If you think tax credits are a good idea, think again.

Tax rebates can be dangerous to the economy and financial-market performance. Tax rebates are a refund of a portion of taxes already paid. A typical rebate would be, say, 10 percent of your last year's tax bill, or simply up to $500 per taxpayer. Usually, tax rebates are given in the hope of spurring economic activity by increasing demand.

By their nature, tax rebates are based on past economic activity. When rebates are financed out of government surpluses, they at least transfer resources from government to the private sector. However, when rebates are financed by government borrowing, they simply shuffle money from one pocket to the next.

In the first step of a deficit-tax rebate, the government borrows money from its citizens. In the second step, it gives the money back based on some politically negotiated formula. Such tax rebates reveal politicians' complete lack of understanding of how high tax rates interfere with real economic growth and the creation of prosperity. Tax rebates, like tax credits, leave in place the tax barriers to commerce. Returning borrowed money to the citizens of a country has no redeeming economic value at all. Worse, since tax rebates are used as substitutes for real tax-rate reductions, they increase the public debt and the potential tax rates into the future.

Tax rebates were most recently tried in Japan to stimulate economic activity by increasing consumer demand. Those who invested believing that rebates would stimulate the economy and be good for the stock market lost money.

Under a 1998 stimulus plan, 3 trillion yen in bonds were sold to the Japanese people. The money was then given back to them based on their 1997 tax liabilities. The advocates of the rebate thought that by putting the money in the pockets of consumers, more money would be spent. But since the equivalent amount of money had to be taken out of Japanese pockets when they bought the bonds, there was no stimulus, only an increase in the deficit, which was then used to argue against permanent tax-rate reductions. The recession in Japan deepened, and unemployment continued to rise. What happened to the Japanese stock market? It fell by a third. By contrast, the passage of across-the-board income tax-rate reductions during the first quarter of 1999 led to a better than 20-percent gain in the Japanese stock market.

When politicians start promising tax rebates instead of tax-rate reductions, it's time to worry about the outlook for the economy and the stock market.

Higher tax rates on higher incomes hurt the middle class and the poor far more than the rich. You must be asking: How can that be? Don't higher tax rates force the rich to pay more?

Sometimes. But even if the "rich" do pay more, does that mean that they suffer the consequences of the higher taxes?

If you say yes, you are assuming that those who pay the higher taxes are passively accepting a decline in their standard of living rather than attempting to pass the cost of the tax onto others.

I discovered this fact when, after both the Bush and the Clinton tax increases, I noticed that my dentist increased his fees just enough to cover the now higher tax rates. Sure, the Internal Revenue Service data show that my dentist is paying a higher tax bill, but he was able to pass the cost or consequence of this tax onto *me* and his other customers.

The next time you hear a politician defending a tax increase because it is targeted at those with high incomes, or attacking a tax cut because it unfairly helps the rich, remember that this is a political sleight of hand that disguises the true consequences of changes in tax rates.

To see what is really likely to happen, think of a tax increase as a game of hot potato in which those targeted with the tax, who start holding the hot potato, attempt to pass it to other players in the economy. Unlike hot potato, this is not a game of chance. The winners in the game of "tax potato" are those who have more options for employment, or more control over their enterprises. Those with fewer options will be left holding the tax potato and will suffer a decline in their standard of living.

Who do you think has more power to shift the tax: those with high incomes, the middle class, or those with low incomes?

Data on hourly wages adjusted for inflation provide evidence that my dentist was not the only high-income individual who was able to pass on the cost of a higher tax bill. Between 1989, the year before the Bush tax increase, and 1997, the top personal income-tax rate was increased to 39.6 percent from 28 percent. Tax rates on lower incomes were unchanged. A study by the Economic Policy Institute shows that during this period, hourly workers, those in the lowest 20 percent, saw their wages after adjustment for inflation rise. However, that was due in large measure to the increase in the minimum wage. The third and fourth deciles saw no change in average wages. *But the heart of the middle class, those in the fifth, sixth, and seventh deciles, saw a decline in their wages of between 1.2 percent and 1.7 percent,* while the eighth decile was unchanged. The ninth decile, those making between $18.82 and $24.73 an hour, experienced a 4.0 percent increase in wages.

Who lost the Bush game of tax potato? The middle class.

As Figure 2–4 shows, the ability of those with the highest incomes to shift the tax potato is even more striking. During the 1990–1991 reces-

FIGURE 2–4 Tax the Rich, But the Middle Class Pays

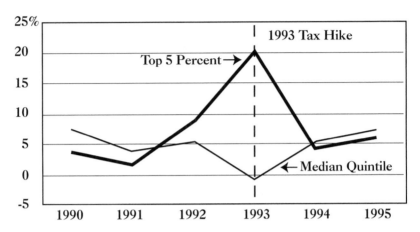

Source: Statistical Abstract of the U.S.

sion, the aggregate income of the top 5 percent of families increased somewhat less than that of the median quintile. But then, in 1992, with the likelihood of a 1993 tax increase rising, the income of the top 5 percent of families increased 9 percent. In 1993, the year the Clinton tax increase on the "rich" became effective, the income of the top 5 percent of households jumped an average of 20 percent—precisely enough to offset the 20-percent increase in marginal tax rates to 39.6 percent from 33 percent.

This means that in aggregate, those with high incomes were able to do exactly what my dentist did—pass the cost of the tax onto the rest of us, especially the middle class. As it turns out, the income of the middle quintile in 1993 fell 1 percent (Figure 2–4).

That's right. The aggregate data show that those with the highest incomes were able to shift the entire consequence of the Clinton tax increase onto the rest of the population. They also show that the increase in wage disparities during the Clinton administration that worries most economists and policy makers can be tied directly to the increase in marginal tax rates on those with the highest incomes.

Who lost the Clinton game of tax potato? The middle class.

The fairness argument is a clever way to keep tax rates higher than they otherwise would be. The truth is, high tax rates hurt the rich, the poor, and especially the middle class. High tax rates divide our society into

40

opposing camps. They separate suburban wealth from inner-city poverty just as surely as 40-percent tariffs would separate the United States from every poor country in the world. And with technology reducing the demand for middle management and other bastions of middle-class incomes, the middle class got hit the hardest by both the Bush and Clinton tax increases.

To add insult to our lower standard of living, high tax rates also appear to have little effect on total government revenues. Since 1950, the top tax rate has ranged from a high of 92 percent to a low of 28 percent. Yet, over this entire period of time, and under all of these various tax schedules, total Federal Revenues as a share of Gross Domestic Product generally have remained in a narrow range between 17 and 19 percent, with an average of 18 percent (Figure 2–5). Whatever advocates of targeting higher tax rates at the rich may claim, the overall results say there are few, if any, benefits to offset the losses produced by high marginal tax rates.

Positive Signs

This does not mean that all taxes should be abolished. Our government was formed to secure life, liberty, and the pursuit of happiness to ourselves and our children. Few would argue with our founding fathers and advocate that we would be better served by no government. Taxes exist because governments exist. Governments exist because, as a society, we choose to pool our resources through government to take care of a variety of our concerns, from providing national defense and domestic tranquility, to protecting the environment and providing some income security in retirement.

The question of the size and scope of government is central to the democratic process. Given the size of government, however, a tax system with the lowest possible tax rates across the widest possible tax base would produce the highest level of domestic trade, that is, employment, output, and economic growth.

The growing debate over the structure and complexity of the Federal tax system is one of the most exciting developments as we consider the outlook for economic growth and financial markets in the decade ahead. The positive signs to look for on the road ahead include

- An increase in the current income threshold for each tax rate
- Across-the-board personal income-tax rate reductions
- A shift to a simpler tax code with lower tax rates

- Reform of the Social Security system, including introduction of an option to invest a portion of the money you are now sending to the Social Security Administration in your own Roth IRA. Such a reform would reduce a portion of the payroll tax by transforming it into a forced savings plan
- Requirements for "supermajority" votes to increase tax rates
- Reductions in state income and sales-tax rates
- Tax-rate reductions elsewhere in the world

To the extent the tax debate leads to lower tax rates, we can anticipate above-average economic growth: so, too, if Social Security reforms include the option of partial privatization. As the barriers to domestic commerce fall, we can anticipate more opportunities to expand our businesses. More innovation and competition are also in the offing as we and others seek to reach and satisfy now more available customers. Specialization and outsourcing can be expected to increase as ever more

FIGURE 2–5   The Top Tax Rate and Total Revenue 1950–1998 (as a Percentage of GDP)

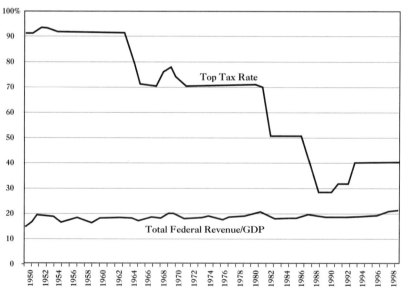

Source: Joseph A. Pechman, Federal Tax Policy, The Brookings Institution, 1987; Price Waterhouse; *The Economic Report of the President*

complex sets of mutually satisfactory exchanges become possible and are realized.

Employment opportunities will also expand. Those opportunities will give urgency and drive to efforts on the part of individuals and businesses alike to increase the skills and abilities of America's workers. The demands on our public educational system will surely increase as we become ever more aware of the value of the potential contribution of each of our fellow citizens. Investment opportunities will expand. As more commerce is committed, incomes and corporate profits will rise. As corporate profits rise, and the prospects for future corporate profits improve, the stock market will rise to new highs.

Lower tax rates alone are insufficient to get us to Dow 100,000 by 2020. But the likelihood of lower tax rates is an important source of our confidence that we are at the beginning of a Great Prosperity that will produce such a lofty result.

NOTES

1. Will Durant, *Caesar and Christ, The Story of Civilization III*, Simon and Schuster, New York, pp. 643–644.

2. Victor Canto, Charles W. Kadlec, and Arthur B. Laffer, "The Financial analyst's guide to fiscal policy," *Praeger*, pp. 189–218.

3. Richard Vedder, "On Tax Reform, Learn from the States," *The Wall Street Journal*.

4. Jude Wanniski and David Goldman, "A Flat Tax Would Produce Explosive U.S. Economic Growth," Polyconomics, March 31, 1992.

CHAPTER THREE

SIGNPOST #2:
THE DIRECTION
OF INFLATION

LET ME ASK YOU A QUESTION: IS IT EASIER OR HARDER TO DO BUSINESS WHEN prices are stable or when they are unstable, such as periods of high inflation or deflation?

The answer is intuitively obvious. Clearly, it is easier to do business with stable prices.

By "stable prices," I do not mean that all prices are fixed. Price stability occurs when, on average, the price level over time is virtually unchanged. During such periods, when some prices go up, other prices go down, wages and living standards rise as the value of what individuals produce goes up.

The reason price stability makes it easier to do business is as simple as it is fundamental to a well-functioning economy: Less time needs to be spent in negotiating the terms of a transaction to protect sellers and buyers from potential windfall gains or losses from unexpected price increases or, in the case of deflation, price declines.

Inflation: Prosperity's Enemy Number One

Inflation is prosperity's enemy because it offers the illusion of giving everyone more money. Who doesn't want a higher income for themselves, and what company would not like to be paid more money for its products? But with inflation, all prices and costs rise. The hoped-for prosperity never appears. This was the lesson of the Great Inflation of the 1970s.

Inflation makes it more difficult to do business and increases conflicts between employers and employees. If you are a manager, you lose control of your costs, aren't sure what to pay your employees, and do everything you can to raise prices to keep up with your increase in costs. If you are an employee, you fear falling behind a rising cost of living. You try to protect yourself by demanding bigger and more frequent pay increases. This combination is a recipe for conflict, increased strikes, and work stoppages.

What made a bad situation even worse during the high-inflation 1970s were two hidden tax increases. Wage gains needed just to keep up with the higher cost of living pushed workers into higher marginal tax rates, a consequence that came to be known as "bracket creep." "Stagflation," a condition of stagnation and inflation, afflicted the economy. Inflation and unemployment both went up. The economic contraction of 1973 and 1974 was the worst since the Great Depression. So was the decline in the Dow Jones Industrials, which fell 46 percent, from a high of 1051 in January 1973 to a low of 578 in December 1974.

If this wasn't bad enough, the top effective capital-gains tax rate was increased to 49.1 percent in 1976 from 25 percent in 1967. During the high-inflation 1970s, the price level doubled in eight years. Property and other hard assets kept pace, but the price of stocks generally rose less than the increase in inflation. Even worse, when financial assets were sold, the nominal gains were subject to the capital-gains tax even if the real, inflation-adjusted value of the stock had declined.

The combination of a higher capital-gains tax rate and the illusory profits created only by inflation produced effective tax rates of more than 100 percent, virtually eliminating the opportunity to invest for the long term. Potential entrepreneurs were cut off from venture capital. Fewer businesses were started. More businesses failed. Less trade took place. Stock prices went down.

Inflation also interferes with our ability to borrow money to finance our businesses or for the purchase of a home or car. Lending and borrowing are another form of trade among human beings. When we borrow, we effectively exchange goods that we will produce in the future for goods, such as a house, that we purchase today. Hence, the ability to lend and borrow opens the dimension of time for trade with other human beings.

When individuals are concerned about inflation reducing the future buying power of their money, interest rates rise and become more volatile. Lenders become less willing to lend money over longer periods of time. Fixed interest-rate mortgages disappear, replaced by floating-rate mortgages that provide at least some protection to lenders against unexpected increases in inflation. The availability of credit declines. Fewer businesses are started or expanded. Fewer houses get built. Fewer people are employed. Less trade takes place. Stock prices go down.

Inflation also creates new uncertainties for borrowers, who may now face unexpected increases in the cost of their mortgages. Inflation inevitably breeds hoarding and speculation as individuals are driven to protect themselves against the loss in value of money and savings accounts, and as they seek to take advantage by increasing their leverage with the hopes of paying off their loans in cheaper dollars. The comity of the marketplace is displaced by fear, distrust, and envy. Cleverness becomes more highly rewarded than do hard work and honest offers. Financial manipulation and windfall gains or losses from unexpected increases in the price level interfere with the possibilities for fair exchanges.

Prosperity becomes but a memory. During the 1970s, malaise was the mood that had settled over the economy as the opportunities to enter into mutually beneficial exchanges continued to shrink. By the end of the decade, President Jimmy Carter worried that "a majority of the American people believe that the next five years will be worse than the past five years."[1]

Today, personal-income tax brackets are indexed to inflation. However, the rise in the price of an asset or stock is not adjusted for the concurrent increase in the price level. Today, inflation is low. But any increase in inflation would lead to higher effective capital-gains tax rates, higher interest rates, less trade, less economic growth, lower corporate profits, and a declining stock market.

Deflation: Prosperity's Enemy Number Two

Deflation, or falling prices, also brings conflict to the workplace as management strives to bring costs in line with the lower prices they can now receive for the companies' products and services. Employees are asked to take pay cuts. They understandably resist, leading to layoffs and strikes.

Producers of raw materials and agricultural commodities feel the full brunt of the deflation, as the market price of their output falls. Their ability to meet their fixed commitments, from the monthly payments on their mortgage to their car payments, shrinks. Defaults lead to widespread bankruptcies and the loss of many a farm and home. The deflation of the 1930s, for example, was associated with massive layoffs and idle factories as the entire economy attempted to adjust to the rapid fall in price. The anguish and despair produced by the destructive force of deflation was captured by Steinbeck in his novel, *The Grapes of Wrath*.

Deflation interferes with the functioning of the capital markets. A sharp decline in the price level makes the true cost of paying off debt more expensive, as the value of each dollar rises. Lenders are put at risk. What had been good loans turn bad as borrowers can no longer meet their obligations and are forced into bankruptcy. Banks, unsure of the future value of collateral, restrict access to credit or, because of loan losses, themselves go bankrupt. Cash becomes king. The highly leveraged perish, as do many of their lenders. Most are worse off. The few who prosper are viewed as unworthy of their success and find themselves subject to political retribution.

Deflation, like inflation, interferes with our ability to coordinate our actions in a community of mutually beneficial exchanges. It disrupts our commercial contacts, reduces trade, increases unemployment, decimates corporate profits, and drives stock prices down. Monetary instability, whether in the form of inflation or deflation, isolates us in a community of distrust. It thereby reduces not only our fortunes, but our humanity as well.

That is why monetary policy is signpost #2 in answering the question: Dow 100,000, Fact or Fiction?

A Steady Course: Stable Prices

Why is it easier to do business when prices are stable?

For one thing, stable prices reduce uncertainty as an obstacle to doing business. Agreements, from wage rates to building contracts, remain valid because the payments and prices specified today provide the same rate of exchange into goods and services tomorrow.

Stable prices also increase the possibility of entering into contracts that span time. Horizons lengthen. This phenomenon is captured in the lower interest rates that are associated with stable prices. As inflation has come down from double-digit levels in the early 1980s to mid-single-digit levels in the mid to late 1980s, to less than 2 percent today, interest rates have fallen as well. Many of us have experienced the positive result of this by refinancing our home mortgages at much lower interest rates, dramatically reducing our monthly payments. (Others have experienced the negative side of lower interest rates as income from their fixed-income investments declined, when their bonds or certificates of deposit matured and the money was reinvested at the now lower interest rates.)

Overall, however, lower interest rates make possible transactions that otherwise could not have taken place. Suddenly home ownership becomes more affordable, and more houses get built. Companies find it easier to raise capital to finance the growth in their business. The demand and supply of plants, machinery equipment, computers, and the like, expand. Automobile sales expand. More trade takes place. Production and employment increase. Stock prices go up.

But the benefits of stable prices go beyond these rather matter-of-fact benefits by increasing the notion of what is possible. During periods of stable prices, individuals are more willing to forsake chasing short-term wins in favor of investing and engaging in business strategies that promise long-term gains. It's the difference between hoping to get rich quick by playing any of life's lotteries and investing with the ambition of building a better life over time. Comity returns to an expanding marketplace of increasing possibilities for exchange. More trade takes place. The economy grows. Output and employment expand, incomes and consumption rise, corporate profits increase. Lower interest rates and increased confidence increase the present value of anticipated future profits as well. Stock prices go up.

Those who argue that above-average growth causes inflation have it backward! Stable prices permit above-average growth.

I know this is a bold claim, that it flies in the face of conventional wisdom, and that it contradicts the opinions of leading economists, including members of the Federal Reserve Board, who have the power to set monetary policy.

So let's take a look at the historical record and see if your intuitive response to my question is backed up by the economic data. For the purpose of this historical review, I will use the following definitions:

- **Deflation** is any year in which the Consumer Price Index (CPI) falls by more than 2 percent.
- **High inflation** is any year in which the CPI rises by more than 5 percent.
- **Low inflation** is any year in which the CPI rises between 2 and 5 percent.
- **Price stability** is any year in which the change in the CPI is within a "band of stability" of plus or minus 2 percent.

What the Record Shows

We begin in 1926, the first year of the S&P 500. For the next four years, consumer prices remained within the zone of stability, and the economic growth averaged 3.2 percent a year. The 1930s began with the Great Deflation, which we associate with the Great Depression, as consumer prices fell by more than 2 percent in 1930, 1931, 1932, and 1933, and real economic growth contracted at an average annual rate of 7.6 percent.

During the rest of the 1930s, periods of low inflation and price stability coincided with economic recovery, and the return of deflation brought with it economic contraction. Low inflation prevailed in 1934 and 1935, and the economy, admittedly coming off a small base, recovered, with growth averaging 10.0 percent. The following year was a year of price stability, and economic output increased an incredible 13.2 percent. Growth continued in 1937, a year of low inflation. But in 1938, prices fell more than 2 percent, and economic output fell 3.6 percent. The decade closed with consumer prices falling a relatively small 1.4 percent, and the economy expanding 8.2 percent.

The 1940s were dominated by World War II and the imposition and then the repeal of price controls. As a consequence we omit this decade from our analysis.

The post-World War II era was generally a period of price stability or low inflation, and above-average growth. One year, 1951, was an exception, with inflation soaring over 5 percent, as the economy advanced 7.6 percent. This was primarily due to the outbreak of the Korean Conflict. During 12 of the next 16 years, the change in the Consumer Price Index was within the zone of stability, and for the other four, inflation never went above 3.4 percent. During those 16 years of prosperity, economic growth averaged 3.8 percent a year and the standard of living of the average worker rose 40 percent.

In 1969, however, inflation rose above 5 percent for the first time since 1951. Inflation eased back to below 5 percent in 1971 and 1972. But the Great Inflation of the 1970s took hold in 1973 and 1974, when the CPI rose 6.2 percent, and then soared to 11.0 percent. It would last for eight more years, ending in 1983, when advances in the CPI fell back below 5 percent for the first time in nearly a decade. During this 10-year Great Inflation, economic growth became highly volatile and averaged only 2.2 percent a year.

The remainder of the 1980s and the first half of the 1990s saw an extended period of low inflation, remaining generally in a band of between 2 percent and 5 percent a year. In 1986, inflation slowed to 1.9 percent as energy prices collapsed and, in 1990, it accelerated to 5.4 percent in part because of a surge in energy prices associated with Iraq's invasion of Kuwait and the subsequent Gulf War. During this period of low inflation, economic growth accelerated to 3.1 percent.

In 1998, price stability was restored as the CPI rose only 1.6 percent. Just as we expected, the economy grew at a well-above-average 3.9 percent, in spite of a sharp contraction in Asian economies brought about by the monetary and price instability of the international currency crisis.

For the entire period, 1926 through 1998 (excluding the 1940s), the economy expanded at a 3-percent average annual rate. The absence or presence of price stability made a big difference in the growth rate during this time (Figure 3–1). The economy contracted or grew at an average annual rate of

- –6.8 percent during years of deflation
- 2.4 percent during years of high inflation
- 3.9 percent during years of low inflation
- 4.8 percent during years of stable prices

Stable prices make it easier to do business. As a result, more business gets done. The longer the Federal Reserve maintains a stable price environment, the longer you can anticipate above-average growth in the U.S. economy. That is why restoration of price stability marks the beginning of the Great Prosperity. Spread stable prices around the world and you will get a Great Prosperity with the potential of encircling the globe.

FIGURE 3–1   Price Stability vs. Economic Growth, 1926–1998*

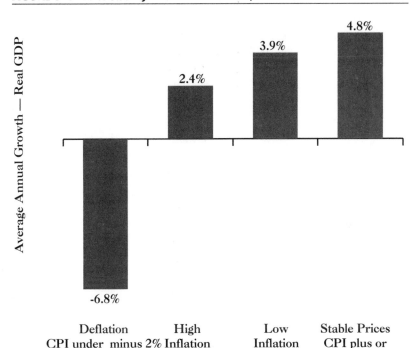

*Excludes 1940–1949 because of distortions caused by World War II. Average annual growth for entire period (excluding the 1940s) was 3.0%.

Source: National Income and Product Accounts; Stock Val

Price Stability and the Stock Market

We would expect price stability and instability to have a similar effect on the stock market. We have to be aware that the stock market anticipates future developments as much as it responds to current events. A truly scientific approach would have attempted to parse out the leads and lags and other factors that were influencing the stock market on a year-to-year basis. However, our purpose here is to check the historical record to see how price stability and instability change the general direction of financial markets.

In this chapter, we are going to focus on the changes in the total return of the S&P 500 instead of the movements in the Dow Industrials. The direction of the results are the same, but in this review, we will also take into account dividend payments.

51

Here is what the record shows:

We begin in 1926. The bull market of the twenties is well underway, ending with the stock-market crash in October 1929, which reduced that year's total return to a loss of 8.4 percent. However, price stability continued through 1929. And, in spite of that year's loss, for the 1926–1929 period, the S&P 500 produced an average annual total return of 19.2 percent.

The next four years of falling prices produced the worst economic and financial market results. If you had invested in the S&P 500 at the end of 1929 and had reinvested your dividends, the value of your investment by the end of 1932 would have fallen by 61 percent. In 1933, the market rallied 54 percent off those depressed lows. Nonetheless, the average annual total return for the four years of falling prices ending in 1933 was –11.9 percent.

The stock market remained highly volatile for the rest of the decade, advancing 48 percent in 1935 and falling by 35 percent in 1937. Still, the pattern of stock-market returns and price stability is evident. During 1934, 1935, and 1937, inflation was low and the average annual total return was –1.9 percent. By contrast, during 1936 and 1939, the CPI was within its zone of price stability, and the total return of the S&P 500 averaged 15.5 percent a year. In 1938, the CPI declined by 2.08 percent, just enough to put that year in the falling-prices column. That year, the S&P 500 registered a total return of 31.1 percent.

Overall, during the 1930s, we have probably understated both the downside risk of deflation on the stock market and the upside potential when price stability is restored.

Once again, we omit the decade of the 1940s and turn our attention to the postwar period beginning in 1950. Overall, 1950 through 1965 was a period of price stability during which the S&P 500 produced an average total return of 16.2 percent a year. During the two years of low inflation, the S&P 500's average annual total return was 13.1 percent. In 1951, the CPI increased 7.9 percent, yet the S&P 500 produced a strong 24-percent total return.

As inflation began to accelerate above 2 percent in 1966, average annual returns declined to 7.4 percent. Then, in 1969 and 1970, consumer prices rose more than 5 percent a year, and the S&P 500 recorded a negative total return of –2.4 percent a year. A return to low inflation in 1971 and 1972 triggered a rally, with an average return of 16.6 percent. But as high inflation took hold in 1973, stock-market returns suffered, as the S&P 500 posted its three biggest one-year declines in the post-World War II era. The total return of the S&P 500 was

- −14.7 percent in 1973
- −26.5 percent in 1974
- −7.2 percent in 1977

Taken together, the 10 years of high inflation that ended in 1982 produced a 6.7-percent average annual total return for the S&P 500.

As price stability began to be restored, better stock-market performance returned. During the first three years of low inflation, 1983–1985, the S&P 500 produced an average annual return of 19.8 percent. A sharp fall in oil prices brought the increase in consumer prices down below 2 percent in 1986, and the market posted a strong 18.6-percent advance. Low inflation returned for the next three years, and the above-average market returns continued, with the S&P 500 producing a 17.4-percent average annual return.

The CPI rose back above 5 percent in 1990, as Iraq invaded Kuwait, and oil prices shot up to $40 a barrel. That year, the S&P 500's total return was a negative 3.2 percent. But low inflation persisted during the next seven years as inflation was gradually reduced. Once again, strong stock-market performance returned, with an average annual total return of 19.8 percent. And, in 1998, the first year of price stability in more than a decade, the S&P 500 posted a total return of 28.6 percent.

Overall, the historical record shows that the S&P 500 produces an average annual total return of

- −4.6 percent during years of deflation
- 5.7 percent during years of high inflation
- 13.9 percent during years of low inflation
- 17.2 percent during years of stable prices

For all the year-to-year vagaries and the lack of scientific precision, the pattern is clear. Price stability is good for stock-market performance. Price instability is bad for stock-market performance (Figure 3–2).

If you have ever wondered why the statements of Federal Reserve Chairman Alan Greenspan are analyzed with such care or been puzzled by the stock market's strong rally or gut-wrenching decline in response to a change in monetary policy, now you know the answer. Monetary policy

FIGURE 3–2   Price Stability vs. the Stock Market, 1926–1998*

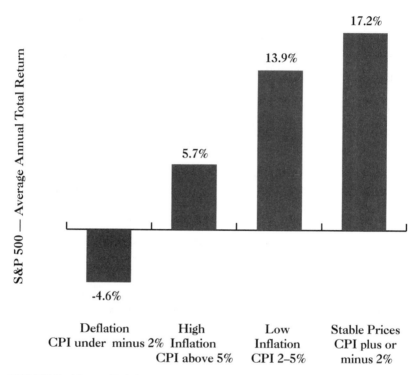

Deflation	High	Low	Stable Prices
CPI under minus 2%	Inflation	Inflation	CPI plus or
	CPI above 5%	CPI 2–5%	minus 2%

*S&P 500 Total Return; Excludes 1940–1949 because of distortions caused by World War II. Average Annual Total Return for entire period (excluding the 1940s) was 11.5%.

Note: An investor cannot invest directly in an unmanaged index, such as the S&P 500. Past performance is no indication of future results.

Source: Compustat; Stock Val; Factset

is one of the most powerful determinants of economic activity and stock-market performance. It is pervasive. There is almost no escape from high inflation or falling prices. And, there are few environments as constructive for human beings to discover new ways to trade with one another as a stable price environment.

That's why in anticipating the future direction of the economy and the stock market, we need to pay particular attention to "Signpost #2," the direction of monetary policy. To do that effectively, we need to reveal some of the myths that cloud our understanding of monetary policy and, in some horrible cases, produce monetary policy errors.

The Myths of Inflation and Deflation

When it comes to explaining inflation and deflation, economists can be confusing, and may themselves be somewhat confused. As it turns out, following conventional wisdom can be particularly dangerous to our financial well-being. So, let's take a closer look at some of the myths that surround discussions about monetary policy and that interfere with our ability to read "Signpost #2."

Unemployment and Inflation

One of the hallmarks of traditional economics, for example, is that there is a trade-off between unemployment and inflation known as the "Phillips Curve." You may not know what the Phillips Curve is, but you have probably heard economists express their concerns that as the rate of unemployment goes down, the risk of inflation goes up. Many economists today, including several members of the Federal Reserve Board of Governors, worry that today's low level of unemployment is a threat to price stability. Last May, for example, Federal Reserve Chairman Alan Greenspan told a Federal Reserve Board Conference in Chicago that "At some point, labor market conditions can become so tight that the rise in nominal wages will start increasingly outpacing the gains in labor productivity, and prices inevitably will begin to accelerate."[2]

I call this a monetary myth because it isn't backed up by experience. The top chart in Figure 3–3 shows what economists say. As unemployment rates fall, that is, move to the left along the horizontal axis, the rate of inflation should rise along the vertical axis. The relationship should thus look something like a line sloping down from the upper left-hand corner to the lower right-hand corner of the chart.

Well, that's what economists say. But to see what the economy actually does, look at the chart on the bottom of Figure 3–3. Can you see any evidence of what economists worry about? Neither can I. The scatter plot of unemployment rates and inflation rates shows that whatever trade-off exists between inflation and unemployment, it is tenuous at best.

Moreover, the whole notion that shortages of labor will produce rising wage rates that will cause a generalized increase in the price level is, itself,

FIGURE 3–3 Inflation vs. Unemployment 1950–1998

What Economists Say

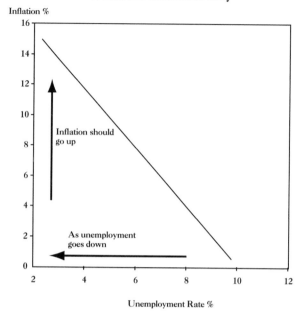

Unemployment Rate %

What the Economy Does

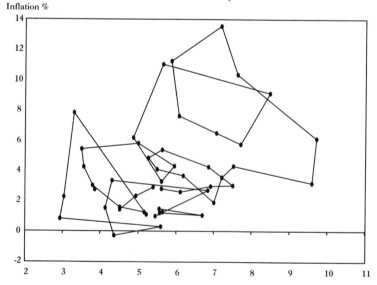

Source: Stock Val.

based on a false premise. Rising wages may be a symptom of an acceleration in inflation, but they cannot be the cause of a general rise in the price level. When you take away all of the economic jargon, the argument that low unemployment or rapid economic growth causes inflation boils down to this claim: Rising prices cause inflation.

Take a moment to think about that statement. How can rising prices *cause* inflation? Rising prices *are* inflation. *Blaming inflation on rising prices would be like the weatherman blaming the rain on falling water.* No doubt, when water falls out of the sky, we know that it is raining. In the same way, when all prices are rising, we know that is inflation.

Shortages and Inflation

Another favorite scapegoat for inflation is shortages. But saying that shortages cause inflation ignores one of the basic facts of the human condition, that few of us can buy everything we would like to have. Scarcity is part of human existence. At amusement parks, long waits ration the shortage of seats on the best rides, while the less exciting exhibits are readily available. Mr. Greenspan's warning that a shortage of labor would inevitably lead to inflation confuses a possible increase in the price of labor *relative* to other goods and services with a general increase in the price level. But in a stable price environment, when some prices go up, other prices go down. On average, prices remain unchanged.

Let me give you a real-world example of a shortage that produced a notable price increase but not an increase in inflation. In early 1999, the combination of stronger world growth, which increased the demand for oil, and efforts by major oil-producing nations to reduce the supply of oil led to a relative shortage of oil and a sharp increase in its price.

In March alone, the price of energy imports jumped 17.7 percent. But the price of all imports, including energy, rose a scant 0.1 percent. Why? Because the price of a wide range of other imports fell, including the price of imported capital goods (down 0.8 percent), nonauto consumer goods (down 0.5 percent), and nonpetroleum industrial materials and supplies (off 0.3 percent).

Here is the way it works. When we have to spend more money for something, such as oil, we have less money to spend on everything else. That is how prices and the marketplace function to allocate scarce resources. In a stable price environment, when scarcity produces an

57

increase in the price of a single item, such as oil or labor, the prices of other items fall. *On average, prices remain unchanged.*

Budget Deficits and Inflation

Another myth is that budget deficits cause inflation. People who have built their investment strategies around this idea have lost money and, perhaps even worse, missed some of the great stock-market advances in history.

I admit that, theoretically, budget deficits should lead to a rise in inflation, but as a practical matter, other factors usually are far more important than this theoretical effect. For example, the doomsayers of the early 1980s predicted that the Reagan tax cuts would lead to record deficits and that those deficits would lead to increased inflation and higher interest rates.

They were right about the deficits. But they were dead wrong about the direction of inflation and interest rates, and hence the stock market. Anyone taking their advice would have sold all of their stocks and bonds and invested in cash or hard assets, such as gold, when the Reagan tax cuts were signed into law in 1981. But inflation slowed, and interest rates trended down. The price of gold? It fell from a peak of $875 in January 1980 to less than $290 in March 1985. If you believed that budget deficits cause inflation, you would also have missed the beginning of the bull market of the 1980s, and the biggest increase in the price of U.S. government bonds in history.

The experience of the 1980s is not an isolated example. The Federal budget deficit soared to 4.7 percent of Gross Domestic Product in 1932 even as the price level plunged. By contrast, the last half of the 1970s saw reduced budget deficits amidst rising prices. The budget deficit was brought from a 30-year high of 4.1 percent of GDP in 1976 to 1.6 percent in 1979, while inflation *doubled* over the same period.

During the late 1950s, the Federal budget swung from a modest surplus to the largest deficit since the end of World War II, but inflation went down, not up. In the late 1980s, the deficit as a share of GDP was cut nearly in half. But this time, inflation went up, not down. By contrast, the movement toward a balanced budget in the nineties has coincided with restoration of stable prices. Sometimes reducing deficits coincides with lower inflation. Sometimes it doesn't. Over the entire period (excluding the 1940s), there is no correlation between budget deficits and inflation (Figure 3–4).

58

FIGURE 3–4   Inflation vs. Budget Deficits 1929–1998*

What Economists Say

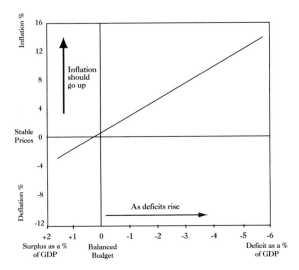

What the Economy Does

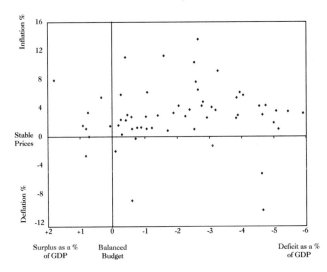

*Excludes 1940–1949 because of distortions caused by World War II.

Source: Stock Val; National Income and Product Accounts; Congressional Budget Office

Deflation

More recently, investors, economists, and pundits have begun to be concerned about deflation. Once again, there is a tendency to blame deflation on falling prices, from semi-conductors to commodities.

But the truth of the matter is the same as for inflation. Falling prices cannot *cause* deflation. Falling prices *are* deflation.

Certainly, a surplus of a good, such as a bumper crop of apples or wheat, can lead to a fall in that item's prices, and there is little doubt that the sharp economic contraction in Asia in 1998 so reduced the demand for energy that it led to a decline in oil prices.

However, blaming an overall decline in the price level on a surplus of output belies the fact that human beings have an insatiable appetite for improving their standards of living. What we call progress speaks loudly and clearly to the point that as human beings, we can always find new ways to use the abundance of the Earth to improve our sense of comfort, adventure, entertainment, or well-being. In a stable price environment, when some items are in surplus, their prices fall, freeing income to purchase other goods and services, whose prices tend to rise. *On average, prices remain unchanged.*

How to Anticipate Price Instability

What, then, causes price instability?

Before I answer this question, I am going to ask you to do something that may be difficult. I want you to put aside everything that you *know* you know about inflation and monetary policy. At the end of this section, you can decide to agree or disagree with what I have written. My purpose is not to win an intellectual debate. My purpose is to help you increase your wealth by investing wisely. To do that, you need to be able to detect the real danger signs of monetary instability. To a large extent, that requires ignoring conventional wisdom, much of which may have made sense in the 1970s, but that can lead to bad investment decisions in today's environment.

Let's start out with this single claim: Price instability is always first and foremost a monetary phenomenon.

What do I mean by that? I mean that unstable prices are evidence of *an imbalance between the supply and demand for money.* In the case of the United States, that means our central bank, the Federal Reserve, is either providing too much or too little money relative to the demand for money.

Economists for years have talked about the importance of money supply. To track the supply of money, they follow data series called "M1," "M2," "M3," and the like. We are not going to go into the details of these different Ms. That's because this is a book to help you be a strategist, not an economist.

What economists have not spent much time talking about is the *demand* for money. This is an important omission. As you will see, the demand for money can be as important, and in many cases more important, than the supply of money. But I digress. Let's get back to my question: What causes price instability?

Inflation occurs when the supply of money is greater than the demand for money. When a central bank prints or supplies more money than people need to enter into transactions in the marketplace, the surplus is used to bid up the price of all goods and services. In this way, the excess supply of money is absorbed by requiring more money for every transaction. When more money is required for every transaction, that is recorded as an increase in the general price level, or inflation.

Deflation occurs when the supply of money is less than the demand for money. If a central bank provides less money than people need to enter into transactions in the marketplace, prices fall until there is enough money to go around. When less money is required for every transaction, that is recorded as a decrease in the general price level, or deflation.

A change in the demand for money can be as important as a change in the supply of money to producing an unstable price environment. While the supply of money is generally in the hands of a country's central bank, the demand for money is in the hands of you and me and everyone else who uses money.

Most economists and commentators assume that the demand for money is relatively stable. Nobel Laureate Economist Milton Friedman, the leader of the monetarist school of economics, for example, advocates that the money supply be allowed to grow by a fixed percentage amount each and every year. His implicit assumption is that the demand for money grows in a constant proportion to the output of goods and services.

Experience, however, shows that the demand for money can change far more rapidly than its supply. Frequently, monetary policy errors occur because too little attention has been paid to what factors determine the demand for money. During the Asian currency crisis of 1998, the

Mexican peso devaluation of 1994, and the Great Inflation of the 1970s, shifts in the demand for money were at least as important as changes in its supply in producing the subsequent period of unstable prices.

Economists aren't very helpful here. Most economists don't even try to track the demand for money, perhaps because it is outside the control of government or any other institution.

The Role of Trust

To help you understand what drives the demand for money, let me ask you another question:

Why do you accept money, say dollars, in exchange for your hard work? Why does the butcher or baker accept some combination of 5-, 10-, and 20-dollar bills in exchange for the meat they prepare or the bread they bake?

The answer, of course, is that you and your butcher or baker expect or *trust* someone will accept those 5- and 10-dollar bills in turn for an equivalent amount of goods and services.

We work to produce satisfied customers so that we may obtain the income—the money—to demand satisfaction in turn. Money is at the center; it makes possible the incredible variety of jobs and occupations that exist in our modern economy. Without money, there would be the opportunity only for the primitive exchanges provided by barter.

Money is an incredible human invention for the purpose of increasing our capacity to enter into mutually beneficial exchanges. Every time we accept money, we do so trusting that someone else will take it in turn.

The more we trust that money will continue to be true to its promise of being this wonderful tool of commerce, the greater its usefulness, and the more it is used. If we are given reason to doubt that the money we have earned will be accepted in turn for an equivalent amount of goods and services, then its usefulness declines. As we doubt more and trust money less, we begin to avoid it as much as possible. It becomes a risky asset. The demand for money falls.

As soon as we trust money less, it becomes worth less. The less we trust money, the more we demand for the same amount of goods and services. If the distrust is shared, the buyer, eager to avoid the risk of holding money, willingly pays more for the now more valuable goods and services. All prices rise. Inflation appears.

Moreover, as we lose trust that the dollars we lend will be repaid in dollars with the same buying power, we demand higher future payments, hoping to earn a return after inflation. Interest rates rise. *The less we trust the future buying power of money, the higher interest rates are; the more we trust, the lower are interest rates.*

Let me give you a real example of this phenomenon. This is a story of a Russian citizen who was shopping for a vacuum cleaner in Moscow the day the Russian government announced that it was going to devalue the Russian currency, the ruble, in August 1998. Earlier in the day, he had visited an appliance store and had been offered a discount to purchase a nice vacuum cleaner made in Sweden. However, he decided to think about it and went to a store selling housewares down the street.

Shortly after he arrived in that store, however, there was a commotion behind the counters. He feared there had been a terrorist attack. Then he heard the manager say that the ruble was being devalued. Before he could engage a salesman, the door to the store was locked and he was informed that they were "closing for an afternoon break."

Within minutes, there were other people at the door, demanding to be let in, but to no avail. The Russian was let out of the store and ran to the place he had been in the morning, hoping against hope that the offer to sell the vacuum would still be there. When he arrived, that store, too, had closed. Other Russians were also pounding on the windows, demanding to be let in so that they could exchange their rubles for whatever was in the store.

If the stores had opened that afternoon, Russians would have gladly paid 10 percent or 20 percent more for the merchandise. It would have been a good buy, since the value of the ruble fell nearly 245 percent over the next three weeks. But, no one was willing to exchange goods for the money. They no longer trusted that someone else would take it in turn.

In the moment that distrust appeared, the demand for money fell and it became worth less. With trust in the Russian ruble collapsing, interest rates rose to nearly 140 percent.

Why did I tell you this story? To emphasize that in tracking monetary policy, you need always to be asking: What policies or actions will maintain or increase trust in the dollar, or the currency in your country? And what policies, actions, or event might reduce trust so much that they would threaten the price stability that has only recently been restored, for example, to the U.S. economy?

There are several factors that can reduce our trust of money and, therefore, our willingness to accept it in exchange for other goods and services. These are the early warning signs of increased inflation and the threat of poorer financial-market performance ahead.

1. The central bank provides more money than people are demanding, and we see prices begin to rise. As trust decreases, the pace of inflation tends to accelerate as individuals and companies alike begin to reduce their cash balances, which are losing value, and rush to purchase things before prices rise again. As money circulates faster, the pace of price increases accelerates more than the increase in the quantity of money. This process may look like excess demand is pushing prices higher. Instead, a flight from money is pushing the value of money lower.

2. Budget deficits so large that people begin to question the government's ability to pay off its debts. As a consequence, they begin to fear that the government will simply print new money to pay its bills and the debt. The consequent fall in trust, to say nothing of an actual excess supply of money to pay off the bonds, can both produce the feared inflation.

3. Talk of devaluation, or a weak currency policy. Governments reduce, and in some cases destroy, trust in money when they announce a devaluation of their currency. Imagine for just a moment a corporation in which you owned stock announcing that it was engaging in activities that would reduce the price of its stock by 10 percent. How long would it take you to call your broker and sell the stock? As individuals, like the Russians in the preceding story, scramble to get out of the money that is now worth less, the demand for money continues to fall. As a consequence, so does its value. In the moment in which we are less willing to accept money, inflation appears.

Ignoring this fundamental characteristic of money led the International Monetary Fund in 1997 to recommend that Thailand devalue its currency, igniting the currency crisis of 1998. This same ignorance was at the foundation of the Great Inflation of the 1970s.

Case Study: The Great Inflation In order to improve your ability to read the signs that point in the direction of inflation, let's quickly review the monetary-policy errors that were at the center of the Great Inflation that brought the go-go-sixties, the last period of U.S. prosperity, to a crushing end.

Many of the myths and errors mentioned here coalesced in the late 1960s and early 1970s to create what became the Great Inflation of the seventies. It is convenient to blame this Great Inflation on the Arab oil embargo and the quadrupling of the price of oil in 1973. Such a view, however, pretends that U.S. monetary policy had nothing to do with an acceleration in inflation to double-digit levels. In short, most commentators blame the Great Inflation on rising prices, in this case the price of oil, but also the price of wheat and all other traded goods.

At the center of the Great Inflation, however, was a series of policy errors that reduced, and almost destroyed, trust in the dollar.

The trigger for the Great Inflation was President Richard Nixon's decision in August 1971 to *devalue* the dollar, that is, to make it worth less in terms of gold and most of the currencies of the world. The devaluation of the dollar, we were told, would make the U.S. economy more competitive by lowering the cost of production in the U.S., especially the cost of labor. The inflationary implications of the dollar's devaluation, we were assured, would be minor.

What happened next, however, shocked the world. Dollar holders all over the world began to trust the dollar less. Not only did they begin to switch into more trustworthy currencies, including the German mark and the Swiss franc, but Americans began a flight out of money into hard assets, including real estate, antiques, Persian rugs, and luxury cars.

Recorded inflation was at first suppressed by wage and price controls. But as the controls were removed, recorded inflation accelerated to 6.2 percent in 1973 and 11.0 percent in 1974.

At that time, just like today, oil was priced in dollars. To a significant extent, the price of oil was administered by the Organization of Petroleum Exporting Countries (OPEC). Thus, when President Nixon devalued the dollar against gold, he effectively reduced the purchasing power of oil producers as well. Five weeks after the United States closed the gold window, OPEC met in Beirut and adopted a resolution directing the member countries to take the actions necessary "to offset any adverse effects on the per barrel real income of Member Countries resulting from the international monetary developments as of 15th August, 1971."[3]

The quadrupling of the price of oil in late 1973 did not cause the Great Inflation. In fact, the price of oil was one of the last commodity prices to rise. Keeping more oil in the ground by reducing its output was just another form of hoarding, a way to hedge against the risk of inflation. The price of oil did rise relative to other goods and services. And since the U.S. is a net importer of oil, that, too, contributed to a general decline in our standard of living.

Inflation peaked in 1980, when consumer prices advanced 13.6 percent, the prime rate hit a high of 21.5 percent, and the yield on the 90-day T-bill reached 16.7 percent. The rate of advance in consumer prices was slowed to 10.3 percent in 1981 and 6.1 percent in 1982, before falling back below 5 percent in 1983.

Trust, once destroyed, is restored very slowly. Although low inflation was restored quickly, interest rates returned to their former levels only slowly. In 1983, the rise in consumer prices slowed to 3.2 percent, but the interest rates on 10-year government bonds remained above 10 percent for three more years. Recurring success builds trust, and as the Fed maintained a low-inflation environment, interest rates followed a downward trend, punctuated by upward spikes as fears of future inflation would arise.

All told, it took 16 years to restore price stability, an era that was known as disinflation. At the beginning of those 16 years, many wondered if the U.S. would ever again be able to compete in world markets. It was a wrenching 16 years in which corporations downsized and right-sized, closing factories and laying off workers, a period in which corporate restructuring remade the face of business in America. It was also a period in which tax rates were reduced and economic growth returned. An era in which malaise gave way to hope and ambition. An era in which innovation and the creation of businesses created 18 million new jobs, even as the largest 500 corporations shed nearly two million workers. Microsoft and Compaq computers were both born in the 1980s, while Intel achieved its dominant role in the production of microprocessors, setting the stage for the technological revolution of today.

Positive Signs

Nineteen ninety-eight was the first year since 1986, and only the second year since 1965, in which the rise in consumer prices fell back below 2 percent. Price stability has been restored. A cornerstone of the Great Prosperity has been put in place. The positive signs to look for on the road ahead include:

Formalization of the policies that the Federal Reserve uses to maintain a stable price environment. As things stand, the trust in U.S. monetary policy rests disproportionately on the shoulders of a single individual, Federal Reserve Chairman Alan Greenspan. Along with his predecessor, Paul Volcker, Mr. Greenspan has brought back a stable price environment. But Mr. Greenspan's term as Federal Reserve governor is up in June 2000. Even if he is reappointed, he is unlikely, because of his age, to remain Fed chairman after that term would expire in 2004. That inevitable departure leaves open the question of how a stable price environment can be assured beyond Mr. Greenspan's tenure.

As the myths that growth causes inflation, or that unemployment causes inflation continue to be undermined by experience, look for the Federal Reserve to begin to target the price level directly in deciding how much or how little money to supply to the economy. A shift toward Price Level Targeting (PLT), as it is becoming known, would be a positive sign on the road to 100,000 on the Dow.

Restoration of an international monetary system. This is the last, great piece of unfinished business from the Great Inflation of the 1970s. Can you imagine a world of stable prices, not only within countries, but also across borders? Probably not. That tells you that such a possibility is not yet reflected in today's stock prices.

Restoration of an international monetary system that would give all who joined the benefits of a stable price environment would make it significantly easier to do business everywhere in the world. Global price stability would bring with it increased trade, more rapid economic growth, and increased profit opportunities everywhere in the world. The benefits of such a rise in corporate profits would lead to sharp increases in the prices of international equity markets. They would also contribute to U.S. prosperity and financial-market returns. About 40 percent of the profits of the companies in the Dow Jones Industrial index and the S&P 500 come from their operations outside the United States.

Maintaining a stable price environment in the United States is crucial to the longevity of the Great Prosperity and to reaching 100,000 on the Dow by the year 2020. Producing global price stability would dramatically increase the prospects of reaching this benchmark even sooner than now seems possible.

NOTES

1. President Jimmy Carter as quoted in Robert Bartley, *The Seven Fat Years* (New York: The Free Press division of Macmillan, Inc., 1997), p. 41.

2. David Wessel and Gregory Zuckerman, "Fed Chief Warns of Inflationary Pressures," *The Wall Street Journal*, May 7, 1999, p. A2.

3. Conference Resolution XXV.140, as quoted in Robert L. Bartley, *The Seven Fat Years*, p. 31.

SIGNPOST #3: THE DIRECTION OF TRADE POLICY

THE THIRD KEY ROAD SIGN OR POLICY VARIABLE THAT IS ESSENTIAL TO ANTICIPATING the direction of the economy and choosing between fact and fiction is the direction of trade policy. There are few policy variables that are as poorly understood and as fraught with risk.

In the case of trade policy, our intuition can be misleading. Restricting the ability of foreigners to compete in our market at first blush looks as if it could only help our fellow citizens. It even *feels* good. What people wouldn't want to put the well-being of their neighbors and friends ahead of unknown strangers from different parts of the world? Imposing trade restrictions is frequently championed in the name of helping out a local company, or local jobs, the "home team" if you will.

But, before you jump up and cheer for those supposed benefits, I suggest you consider the danger of trade restrictions.

When we think of trade as a game between the foreign team and the home team—as a win, lose, zero-sum game—we are forgetting that all of trade is produced by mutually beneficial exchanges. As long as the trade is voluntary and not fraudulent, it is by its nature a positive-sum game. If it were not a positive experience for both parties to the trade, the trade would not continue to take place. *Thus, anytime we restrict trade, we are denying our fellow citizens an opportunity to improve their well being. In so doing, we make them worse off.*

The truth about the benefits of free trade can be found in the experience of our everyday lives. Because humans have the capacity to enter into mutually beneficial exchanges with others, we are free to concentrate our energies and talents on our dreams and ambitions. *The only true isolationists are hermits, choosing to do everything themselves rather than to enter into the world of commerce.* This is so obvious that most of us take for granted that we can earn a living in a profession or business and use that income to trade for food, shelter, medical care, entertainment, travel, education for our children, and for the many other concerns of our families.

International trade is merely an extension of this practice across political boundaries. *By enlarging the community within which we are able to trade, free trade increases the markets for our skills and products, while increasing our choices on how best to take care of our economic concerns.*

Free Trade and Prosperity

The case for free trade has been known since Adam Smith wrote *The Wealth of Nations* in 1776. The basic element of trade, a mutually beneficial exchange, was first shown in its entirety by David Ricardo and was given the name of "comparative advantage."[1] Imagine there are two countries. The first has rich soil for producing wheat inexpensively, but can produce steel only at great expense. The second country has mountains that are rich in iron ore. As a result, it can produce steel cheaply, but wheat only at great expense. The people of both countries can be better off by trading the product in which they have a comparative advantage for the one that they find expensive to produce: wheat for steel, and steel for wheat.

The vast majority of economists agree that free trade brings with it rising living standards over time. A recent study of global patterns of economic growth during 1965–1990 by the Harvard Institute for International Development, for example, concluded, "openness was decisive for rapid growth." According to the study, open economies grew 1.2 percentage points per year faster than closed economies.[2]

An extra 1.2 percentage-point increase in the size of an economy may not be noticeable over one year. But over 20 years, increasing growth by 1.2 percent a year would increase incomes by about 25 percent, creating untold business, profit, and investment opportunities that would not otherwise have been possible. Just because trade occurs across an international border does not reduce its power to produce economic growth, higher corporate profits, and rising stock markets.

One of the reasons the United States has grown to be the dominant economic power in the world in less than 200 years is because the Constitution prohibits the states from interfering with trade among their respective citizens and citizens of any other state. This Constitutional protection created what was to become the largest free-trade area in the history of the world.

In the absence of political barriers to trade, much of American history is the story of humankind's success in overcoming the physical barriers to trade that spanned a vast and rugged continent. The building of the earliest turnpikes, the digging of the Erie Canal, the creation of the Pony Express, and the construction of the Transcontinental Railroad and the Panama Canal all testify to our extraordinary desire to realize the benefits of increasing the amount of trade we can do with other human beings. Two mountain ranges, wide rivers, a vast desert, the threat of treacherous weather conditions all failed in the end to deter this desire and fell instead to humankind's ambition and ingenuity.

What, then, is the source of opposition to free trade? Enlarging the community of trade produces not only new customers and new suppliers, but also new competitors. As consumers, we prefer competition. Who doesn't shop for the best deal when purchasing a car or television? As producers, however, it is only natural for us to prefer as little competition as possible. We like to be secure in our jobs and to know our businesses will thrive. And few of us like to change.

Yet, trade brings with it new competition, some of it unexpected and almost all of it unwanted. Competition challenges our habits and frequently forces us to change our ways—in some cases, even to change our business or jobs.

Even with all of its challenges and inconveniences, competition is good. It is what gives the individual consumer power over what otherwise would be the dictates of big business. Competition is also an agent of change. It brings forth innovation and excellence. In sports, it makes possible the four-minute mile. In the marketplace, the individual consumer, by choosing what to buy and what not to buy, guides competitors toward producing increased levels of customer satisfaction. *Does anyone doubt that Japanese competition has increased the quality of every car that is built in the world today?*

Trade also exposes us to the vagaries of the entire world economy. It exposes the illusion that we can control the ever changing world in which we live. That can make us uncomfortable. The sharp contraction in the

71

economies of Asia in 1998 showed up in the form of an increase in the U.S. trade deficit. Exports from these countries into the United States grew somewhat, but because of the collapse of economic activity in their economies, exports from the United States to these countries fell sharply. As a consequence, TV news reporters showed us pictures of container ships arriving full into U.S. ports, but leaving empty on their return trip to Asia.

I have yet to meet anyone who complained about the abundance of goods at very reasonable prices that are found at the malls during the holiday shopping season. The money you and I and everyone else saved on those imported goods meant we had more money to spend on domestically produced goods as well. During the fourth quarter of 1998, for example, domestic auto sales were headed for a near-record quarter, and overall, it was the best quarter for the U.S. economy in more than two years.

Nevertheless, many financial advisers and individuals to whom I talked were concerned that those empty, outbound ships might put American jobs and prosperity at risk. In fact, in the fall of 1998, the Federal Reserve began to lower U.S. interest rates in part because of the risk that a spread of the Asian currency crisis to South America could trigger a recession in the U.S. economy. In addition, the U.S. government, working with other industrialized nations and the International Monetary Fund, put together a $41.5 billion loan facility to assist Brazil in stabilizing its currency, thereby bringing the currency crisis that had begun in Asia to an end.

Like it or not, each of us, directly or indirectly, is connected to the successes and failures of people everywhere in the world. Most of the time, the consequences are imperceptible, like the contribution any one action has on the success of a company or the soundness of a family, but the cumulative effects of our actions shape the world in which we live. While we are told to worry about the exports of other nations to the United States, we forget to celebrate that the United States sells more goods to the rest of the world than any other country. More than 10 percent of U.S. jobs can be tied directly to exports, and more than 25 percent of U.S. economic activity is related to international trade.

The "Job" Myth

But don't trade deficits cost Americans jobs?

This claim, that a trade deficit means we are "exporting" jobs, is one of the most dangerous myths to our overall prosperity and financial well-being.

When Americans sell less to foreigners than we buy from them, it looks as if we are moving employment outside the United States. Certainly, some jobs that once were done in the United States are now done by workers outside the United States. Following this logic, we would expect a rising trade deficit to be associated with high levels of unemployment, and a narrower trade deficit or a larger trade surplus to be associated with low levels of unemployment. The chart on the left side of Figure 4-1 would describe such a relationship.

However, as the chart on the right of the figure shows, the claim that exporting jobs leads to unemployment is only half of the story. As often as not, the greater the trade deficit, the *lower* the level of unemployment. Right now, for example, the United States is running some of the largest trade deficits in its history, yet the unemployment rate is the lowest it has been since 1970.

I hope you are asking: "How can this be?"

Well, first of all, when unemployment rates are low and more Americans are working, times are good. During such periods, the U.S. economy and income growth tend to accelerate relative to the rest of the world. As a result, we tend to purchase more of what we produce and more of what the rest of the world produces. So we export somewhat less, and import somewhat more, increasing the trade deficit.

Second, an expanding economy attracts foreign investment. To get their capital inside the United States, foreign entities have to sell more to U.S. consumers than they purchase from U.S. producers. The difference is the increase in their capital, or savings, located in the U.S. economy. This money is not taken back home, but is spent in the United States, either by investing in financial assets such as stocks or bonds or by investing in real estate or by building new factories and offices or otherwise investing to expand their U.S. operations. Strange as it may seem, when trade deficits arise out of private actions, more often than not they are a sign of an increase in a country's economic growth and standard of living relative to the rest of the world.

The Cultural Aspects of Trade

As important as these economic and commercial advantages are, resting the case for free trade solely on better living standards risks trivializing its importance. International trade deepens our humanity by putting us in touch with an entire world of innovations and ideas. To this day, we

FIGURE 4–1   Trade Deficits vs. Unemployment 1950–1998

Intuitive Relationship

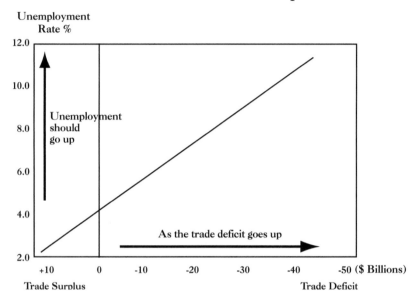

Actual Relationship

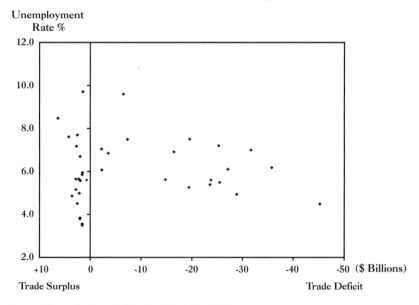

Source: Economic Report of the President; Stock Val

celebrate the great explorers for the discoveries that increased our world of possibilities and, in so doing, increased our humanness. Marco Polo for discovering China. Magellan for circumnavigating the world. Columbus for discovering an entire "new world." Lewis and Clark for opening the West.

The benefits of exposure to other peoples with different customs, cultures, histories, and skills may be the least appreciated gain from trade with other nations. This benefit cannot be measured directly. Frequently, they seem trivial within time spans of a year or less. Yet here, too, the cumulative effects can be and have been monumental.

Wherever geography isolates people, we find societies that are technologically backward and relatively poor in economic terms.[3] The indigenous tribes recently discovered in the Amazonian rain forests have been isolated from the rest of the world since the beginning of their histories. Today, their existence can be characterized as primitive, with no running water, no sanitary systems, no antibiotics or other forms of modern medicine. Even so, at their earliest discovery, we begin to seek ways to trade with them.

Think of it in our own country. Geographical areas that are isolated by mountains or deserts or lack of cheap transportation may be charming. But they almost always lag behind the commercial centers in average incomes, the number of high-paying jobs, and in economic opportunity. Wealth creation always shows up at the intersection of commercial thoroughfares: regional, national, or global. Throughout history, prosperities and cultural flowerings have been associated with and located in cities that were great commercial and financial centers, places that were open to and became the common meeting ground for their worlds. In ancient times, there were Athens, Rome, and Cairo. In European history, they include Venice, Amsterdam, London, and Paris. In our own time, New York, Los Angeles, London, Tokyo, and Hong Kong are those kinds of commercial and cultural centers.

Trade and the Creation of Wealth

To see why no society in history has become powerful by remaining isolationist, try this experiment:

Imagine two professional football teams. The first competes all year, winning its slot to play for the world championship in the Super Bowl. The second, at the beginning of the season, wins the right to play in the

75

Super Bowl by lottery. All year it practices its plays and works to perfect its game, but never competes in an actual football game.

Which team would you bet on to win the Super Bowl?

The answer is obvious—the team that actually spent the year winning games, all the while refining its play and improving the skill of its players.

Trade restrictions can be as effective as geographical barriers in isolating a country and its economy from the rest of the world. As noted economist Thomas Sowell points out, China in the fifteenth century was far ahead of Western Europe in its exploration by sea of adjoining territories, and it enjoyed a far higher standard of living. But near the end of the fifteenth century, those who ruled China were able to burn all of the ships and force a cessation of "foreign" exploration and trade. Within 300 years, European wealth and power would far exceed China's.[4]

A similar scenario was acted out in the post-World War II era. Mainland China, under the rule of the Chinese Communist Party, chose isolation and a centrally directed economy. Taiwan chose trade and a market-oriented economy. Thirty years later, in 1978, the per-capita income of the Chinese who lived in Taiwan was 24 times those who lived in mainland China.

Since then, China has once again begun to open its economy and culture to the rest of the world. And, for the past 20 years, its economy has grown at near double-digit rates, and the per-capita income of its citizens has increased five-fold to $860 per person.

Finally, the freedom to trade is fundamental to our liberty. Not only does free trade increase the scope of our economic and commercial interests, but it also constrains the power of government to impose ill-conceived policies on its citizens. Perhaps it is this constraint that the politicians and those who desire to use their political power to win advantage in the marketplace dislike most about unfettered international trade. When trade is an option, even the most powerful corporations will sooner or later be brought to account by the consumer. That was the lesson that U.S. automakers learned when, in the early 1980s, they refocused their efforts toward improving the quality of U.S.-made cars and satisfying U.S. consumers.

When free trade is an option, elected officials and government bureaucrats, too, become more accountable. Poorly conceived economic policies, confiscatory taxes, or undue regulations will drive production and employment out of the political jurisdiction, forcing a change in policy. That is why governments that seek to control their economies and that deny their citizens the freedom to enter into mutually satisfying exchanges inevitably close their borders to the rest of the world and frequently resort to terror to maintain control. All their people must be held captive. That was one of the lessons of the Berlin Wall and the Iron Curtain.

Trade, the Economy, and the Dow

Before World War I, tariffs were the major source of tax revenue for the Federal government. From the earliest days of the nation, the level and form of tariffs had been a major source of friction between the industrial North, which preferred high tariffs on its foreign, mostly European competitors, and the South, which depended on exports, especially to Europe, for a good deal of its income. After the Civil War, tariffs tended to fluctuate based on the party in power. The Republicans during this time favored higher tariffs, and the Democrats, lower tariffs.

We pick up our analysis in 1926. Tariffs had been increased four years before. The negative consequences of this tariff increase on international commerce, however, were more than offset by the dramatic reduction in barriers to domestic commerce through the significant reductions in personal income-tax rates.

Tariffs were left unchanged for the rest of the decade, even as personal income-tax rates continued to fall. The ensuing economic boom benefited all sectors of the American economy. And, as we have already seen, the Dow, in the late 1920s, was advancing at an above-average rate.

The importance of tracking trade policy is amply demonstrated by the events of October 1929, when the Dow began its historic fall even though income-tax rates had just been reduced and prices were stable. During the final quarter of that year, there was a sudden, dramatic, and unexpected increase in support in the U.S. Congress for the Smoot–Hawley tariffs, which would raise duties 17 percentage points and push the average tariff to 55 percent. The Republican Party began to promote higher tariffs to support the farm sector. The allure of higher tariffs, which held the promise of higher prices and profits and less foreign competition, attracted a wide range of businesses to appeal for higher import duties as well.

The Smoot–Hawley tariff bill was not signed into law until June 1930, but the stock market reacted to its progress throughout 1929, rallying when it looked as if the tariff increase would be narrow or would fail, and falling as the bill broadened and new coalitions formed to push its passage. On October 28, 1929, *The New York Times* reported that passage of the bill was virtually assured. Forever more, that day will be known as Black Monday, a day in which the stock market "crashed," falling nearly 13 percent on record volume.[5] At 10,000 on the Dow, *that is equivalent to a 1300-point drop in a single day.*

The stock market is always looking ahead, anticipating the implications of policy changes for the economy in general and corporate profits in particular. In this case, it correctly anticipated that the tariff increases would be ruinous for the U.S. economy in particular, and the world economy in general, that they would trigger a series of events that we now know as the Great Depression.

European governments were furious, seeing the tariff increases as an economic assault on their domestic industries and workers. British India complained that the 1,000-percent increase in the tariff on cashews was unjustified because the United States did not produce cashews. Italy, too, objected to a significant increase in U.S. tariffs on olive oil, another area in which the United States had no production. Throughout Italy, American cars owned by Italians became the target of protests and were vandalized. Worse, Italy responded by imposing duties so high that importing American cars became impractical.[6]

Other countries followed suit, increasing their own tariffs on American exports. As trade among the industrial nations collapsed, the international financial markets came under extraordinary pressure.

Between 1929 and 1932, U.S. imports fell two-thirds. But U.S. exports fell slightly more. A slight trade surplus in 1929 gave way to a balanced trade account in 1932. Total trade, however, was at a fraction of its former level. The U.S. economy was, for all practical purposes, cut off from the rest of the world economy, and, of course, the rest of the world was cut off from the United States.

Factories that had made sense in a world economy were redundant in a purely domestic economy. Specialized skills that could be sold on a world market were no longer in demand in a narrower local market. Factories closed. Unemployment increased. The volume of domestic trade declined. The U.S. economy contracted in both 1930 and 1931, with GDP falling 15 percent. The Dow, which had peaked at 381 on September 3, 1929, fell 35 percent by the end of 1929. That decline was followed by a 34-percent decline in 1930 and an additional 53-percent decline in 1931.

In the face of collapsing revenues and a soaring budget deficit, President Hoover and the Republicans in 1932 committed their second monumental error, raising personal income-tax rates. In an effort to balance the budget, the top income-tax rate was increased to 63 percent from 24 percent. This increase led to more unemployment, more business failures, and less output. The GDP fell an additional 13 percent in 1932. The Dow fell to a low of 41.22 on July 8, 1932, and closed the year at 60, its lowest level in more than a decade. The Great Depression took hold of the entire world. The U.S. banking system would collapse in 1933, as would the international monetary system.

The prosperity of the 1920s was but a memory. The trade restrictions of the 1930s are associated with an increase in the unemployment rate to a peak of 24.9 percent in 1933. All the parties that were to benefit from the tariffs suffered. The prices of farm commodities and industrial products went down, not up. Instead of protecting American farmers and industrialists, the sharp contraction of domestic trade and falling prices spread bankruptcies and economic ruin throughout the land.

The association of the Great Depression with the tariff increases of 1930 have left an indelible mark on the collective memories of the United States and Europe. The power to change tariffs was fundamentally changed by the Reciprocal Trade Agreements Act of 1934, which delegated to the President the authority to reduce tariffs by negotiating foreign-trade agreements. By 1936, 13 trade agreements had been signed, reducing tariffs 6 percentage points. The dollar's devaluation against gold in 1933 also produced an increase in import prices, as well as the general price level. The average tariff fell below 40 percent. In 1936, the economy grew an extraordinary 14 percent and averaged 6.2 percent for the 1934–1939 period.[7] By the end of the decade, the Dow had nearly tripled from its lows, closing 1939 at 150.

In the aftermath of World War II, the United States led a global effort to continue to reduce what by then had become known as the "beggar thy neighbor" trade policies of the 1930s. The goal was to liberate the world of trade, and the consequence would be to integrate the U.S. economy into the world economy as it never had before.

In October 1947, 28 nations gathered in Geneva to sign the General Agreement on Tariffs and Trade. The first GATT negotiations reduced tariffs on two-thirds of the items traded among the countries and contributed directly to the postwar recovery in the United States, Europe,

79

and Japan. Over the next 17 years, the average import duty in the United States, Europe, and Japan was reduced to only 10 percent.[8]

The entire postwar period was one of strong U.S. growth, rising living standards, and falling unemployment. Between 1950 and 1968, the economy grew at an average annual rate of 4.1 percent, while the unemployment rate averaged 4.7 percent and the Dow, which began 1950 at 200, had climbed all the way to 944 by the end of 1968.

Beginning in the mid-1960s, however, U.S. trade policy began to shift toward protectionism. The rebuilding of European and Japanese companies and economic infrastructure that had driven years of U.S. trade surpluses was largely complete. Now, U.S. businesses and labor unions were facing increased foreign competition. Foreign companies were also increasing their rate of investment in the U.S. economy. Although exports continued to grow, imports were growing even faster. Concerns also increased about the U.S. commitment to maintain the value of the dollar at $35 per ounce of gold as called for under the Bretton Woods agreement.

In 1969, the shift toward protectionism was signaled by the Nixon administration's decision to negotiate "voluntary" import restraints that limited meat and steel imports. In 1973, OPEC embargoed the export of oil to the United States. In 1974, the United States imposed restrictions on textile imports and embargoed the *export* of soybeans to the rest of the world.

The last half of the 1970s continued the trend toward non-tariff barriers. The United States skirted its international commitments by negotiating a series of agreements with foreign governments under which they would "voluntarily" restrain their exports to the United States. Between 1975 and 1979, such agreements were used to restrict imports of meat, nonrubber footwear (from Korea and Taiwan), specialty steel, color televisions (from Japan), and industrial fasteners. In 1978, an embargo was also imposed on the sale to the Soviet Union of wheat, superphosphoric acid, and other products.[9]

The protectionist wave crested in 1980 with the restraints on the imports of Japanese cars, the imposition of a 25-percent tariff on lightweight chassis trucks, and an extension of import restraints on color televisions to Korea and Taiwan.[10]

During this period of rising trade restrictions, growth slowed, inflation accelerated, and unemployment rose. Between 1969 and 1980, economic growth averaged 2.8 percent as the United States experienced its worst recession since the Great Depression. Unemployment rose to a peak of 8.5 percent in 1975 and stood at 7.2 percent in 1980.

Over those 12 years, the advances in the Dow failed to offset the losses posted in 1969, 1973, 1974, 1977, and 1978. At the end of 1980, the Dow stood at 964, only 20 points above where it had been at the end of 1968. During those same 23 years, consumer prices, however, had gone up 136 percent. So, in inflation-adjusted terms, the Dow Index had fallen 57 percent. Just as in the 1930s, trade restrictions and monetary instability proved to be a lethal combination for the stock market.

By the end of 1980, cracks began to appear in the protectionist wall, and the shift toward freer trade became clear in 1981. The embargo on U.S. exports to the Soviet Union was ended, and the restraints on imports of nonrubber footwear expired. In 1981, price controls were ended on crude oil and refined products. The administrative and other measures that interfered with and regulated energy exports and imports lapsed. The price of oil, which those that advocated the restrictions warned would triple to $100 a barrel, instead began its long decline.

The 1982 recession forestalled further liberalization. The Reagan tax cuts, which began to take effect in 1983, reduced barriers to domestic trade and paved the way for reducing the barriers to international trade as well. Restraints on Japanese car imports became moot as production at their U.S. plants rose to meet a growing share of U.S. demand.

In the mid-1980s, the United States again began to actively promote increased world trade. A free-trade pact with Israel was signed in 1985. The U.S. and Canada signed a historic, free-trade pact in 1988. That was broadened to include Mexico in a North American Free Trade Agreement (NAFTA) which was implemented in 1994. That year negotiations begun in 1986 to further reduce tariff and nontariff barriers cut the average tariff imposed by the United States and other industrial countries to 2.5 percent. Tariff and nontariff barriers to trade in agricultural products would be reduced over the next 10 years, and agreements were reached that reduced barriers to trade in services, such as tourism, banking, health, and transportation. Intellectual property rights, including patents and copyrights, also were provided multilateral protection. Finally, a successor organization to GATT, the World Trade Organization (WTO), was created and given expanded powers to arbitrate and adjudicate trade disputes among member nations.

The movement toward free trade was given further impetus in 1997 when WTO members reached agreements to eliminate all tariff and nontariff barriers by the end of 2002 on technology and information pro-ductions, including computers, semi-conductors, software, and the like, and, in a second agreement, on telecommunication services. Currently, those markets are worth more than $1 trillion and represent the fastest growing part of the world economy.

During this period of trade liberalization, unemployment rates declined even though economic growth remained modest. For the entire 1980 through 1998 period, the U.S. economy expanded at a 2.8 percent annual rate. The total number of jobs increased by 32.2 million. The labor-force participation rate increased to 67.1 percent of the work force, and the unemployment rate ended 1998 at 4.3 percent, its lowest level since 1970.

As for the Dow Industrials: As we know, the bull market that began in 1982 has been the longest on record and the strongest advance since the great bull market of the roaring twenties. Between the end of 1920 and the Dow's high in 1929, the index advanced just over five-fold in just under nine years. The Dow Industrials closed 1981 at 875. Over the next 17 years, it would advance ten-fold, and it closed 1998 at 9181. Within the next three months, the Dow would post its first close above 10,000.

If we look at the entire period since 1926, once again taking out the decade of the 1940s, we find a striking relationship among trade policy, the economy, and the stock market. During this entire period, the economy grew at an average annual rate of

- Only 0.8 percent during periods of rising trade restrictions
- 4.0 percent during periods of trade liberalization (Figure 4–2)

An equally striking relationship exists between trade policy and the stock market. Between 1926 and 1998 (excluding the 1940s), the average annual total return for the S&P 500 was

- 4.9 percent during periods of rising trade restrictions
- 14.8 percent during periods of trade liberalization (Figure 4–3)

Small changes in trade policy usually are not so important as small changes in tax or monetary policy. But a dramatic change in trade policy or a shift in the direction of trade policy have been associated with a change in the direction of the economy and the stock market. That is why the direction of trade policy is "Signpost #3" on the road to 100,000 on the Dow.

FIGURE 4–2 Trade Policy vs. Economic Growth, 1926–1998*

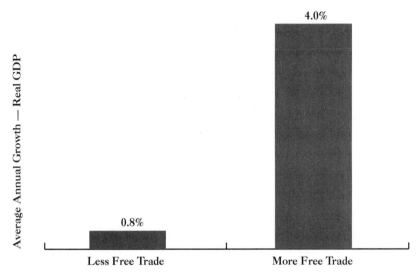

*Excludes 1940–1949 because of distortions caused by World War II. Average annual growth for entire period (excluding the 1940s) was 3.0%.

Source: National Income and Product Accounts

The Curves Ahead

Yet, for all its benefits, political attacks on free trade are on the rise. Even as unemployment rates fall to their lowest levels in 30 years, tolerance for foreign competition seems to be on the wane. Dangerous curves in the road ahead include:

A shift in policy toward increased trade restrictions. Recent polls indicate a growing opposition to free trade. One poll, conducted by *The Wall Street Journal* and NBC News in late 1998, for example, showed that given a choice of statements, 58 percent agreed that foreign trade has been bad for the U.S. economy because cheap imports hurt wages and jobs, while only 32 percent agreed that foreign trade was good for the U.S. economy because it creates foreign demand, U.S. economic growth, and jobs.[11]

There is an element of truth in what these respondents were saying. The opening of trade with China and the lands of Asia, Mexico, and Eastern Europe has increased the supply of hard-working, low-skilled people who are happy to compete with low-skilled American workers to improve their standard of living. Manufacturing employment has

83

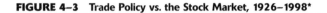

FIGURE 4–3   Trade Policy vs. the Stock Market, 1926–1998*

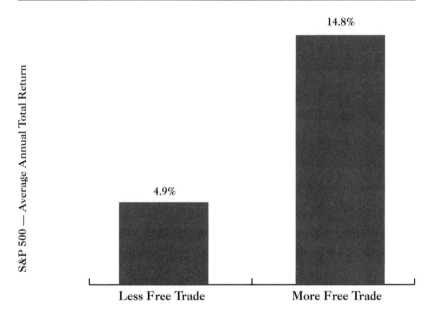

*S&P 500 Total Return; excludes 1940–1949 because of distortions caused by World War II.
Average annual total return for entire period (excluding the 1940s) was 11.5%.
Note: An investor cannot invest directly in an unmanaged index, such as the S&P 500. Past
performance is no indication of future results.
Source: Compustat; Factset

declined even as the manufacturing sector has led the economy in productivity gains. The spread of technology has also brought with it a
growing need to be able to think and to add value to our work through
our knowledge, relative to our ability to work hard through the use of
physical strength. One result is that in the past 20 years, the average pay
of college graduates has increased dramatically relative to those with a
high school education.

The election of a protectionist President. Congress may have become
more protectionist since the passage of the North American Free Trade
Act (NAFTA). Since its passage, Congress has been unwilling to give the
President the authority to negotiate new trade deals under a so-called
"fast-track" authority, which limits Congressional action to either
approving or voting down any agreement. That opposition rests in part

on the concerns of organized labor that fears competition from the vast increase in the number of workers in the world who can work on goods destined for the United States. Environmentalists, too, fear lax standards in foreign lands will erode support for the high standards now imposed on U.S. manufacturing facilities. Denial of "fast-track" authority effectively puts on hold any U.S. efforts to negotiate additional free-trade agreements.

Thus, a President who believed in reducing the freedom to trade would likely find a willing Congress ready to protect favored constituents—from big labor to big business—with new forms of trade restrictions.

An accidental trade war. In its efforts to open foreign markets to U.S. goods and thereby increase freedom to trade, the United States frequently threatens to impose targeted trade sanctions. During the first half of 1999, for example, the United States was engaged in a trade skirmish over European restrictions on bananas, beef, and airliners that used older airplanes whose engines were fitted with noise-reducing mufflers, instead of even quieter modern jet engines. In each case, the U.S. position had been upheld by the World Trade Organization, which is supposed to adjudicate such disputes. Once the shooting begins in either a military or a trade war, however, you can never be sure how it will end.

Positive Signals

Positive turns in the outlook for trade include:

China joining the World Trade Organization. As we go to press, negotiations are underway between the United States and China over the actions that China needs to take to qualify to join the WTO. Chinese agreement to comply with the rules of world trade required for membership in the WTO would extend the "rule of law" to matters of trade between China and the rest of the world. That would increase the prospects for lower Chinese tariffs and increased trade with China. Bringing China formally into the world trading system would benefit China, the United States, and the rest of the world as increased trade would, as it always has in the past, lead to increased prosperity. Integrating China more deeply into the world trading system would also reduce the risks of future military conflicts.

Extending NAFTA to the rest of the Western Hemisphere. Chile has already reached free-trade agreements with Canada and Mexico and seeks free trade with the United States as well. Other countries in Latin America and the Caribbean would also be willing to enter into a free-trade pact with the United States. An expansion of NAFTA would increase prosperity and strengthen democratic forces throughout the hemisphere. One of the most memorable phrases of the 1992 election was presidential candidate Ross Perot's warning of a "great sucking sound" of lost jobs that would head to Mexico if NAFTA became law. Instead, since NAFTA's passage in 1994, U.S. exports to both Canada and Mexico have grown more rapidly than exports overall. Imports, too, increased. And, although some jobs were no doubt lost to Mexican competition, the overall unemployment rate fell to its lowest level in 29 years.

With barriers to trade removed, people find new ways to help one another by entering into voluntary exchanges. Competition has increased in some industries from companies operating in Mexico and Canada, but so have opportunities to sell goods and services to the Mexican and Canadian people. The volume of trade among Canada, Mexico, and the United States has increased, and the three economies have become more integrated.

Expanding the EC to include all of Eastern Europe. The fall of the Iron Curtain and the destruction of the Berlin Wall in 1990 permitted the reunification of Germany. Since then, many of the old trade relations that had existed among the European countries prior to World War II are being reestablished.

Although there are budgetary and other issues, especially surrounding the agricultural subsidies of the European Community (EC), the expansion of the Common Market to include Poland, Hungary, Slovakia, and the Czech Republic would be as important as the expansion of NATO to securing the peace in Europe and spreading prosperity throughout the Northern Hemisphere.

Foreign trade is now a bigger part of our economic life than at any time since before the Great Depression. In 1929, 11 percent of GDP was associated with international commerce. Passage of the Smoot–Hawley tariffs drove down the volume of international trade to only 6.7 percent of a much smaller economy in 1932. In 1950, trade, at 8 percent of GDP, was still a smaller factor in the U.S. economy than it had been in 1929. Today, trade accounts for nearly 25 percent of GDP and more than 12 million jobs are directly attributable to exports (Figure 4–4). We cannot drive down the street or go shopping without engaging in international trade. Not only automobiles, beer, and wine, but also fast-food restaurants (Burger King), convenience stores (7–11), Lipton Tea, and *TV Guide* bring us in contact with foreign-owned companies.

This means that when we shop or invest, we are in some real sense bumping into people from all over the world even as American culture intrudes into every corner of the world. This kind of contact can and does make some of us a bit uncomfortable. It provides fertile ground for those who seek to gain power by exploiting our fears, but the reality is that any effort to significantly decrease our contact with the rest of the world, to disintegrate our markets from theirs, would seriously disrupt our economy. It would put at risk the economic and financial well-being of far more of our friends and neighbors than it would ever help, and in the process, undermine the success and prospects of our own businesses and

FIGURE 4–4 Trade's Increasing Importance as a Percent of GDP*

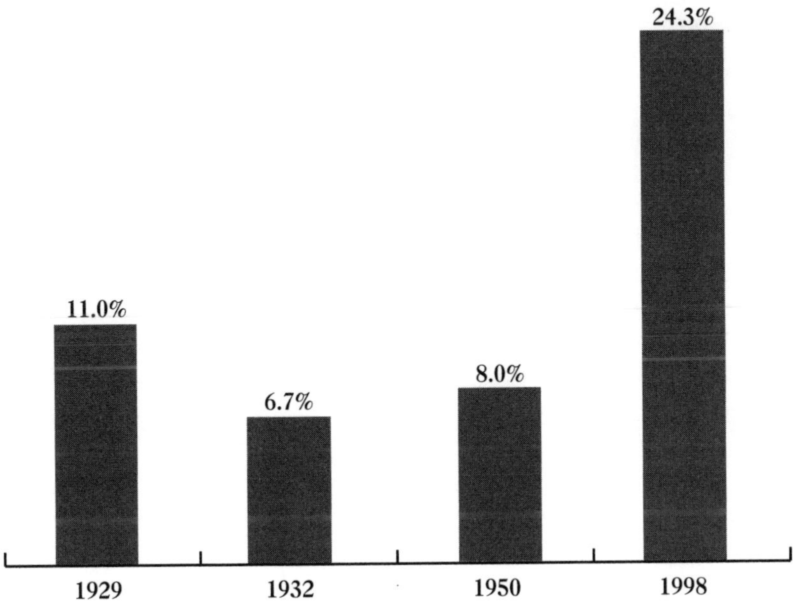

| 1929 | 1932 | 1950 | 1998 |
| 11.0% | 6.7% | 8.0% | 24.3% |

*Exports plus imports divided by GDP.

Source: National Income and Product Accounts

87

investments. A shift toward protectionism as occurred in 1929, or even in 1969, would put at risk the Great Prosperity that lies before us.

By contrast, increased world trade will make the dream of a global village a reality. For all of its inconveniences and challenges, open trade not only is an engine of growth and prosperity; it is also the best long-term defense against war and tyranny. That is why avoiding protectionist trade policies and achieving further reductions in the barriers to trade among people of different lands is the final key to the next ten-fold increase in the Dow over the next 21 years.

NOTES

1. David Ricardo, "On the Principles of Political Economy and Taxation," as cited in Douglas A. Irwin, *Against the Tide,* p. 90.

2. Jeffrey Sachs, "Nature, nurture and growth," *The Economist,* June 14, 1997, pp. 19–22. That higher growth rate was identified after controlling statistically for such other factors as physical geography, government policy, and demographic change.

3. See Thomas Sowell, "Race, culture and equality," *Forbes,* October 5, 1998, pp. 144–149.

4. Ibid.

5. Jude Wanniski, *The Way the World Works.* Morristown, NJ: Polyconomics, Inc., 1989, pp. 139–149.

6. Ibid., p. 149.

7. Douglas A. Irwin, "Changes in U.S. tariffs: The Role of import prices and commercial policies," *The American Economic Review,* September 1998, pp. 1015–1027.

8. Victor A. Canto et al., "The Effects of Trade Restrictions on the U.S. Economy," A. B. Laffer Associates, March 1982, pp. 1–6.

9. Ibid.

10. Ibid.

11. Jackie Calmes, "Despite Buoyant Economic Times Americans Don't Buy Free Trade," *The Wall Street Journal,* December 10, 1998, p. A10.

PART II

THE MAP

At any moment in history, there are always secular or historical forces that are guiding and shaping the direction of economic and social policies. Sometimes, those forces are in conflict, producing turbulence and uncertainty. At this time in history, we can identify five historical forces that are aligned, each pointing to a positive environment for economic growth and financial markets. They are

- The end of the 80-year emergency
- The aging of the baby boomers
- The technological revolution
- The spread of freedom
- The emergence of global competition among governments

As these forces unleash social and political pressures for changes in tax, monetary and trade policies, they will shape the direction of the economy and financial markets. When you add them up—take into account their cumulative effect—you can see before us a Great Prosperity.

We turn now to examine each of these historical forces to better answer with conviction the central question of this book: Dow 100,000, fact or fiction?

CHAPTER FIVE

THE PEACE DIVIDEND— AN OPEN ROAD AHEAD

THE END OF THE COLD WAR IS THE FIRST HISTORICAL FORCE WE MUST CONSIDER. It brings to a close a period of 80 years in which we as a country have been in a state of emergency. The end of this 80-year emergency points toward lower tax rates, stable prices, and freer trade, increasing our conviction that Dow 100,000 by the year 2020 will prove to be fact.

Think of it, ever since World War I, we have been faced with one emergency after another. Yes, there was a brief respite in the 1920s. But that gave way to the economic emergency of the 1930s. The Depression was followed by the second World War. Then, no sooner had we celebrated victory in Europe and Japan than we were faced with a new enemy, the Soviet Union, the challenge of communism, and the threat of nuclear war. From our vantage point in 1999, it may seem obvious that we would prevail in the Cold War, but in the aftermath of World War II, when the Russians built the Iron Curtain that divided Europe and closed off the Allied land routes to Berlin, it was far from obvious what should be done, to say nothing about who would prevail. The Berlin airlift started what would prove to be a 43-year war that was shaped and constrained by the threat of nuclear annihilation.

The Cold War was punctuated by conflicts and crises that kept the country on a near wartime footing. The Korean Conflict marked the beginning of the 1950s; the Cuban missile crisis brought the world to the brink of nuclear war at the beginning of the 1960s. Vietnam plunged America into a protracted, debilitating conflict more than halfway around the world that would reverberate through American politics and policies for the next 20 years. With antiwar sentiment strong, the United States began what amounted to unilateral disarmament in the late 1970s, but the Soviet Union increased its strategic forces and arguably had achieved nuclear superiority by the early 1980s. The United States responded with its own military buildup, which included the deployment of new nuclear-armed Pershing and cruise missiles in Europe, and began the development of a strategic defense that offered the chance of at least deterring a missile attack on U.S. cities and military installations.

But then it ended. The Soviet Union collapsed and sued for peace. Its empire disintegrated into a loose confederation of independent states. The wall that divided Berlin was bulldozed in 1989, and the Iron Curtain that had divided Europe fell. On September 27, 1991, President George Bush ordered U.S. strategic forces to "stand down." For nearly 24 years to the day, the United States had had its nuclear-armed forces on 24-hour alert, ready to deliver a retaliatory attack against the Soviet Union within 15 minutes. I remember hearing the President announce the end of the nuclear alert and feeling a weight that I had not even been aware of lifted from my shoulders.

Today, no nation poses a comparable military threat to the United States. We continue to live in a dangerous world. A rogue state or terrorist organization might be able to inflict great damage upon our shores, but the United States is the sole superpower. There exists no military power that can threaten our existence.

The Road to Change

The end of the Cold War marks the end of an 80-year period in which our lives have been dominated by national emergencies. The end of this era of emergencies is important because the presence and disappearance of emergencies unleash powerful social forces that shape the world in which we live.

During emergencies, it is natural to centralize power in the hands of a few who are in a position not only to make decisions, but also to marshal the resources necessary to respond to the emergency. Emergencies are thus "elitist" periods.

By elitist, I do not mean to imply anything negative. Rather, I am describing a social phenomenon identified by Jeffrey Bell in his book, *Populism and Elitism.*

- Elitism is a period in which we trust a few people to make decisions for everyone.
- It implies pessimism about people's ability to make decisions for themselves.

Elitism appears spontaneously during emergencies. Imagine, for example, that you are listening to a radio and an announcer interrupts the program to warn against a tornado approaching your neighborhood. This disembodied voice tells you to take shelter. And you do! You delegate to that person incredible power over your life.

In January 1996, for example, the Northeast was hit by a blizzard. Snow was piled up in drifts five feet high and higher. Roads were blocked. Cars were being abandoned. The governor of New Jersey, Christie Whitman, declared a "State of Emergency" and told us not to drive our cars, and to otherwise stay off the highways. We obeyed her. We trusted that she had the information necessary to make that decision on behalf of all of us.

In a similar fashion, we delegated enormous and ever increasing power to the Federal government during the past 80 years of emergencies. Under the circumstances, it was right and proper to do so. During the 1930s, with economic life at risk, we waived most of the Constitutional restrictions that had contained government spending and created a powerful Federal government to guide the economy. During World War II, with the future of our nation at risk, the Federal government took 44 percent of all the goods and services produced by the entire economy to wage war, and the American people were grateful for the victories produced by that combination of leadership and resources.

During the Cold War, it was right and natural to maintain a strong central government. It is unlikely that the United States would have prevailed against the Soviet Union had we relied on town meetings for making all our decisions. We trusted a few people in Washington to make decisions for all of us. They did, and we won.

But once an emergency recedes, *populism spontaneously appears.*

- Populism is a period in which we trust people to make decisions about their own lives.
- It implies pessimism about the elites' ability to make decisions for everyone else.

Once the danger of the tornado has passed, can you imagine obeying a radio announcer who told you to stop whatever you were doing and go immediately to the basement or some other shelter because he or she thought it was a good idea? Of course not. As emergencies recede, we resist big government or any other central authority telling us what to do or how to lead our lives.

In the same way, once the snow was cleared, and the State of Emergency lifted, Governor Whitman and the people of New Jersey would never have entertained the notion that the role of the governor should be to tell people when and where to drive their cars. In both cases, the power to make decisions that affect people's lives was restored to the individual.

As the 80-year emergency recedes, this same fundamental shift in power from the elites to the individual is taking place. Populism is becoming the central political force of our time. The impulse is not antigovernment so much as it is a shift in the desire of ordinary people to wrest power from the elites and gain more power over their own lives. Revolution is not in the air. Rather, we have set about a period of trial and error as we begin to design anew the role of government from a central to a more benign force in our society.

The almost unbounded faith in the power of government that existed after World War II and throughout the Cold War has been called into question by the experience of the past 20 years, not only in the United States, but throughout the world. Where elites had the greatest power, in the Soviet Union, Eastern Europe, and Communist China, the economic results were uniformly inferior to nations where the powers of elites were checked by democratic political processes. More shocking was the environmental degradation that was tolerated, and in some cases perpetrated, by governments within the Soviet block.

In the United States, the faith in government has also been challenged by practical experience. The prosperity of the 1960s disintegrated into the Great Inflation of the 1970s. Federal jobs programs of the late 1970s failed to create prosperity.

Today, our world is being reshaped by populist forces. A 1997 survey of American social beliefs by the Pew Research Center,[1] for example, found that

- Nearly two-thirds of respondents believe that government is usually inefficient and wasteful.
- Nearly two-thirds also agreed with the statement that "the Federal Government controls too much of our daily lives." That result was down from its peak of 69 percent in 1994, but was still up from the 58 percent of respondents in 1987.
- Only 61 percent agreed that government should take care of people who can't take care of themselves, down from a high of 74 percent in 1988.

Even as confidence in government wanes, self-confidence is on the rise:

- Only one-third of respondents agreed with the statement that "success in life is pretty much determined by forces outside our control." That was down 8 percentage points from its high registered in 1988 and 1993, and the lowest level recorded by the poll since its inception in 1987.
- Only one-third of respondents agreed that "hard work offers little guarantee of success," down from a high of 45 percent registered in 1992.
- A record 71 percent of respondents agreed that "as Americans we can always find a way to solve our problems and get what we want," up from a low of 59 percent in 1993.

Populism and Economic Policy

Populism is now one of the most powerful forces animating our political system. The populist political impulse is pointing all three of the key signposts in a positive direction, and is part of the foundation in our conviction that we are headed to Dow 100,000.

This question should help you see why I say this:

If you want more control over your own life, do you want higher or lower tax rates?

Lower tax rates, because, in the first order, they allow us to keep more of the money that we earn. But even more important, lower tax rates reduce the barriers between us and our fellow human beings. Instinctively, we know that lower tax rates increase the possibility for us to take care of ourselves and our families. They imply optimism over our ability to make decisions about our own lives.

The 1980 election of Ronald Reagan as President can now be seen as the first break toward populism. President Jimmy Carter had deregulated the trucking and airline industries. President Reagan took the radical step of deregulating oil prices and the energy industry. The elites predicted energy shortages and $100-per-barrel oil. Instead, gas lines disappeared even as prices came down.

The Reagan tax cuts reduced personal income tax rates 25 percent across the board. The elites predicted rising budget deficits, soaring inflation and interest rates, rising unemployment, and economic calamity. They were right about the deficit, but wrong about everything else. Instead, on January 1, 1983, the day the tax cuts began to take effect, the economy began what was then the longest peacetime expansion in the nation's history. And the stock market began its historic, ten-fold rise from 1000 to 10,000 on the Dow.

In 1988, George Bush was elected President on his "read my lips" promise of "no new taxes." During his first two years, the Cold War was won and Iraq was thrown out of Kuwait. The United States was the undisputed leader of the world, and President Bush was the most popular President in history halfway through his first term. Two years later, he was defeated in his bid for reelection. His critical error: He broke his promise not to raise taxes.

That populist impulse also gave rise to the instrument of President Bush's defeat in the person of billionaire computer salesman and entrepreneur, Ross Perot. Perot was propelled into national politics when, in response to a question on the *Larry King Live* television show, he said he would run for President if the American people wanted him to. He told the American people that the country belonged to them and that the budget deficit was diminishing the future of their children. In spite of some poor decisions Perot inspired a grassroots uprising and won an astounding 19 percent of the popular vote. As a result, Bill Clinton was elected President.

President Clinton, who had promised to be a "New Democrat," quickly veered to the left. With control of both houses of Congress and the White House for the first time since President Jimmy Carter, the Democrats raised the top income-tax rates. Next, they declared a health-care crisis or emergency and moved to use the secret proceedings of a health-care task force to "solve the problem."

This was elitism writ large. In 1994, the Democrats were voted out of office in record numbers, and to almost everyone's surprise, the Republicans won control of both the House of Representatives and the Senate for the first time since 1954.

In the next two years, President Clinton charted a course to a middle ground between a Republican Party that too often seemed ready to use the power of government to impose its own, elitist ideas, and the left wing of his own party. It was, in all but name, a more populist political thrust. With his own reelection at risk, President Clinton defied the left wing of his party and some of his most ardent supporters and signed a landmark welfare-reform bill. The bill ended the Federal guarantee of welfare benefits and put limits on the length of time an individual may claim welfare benefits. Just as important, it devolved the centralized powers of the welfare state to the individual states.

All over the world, and in all areas of life, individuals are gaining power over their own lives. In the United States, the populist impulse goes beyond taxes, monetary policy, and trade, and includes increased interest in religion, falling crime rates, and a move toward extending the right to choose a child's grammar or high school to all Americans, including those with the least amount of income. The populist impulse is a common thread. Those who embrace it achieve political success. Those politicians who fail to grasp its power lose their power. The implications of the end of the 80-year emergency and the populist forces it is unleashing for taxes, inflation, and trade are immediate and powerful.

Populism and Taxes

During war, during emergencies, people give willingly and voluntarily of their time and resources. But during normal times, people choose to be more self-reliant. When wars end, tax rates typically are reduced. Governments have less need for the money. More important, they have less legitimacy in taking the money. Lower tax rates give people more control over their own lives. During World War I, for example, the top personal income tax rate reached a high of 77 percent. In the first year after the war's end, the top rate was cut to 73 percent. Within seven years of the war's end, it had been reduced to 25 percent.

Tax-rate reductions are a natural, inevitable consequence of the end of the Cold War. Federal tax receipts in fiscal year 1999 are now estimated to be

20.1 percent of GDP. That will be only the third time in history, and the first time since 1945, that Federal receipts will exceed 20 percent of the nation's output. But even this understates the case for tax reductions. State and local tax receipts, too, have been on the rise, propelled in part by the demands of federally mandated programs and, in recent years, by the increase in employment, incomes, and economic activity that have expanded the tax base. Total state and local receipts were under 9.2 percent of GDP in 1960, rose to a peak of 14.0 percent in 1976, fell below 13 percent in 1979, and bottomed out at 12.5 percent in 1988. By 1995, however, they were back to 13.75 percent of GDP. Taken together, total Federal, state, and local receipts were more than 32 percent of GDP in 1998.

The United States has been at peace since 1991, but instead of tax rates being cut, as they were after World War I, the top tax rate on personal income (including the Medicare tax) has been increased to 42.5 percent from 28 percent. The justification was to balance the budget.

Now, the budget has been more than balanced. The tax increases helped, but of far greater importance have been reductions in defense spending, a constraint on overall spending increases, and better than expected economic growth. At the beginning of fiscal year 1998, for example, the Congressional Budget Office was projecting a $35 billion increase in the Federal deficit to $57 billion. Instead, the government achieved a record $70 billion surplus. *That was a $127 billion swing in just 12 months.*

More important, the fiscal year 1998 surplus marked the end of a 29-year string of Federal budget deficits and brings to an end an era in which "the deficit" has virtually dominated the entire discourse and debate over the direction of government policy. The prospect of continued $100 billion-plus surpluses has made inevitable a power struggle to articulate a new "point of the game" for government policy.

Achieving a political consensus on the point of the game for a Federal government running hundreds of billions of dollars of surpluses is pivotal to the outlook for the Great Prosperity. Once accepted, the point of the game acts as the polar star around which all players develop strategies and goals and against which all results are measured.

Pay attention to this debate over what to do with the surplus. It is about far more than money. *The debate over what to do with the surplus is a fundamental struggle over the balance of power between the public and private sectors in the United States.*

The bipartisan agreement to use the surplus to first reform Social Security is acting as an interim point of the game, but the Federal surpluses are almost sure to swamp the effort to hold back the tide of general tax relief. In the Clinton budget presented to the Congress in January 1999, for example, the Federal surplus was projected to be $79 billion in fiscal year 1999 and $117 billion in fiscal year 2000. A year before, the Administration had projected a surplus of less than $10 billion in both fiscal years, and that was before the Congress and the President had approved $23 billion in "emergency spending" in 1999.

But even these projections are based on relatively conservative assumptions. Consider the following:

- At the beginning of 1998, the cumulative surplus for the 10 years ending 2008 was projected to be $655 billion.
- One year of better-than-expected-growth later, the cumulative surplus had jumped to $2.4 trillion, a $1.7 trillion increase in 12 months.

Even by Washington's standards, this is real money. What's more, these projections assume real, inflation-adjusted growth will slow to less than 2.5 percent a year. That is slower than the United States has grown for the 1-, 5-, 10-, 20-, and 50-year periods ending in 1998. Since 1926, through the Great Depression, World War II, Korea, Vietnam, the Cold War, the Great Inflation, the high-growth eighties, and the slow-growth early nineties, the U.S. economy has grown an average of 3.4 percent a year.

The Federal government is lowballing the growth estimate and understating the surplus. *The better-than-expected growth that lies ahead means larger-than-expected surpluses are in the offing.* Wartime levels of taxation with $100 billion-plus surpluses over and above what it takes to "save Social Security" are simply not sustainable in a democracy.

Some of the surplus will surely be used to reform and strengthen the Social Security system. Some will be used to fund existing and new Federal programs. Some of it has already been used for pork-barrel spending and to pay off a portion of the national debt.

The sheer magnitude of the surpluses will put before the American people a fundamental choice regarding the role of government in the years ahead. One possibility is that the American people will choose to turn over more of their money and more of the decisions about their lives and future well-being to government officials—elitism. The other is to claim some of the surplus as their own by insisting on tax-rate reductions, thereby increasing their power to make decisions about their own lives—populism.

History and current experience point to populism. Lower tax rates are on the way. The new point of the game for government will include using at least a portion of the peace dividend to increase the freedom and independence of the American people.

The push to reduce tax rates has already begun. In 1997, the tax bill that became law was the first designed to reduce the overall tax burden on the American people since the Reagan tax-cut bill of 1981 and the first to reduce tax rates since tax reform of 1986. But, with the exception of the capital-gains tax-rate reduction, most of that relief was in the form of targeted tax credits. The wartime level of tax rates was left in place. Across-the-board tax-rate relief will give to all Americans who, after all, funded the Cold War and now deserve to share in the fruits of their victory, a share of the peace dividend.

Already, we can see the populist impulse lead to tax-rate relief at the state and local levels. Since 1995, at least 25 states have cut taxes each year. In 1997, state and local governments were projecting a $37 billion *surplus* for the 1998 fiscal year. Nonetheless, expenditure growth remained under control, clearing the way for 25 states to reduce personal income and corporate taxes for fiscal year 1998 by $4.4 billion.

Thanks to the stronger-than-expected economy, state revenues were 3.6 percent above expectations. That has led 35 states to pass another $7.5 billion in tax cuts for fiscal year 1999, mostly in the form of lower personal income-tax rates. More cuts are already being planned for 2000.

The populist impulse is also forcing a 180-degree turn in fiscal policies among America's cities. The mayor of Detroit, Dennis W. Archer, says his number-one priority is to reduce that city's income tax. And, the liberal legislative branch of New York City government is considering a broad-based tax relief as well.

Continued strong growth in the economy offers the prospects of additional tax-rate reductions at the state and local levels as well. Taxes are coming down. If your state is not planning tax-rate reductions, start asking why. Politicians who stand in the way of this historical phenomenon will lose power, and those who understand it and translate it into sound fiscal policy will continue to gain power.

As tax rates come down, economic growth will remain strong, the outlook for corporate profits will improve, and the stock market will head higher.

Populism and Price Stability

The populist impulse can also be seen in the successful fight against inflation in the United States and Europe.

To see this, ask yourself if you have more power over your own life during periods of stable or unstable prices.

Clearly, the answer is stable prices.

Stable prices are to their core a populist achievement. They shift power away from the elites on Wall Street to the ordinary people who live and work on Main Street. Stable prices shift power away from those who can invent and manage the sophisticated investment and hedging strategies that are necessary in an unstable price environment. Stable prices shift power toward ordinary people. These are individuals who are ready and able to invest their savings, who in a stable price environment can build their business, take care of their careers, and tend to the everyday needs of their families and communities, but who often lack the specialized skills to cope with the vagaries of advanced financial strategies required by unstable prices.

Price stability gives us more control over our own lives. It creates more room for personal initiative, more opportunity for individuals to prepare for their own retirements through current savings instead of relying on government programs that are underfunded and problematic.

During wars, the populist demand for stable prices gives way to the emergency need to finance the war. Monetary standards are abandoned. Inflation accelerates. The channeling of vast resources to support troops in the field and munitions that produce no consumer satisfaction creates shortages.

The Revolutionary War produced hyperinflation in the United States, giving rise to the phrase "It's not worth a Continental" to refer to something that was as worthless as a Continental dollar. The War of 1812 saw consumer prices rise 47 percent. During the Civil War, consumer prices rose 81 percent. During World War I, the CPI more than doubled, and between 1940 and 1948, the CPI soared 73 percent.

The Cold War, which stretched more than 40 years, contributed to the Great Inflation of the 1970s. The United States began to break its promise to maintain the convertibility of the dollar into gold in 1968. Between then and 1997, consumer prices rose nearly five-fold.

Prices fell after the War of 1812, the Civil War, and World War I. In each of these cases, the rate of exchange between the dollar and an ounce

101

of gold was either maintained or, in the case of the Civil War, restored. As the wartime shortages and fear disappeared, the buying power of gold tended to revert to its former levels. Because the buying power of the dollar was linked directly to gold, its buying power, too, reverted to its former levels. That, of course, meant that prices had to fall to their former levels as well.

Prices, however, did not fall after World War II. Instead, they rose to finish the adjustment to the 41 percent devaluation of the dollar that had occurred in 1934. The creation of the Breton Woods agreement then produced stability at this higher price level to the United States and most of the rest of the industrialized world.

When wars end, societies find their way back to a stable price environment. It has taken 17 years and the skills of two great Federal Reserve Chairmen, Paul Volcker and Alan Greenspan, to restore price stability after the Great Inflation of the 1970s. We have yet to reestablish a monetary standard that would codify and perpetuate a stable price environment. But the populist impulse stands as a powerful force in favor of maintaining the stable price environment that was achieved in 1998. It was this accomplishment, as much as any other, that signaled the beginning of a Great Prosperity.

Stable prices will also reinforce the pressure to reduce tax rates by increasing the Federal budget surplus in the years ahead. Stable prices bring lower interest rates. Lower interest rates reduce government spending directly by lowering the interest cost of the debt. The Federal government is the biggest debtor of all, with about $5.5 trillion in debt. *Each one-percentage point reduction in interest rates in due course reduces Federal government expenditures and increases the budget surplus by approximately $55 billion a year.*

Second, stable prices permit increased economic growth. Increased growth increases the size of the tax base, increasing tax revenues and reducing the demands for federal spending on unemployed workers. That, too, will tend to increase the budget surplus above its projected levels.

We have just begun to experience how this combination of stable prices, lower interest rates, and better-than-expected growth produces huge increases in Federal, state, and local surpluses. As we will discuss in the next chapter, using these surpluses to reform Social Security may prove to be one of the biggest tax cuts in American history. Regardless, the surpluses that are now building will prove to be so vast that across-the-board tax reductions in tax rates are all but inevitable in the years ahead.

Finally, the trend toward lower interest rates is associated with higher stock prices relative to earnings, what portfolio managers and analysts call price/earnings ratio. In all three ways—increased growth, lower tax rates made possible by bigger Federal surpluses, and lower interest rates—stable prices will contribute to the stock market's climb to 100,000 on the Dow.

Populism and Trade

The end of the Cold War has also increased the opportunities to trade. The elimination of the Iron Curtain which, in Winston Churchill's memorable words, ran "from Stettin in the Baltic to Trieste in the Adriatic,"[2] reopened the old trade routes between Eastern and Western Europe. Goods and services are once again flowing between Germany and Poland, France, and the Czech and Slovak republics. China, too, has become far more open to trade with the United States, Europe, and the rest of the world.

The economic gains so far are modest. But the direction is clear. More trade will open new opportunities to sell and buy, invest and produce. U.S. exports to Eastern Europe, the former Soviet Union, and China in 1998, for example, totaled $21.7 billion. That is 96 percent above where it was in 1991. In the decade ahead, the volume of trade is sure to continue to grow as the incomes of the people who live in the former Communist bloc rise and we find more opportunities to enter into mutually beneficial exchanges.

The longer-term benefits, however, are in many respects immeasurable. As the economies of our former enemies become integrated with our own, as our commercial contacts lead to an increase in shared economic, cultural, and social interests, the risks of armed conflict, of world war, will recede. Small local wars, such as NATO's action against Yugoslavia, and the military action that pushed Iraq out of Kuwait, may flair from time to time. However, the thought of a European war on the scale of either of the world wars seems remote, if not anachronistic. That means that much of the money and resources spent on military hardware and uniformed personnel can be redirected toward satisfying consumers the world round. That, too, will contribute to the Great Prosperity and the higher stock prices that lie before us.

Global Populism

The end of the Cold War is ending a state of emergency, not only in the United States, but throughout most of the world. The populist political impulse, therefore, should be evident in other societies. And it is.

In Britain, for example, the Labour Party, the party of the left, won control of Parliament in May 1997 for the first time since the Conservatives had been led to victory by Margaret Thatcher in 1979. They won by eschewing their elitist rhetoric of nationalizing large segments of the economy and, instead, appealed to the populist impulse.

Under Thatcher, the conservative Party had reduced Britain's personal-income tax rates to among the lowest in Europe, with a top rate of 40 percent. With those lower tax rates, the U.K. economy had been one of the fastest growing in Europe, with the unemployment rate, at 5.9 percent, among the lowest in Europe. Thatcher's successor, John Major, left the personal tax rates unchanged, but engaged in a series of other revenue-raising measures in part, he promised, to balance the government's budget. During the election, Labour attacked the Conservative party for raising taxes 22 times, which included extending the value-added tax to heating oil, directly increasing the cost of maintaining a warm home. Yet, they claimed, the national debt had doubled under Prime Minister John Major.

Education and economic growth with low inflation were at the top of the Labour Party's "contract." They promised to keep spending within the Conservative Party's budget and not to increase the basic or top rates of income tax. In addition, they promised to work toward reducing by half the lowest personal income tax rate of 20 percent, which currently takes effect on incomes as low as $6,200. Labour justified this potential tax rate by pointing out that as individuals in this tax bracket increase their income, they not only have to pay increased taxes but also lose welfare benefits. When the reduction in welfare benefits is added to their tax payments, these individuals face *effective* tax rates of between 60 percent and 80 percent. Tax-rate relief on lower incomes, therefore, was advocated not for the sake of redistributionist "fairness," but as part of an overall plan to increase labor-participation rates among those now on the dole—giving people more control over their own life: populism.

The commitment to economic growth and price stability was reinforced when in its first initiative, the new government gave the Bank of England independence to operate monetary policy free from direct political control, making clear the government's commitment to a sound currency and a low-inflation monetary policy. In their first budget, the Labour Party *reduced* the corporate income-tax rate to 31 percent from 33 percent, while repealing tax credits on dividend income.

Weeks after the British election, the French electorate overthrew its government for the second time in four years. While heads did not roll, there was an extraordinary shift in power from the Conservative Coalition, which had been swept into office in 1993 and had won the presidency in 1995. The day before the election, the Conservative Coalition held an 80-percent majority in Parliament. After the election, they were reduced to a minority party, with 45 percent of the seats. What had the Conservative Coalition done to deserve such a crushing defeat? They had failed to keep their promise to reduce France's high unemployment and to reduce taxes.

Instead, they had raised taxes and had attempted to reduce spending in order to meet the criteria for membership in the new common European currency. When they promised more of the same austerity policies, the Socialist promise of pursuing jobs and economic growth proved an irresistible alternative. Although the Socialist's policies, including more government employment and a hike in the minimum wage, are unlikely to be successful, they at least articulated a more populist goal.

Democracy's great strength is not found in the electoral process's ability to find great leaders. Rather, the genius of democracy is in its ever present ability to upset the existing political order by "throwing the bums out" without resorting to violence or bloodshed.

Since these elections, the British and French stock markets have been among the strongest in the world.

Nowhere is the shift from elitism to populism more evident than in the former Soviet Union, which has devolved into its constituent states, and in Eastern Europe, most of which has embraced democracy. Economic crisis in Russia now threatens to reestablish centralized authority across its vast territory, but in Eastern Europe, the shift toward democratic institutions and market economic policies made possible by the end of the Cold War has produced rising living standards and growing confidence in democracy.

The Creation of the Euro

Europeans are also leading the rest of the world back to a stable price environment. In Western Europe, successful creation of the euro in

1999 increased the domain of price stability from the United States and Germany to most of Europe. At first glance, centralizing power in a new pan-European central bank might appear to be a shift toward elitism. However, this action eliminated the power of 11 national central banks to manipulate their respective currencies and interest rates. In addition, the new central bank was modeled on the German Bundesbank, known for its success in maintaining a stable price environment. Gaining price stability is, itself, a powerful populist impulse.

The creation of a single currency for the 11 member nations of Euroland radically simplifies the complexity of doing business on a pan-European basis. To get a sense of what it had been like, imagine that each of the 11 Federal Reserve Banks in the United States issued their own currency, which was allowed to float relative to the dollars issued by the other Reserve Banks. A trip from New York to Philadelphia would require exchanging currency. At any moment, payroll and other expenses associated with doing business in the various Federal Reserve Districts could change overnight. Your company would have to arrange to actively hedge its currency exposure across 11 different regions of the country.

The creation of the euro also reduces the barriers to trade among Europeans and thereby increases the power of individuals to shop for the best deal. One of the surprises that greeted the euro's creation was the disparity in prices on consumer goods that had been at least partially hidden by the presence of different currencies. In December 1998, just before the creation of the euro, *The New York Times* reported that a pair of Levi jeans sold for 75.4 euros in Germany, but only 56.5 euros in Italy, a difference of $22. At the same time, a Canon Prima Super 135-mm camera that sold for 300.3 euros in France sold for only 202 euros in Germany, a difference of $124.[3] As the use of the euro becomes part of everyday life of Europe, we can expect consumers to benefit from the ability to more easily compare prices across national borders.

As compelling as these arguments are from the point of view of economic efficiency, they miss the emotional aspect of a common currency. People everywhere want what we in the United States have only recently attained, money that provides a stable price environment and low interest rates. The common currency received public support because Europeans intuitively grasped that it made both their current and future financial situation more secure.

The Fall of "Crony Capitalism"

Faith in the wisdom of the elites and the power of government has long been supported by cultural traditions in Asia. But even in this part of the world, the populist forces are at work. Consider this: The Great Depression of the 1930s was widely blamed on a failure of capitalism. By contrast, the Asian currency crisis of 1998 has given the whole notion of a market economy run by government bureaucrats a bad name. What was once cited as the source of Asia's economic miracle is now disparagingly called "crony capitalism"; that is, the abuse of government power by the elites. Democracies with more than token oppositions have now taken hold in Japan, Taiwan, and South Korea.

There are few places in the world where confidence in the elites's ability to manage the economy was as great as it was in Japan. That confidence was widely shared by elites in the United States as well, but, after nine years of poor economic performance, that confidence is being shaken.

In Japan, the Liberal Democratic Party has lost the absolute hold on power it held during the post-World War II era. In the United States, we no longer hear of the powers and prowess of "Japan, Inc." as a reason to increase the regulatory power of the Federal government or to justify an expansion in government to "manage trade." Those were popular themes in the early 1990s, both among politicians and some leaders of American business. Today, they are widely discredited. Instead, in early 1999, the Japanese government passed significant and permanent Reaganesque across-the-board tax-rate reductions on personal and corporate incomes as well as capital gains realized from land transactions. Populism finally appears.

In China, where political freedoms are severely limited, populist forces are gaining ground. State ownership of enterprises is being transferred to individual shareholders, and, in 1997, the government announced a unilateral reduction in tariffs by an average of 26 percent. Democratic institutions, though limited in scope, are also taking root.

Global populism is bringing with it lower tax rates, increased efforts to provide stable prices, and freer trade. These are the preconditions to a historic increase in global prosperity as well. International equity

107

markets will move to historic highs based on an expansion in their economies and a rise in their corporate profits, throughout the world.

U.S. equity markets, too, will rise on the power of an expanding global economy. U.S. corporations will have increased opportunities to do business, serve customers, and increase profits. This increased economic activity will also feed back into the U.S. economy, adding strength to domestic growth as well. Above-average growth and rising profits are the bedrock of rising stock prices.

The Outlook

The end of the Cold War does not guarantee the Great Prosperity. But the populist forces it has unleashed, and the increased opportunities for trade, increase the odds in its favor. The end of the 80 years of emergency have, if you will, created a more open road to 100,000 on the Dow. The failures of government and the success of the private sector in expanding opportunity and incomes have increased pessimism about the elites's ability to make decisions on behalf of the individual and have increased the trust people have in their ability to make decisions about their own lives.

When asked, "How much do you think you can trust government to do what is right?" about three-quarters of Americans in the late 1950s and early 1960s said "just about always" or "most of the time." That ratio plunged to less than 25 percent in the late 1970s, but rebounded to more than 40 percent during the Reagan era. During the last five years, however, less than one in four Americans say they trust the Federal government to do what is right "most of the time."

During the wage and price controls of the 1970s and the defense buildup of the 1980s, an expanding, more intrusive government was crowding out the private sector. Today, the private sector is crowding out government. No one is calling for a government jobs program. Just the reverse. Since the end of the Cold War in 1991, the private sector has increased its share of the economy to 83 percent from 79 percent. That is worth $300 billion of private-sector activity. At the end of 1998, 74 percent of the work force was employed in the private sector compared to 69 percent in 1991.

Government will continue to lose market share. Its power over our everyday lives is in decline. The end of the Cold War and, with it, the end of an 80-year emergency is bringing forth lower tax rates, stable prices, and increasing trade, not only in the United States, but throughout the world. The implicit increase in freedom is fundamental to creating the Great Prosperity and making Dow 100,000 a fact by the year 2020.

NOTES

1. "American Social Beliefs 1997–1987," The Pew Research Center, April 20, 1998.
2. Compton's Encyclopedia Online; http://comptons2.aol.com/encyclopedia/ARTICLES/01056-A.html
3. Edmund L. Andrews, "Sticker Shocks in Euro Land," *The New York Times*, December 27, 1998, Section 3, p. 1.

THE BOOMERS—
THE ACCELERATOR

In the United States, the end of the 80-year emergency is being amplified by the aging of the baby boomers. There are few things that are as predictable as demographic trends and few forces as powerful as the economic activities and concerns of the baby boomers.

The boomers number nearly 80 million, or 30 percent of the U.S. population. They were born between 1946 and 1964. In 1999, the youngest boomers are age 35; the oldest, 53.

One consequence of the aging of the boomers is a dramatic increase in the average productivity of the overall work force. When the boomers were young and just entering the labor market, their skills were undeveloped. As they piled into the lower end of the work force, their sheer numbers dragged down the overall average increase in productivity. In 1970, the boomers accounted for 22 percent of the work force. By 1980, that had grown to 51 percent. During this period, productivity as measured by output per man-hour in manufacturing increased by a paltry 2.6 percent per year. Productivity for the overall economy, including services, advanced at only 1.8 percent per year. Both were significantly below the average of the prior 20 years.

Today, however, the boomers are in their most productive years and make up 48 percent of the work force. Partly as a result, productivity improvements are soaring. Since 1995, productivity increases in manufacturing have averaged 4.4 percent, and for the entire economy, including the hard-to-measure service industry, output per man-hour is now increasing at a 2.4-percent annual rate.

Increased productivity alone contributes to higher living standards and a general increase in prosperity. As our productivity increases, our capacity to produce satisfied customers also increases. The result is a rise in income. Businesses participate by producing more goods and increasing sales. Profits rise, leading to higher stock prices.

What makes the aging of the boomers even more important, however, is the simple fact that ever since they were born, their concerns have dominated the American culture. When the boomers began to appear in the late 1940s, suburbs were built to house the millions of newly formed families. Dr. Benjamin Spock wrote a book for their mothers, a best seller, which guided an entire generation of child rearing.

In the 1950s, the boomers were captivated by rock-'n-roll, epitomized by the first, partially censored appearance of Elvis Presley on the Ed Sullivan show. The established order was appalled, even as rock-'n-roll took over one AM radio station after another. Meanwhile, the boomers' parents continued to move to the suburbs. They built the schools necessary to educate their children as school enrollments increased 52 percent between 1950 and 1960. During the 1950s, governments began to build modern freeways with the goal of easing the drive from those suburbs to the office complexes in the center cities.

In the 1960s, it was the Beatles and the Beach Boys, which gave way to the beginning of the social revolutions that were to come in the next decade. College enrollments surged, and second-level state colleges became regional universities in their own right. In the 1970s, it was the antiwar movement, drugs, and the sexual revolution as the boomers came of age. The real-estate boom set off by the boomers' demand for housing and office space remade the skylines of virtually every city in America, while at the same time the center of economic power shifted from center cities to suburbia and their mega malls.

In the 1980s, the boomers were known as yuppies, with their taste for fast money and conspicuous consumption. They gave birth to a whole new industry in a garage near San Francisco with the creation of the first Apple computer. The technological revolution was under way. Now, their concerns, and their abilities, moved to the forefront of the American economy.

In the 1990s, in ever greater numbers, they began having children, and their taste in cars went to minivans and Jeep Cherokees. Today, not only Ford, Chevrolet, and Plymouth focus on making sports-utility vehicles, but Lincoln, Lexus, Mercedes, and Cadillac have joined the ranks as well. Because of their sheer numbers, the concerns and desires of the baby boomers always show up as huge market opportunities, which inevitably are met. The economy literally is warped by the pull of the boomers' appetites.

What's up next for the boomers? Paying for their children's college education and getting ready for retirement.

The major obstacle in both cases: today's high marginal tax rates.

This is one reason the boomers are a political force that demands our attention.

A private-college education can cost $25,000 or more per year. That is what you have to pay. But to have that much money after tax, how much do you have to earn? This is similar to the calculation we did in Chapter 2 when we looked at how much you had to earn before taxes to get $10,000 into your contractor's pocket.

To calculate this number, we have to add up your Federal income-tax rate, the Medicare payroll tax, and, of course, state and local income taxes. If you earn a high income, then those three taxes are likely to add up to as much as 48 percent (39.6 percent, 2.9 percent, and 5.5 percent respectively) of your gross pay. That means to pay $25,000 to the college or university of your son's or daughter's choice, you would have to earn $48,077.

If the top tax rate were reduced to its tax-reform low of 28 percent, and state and local tax rates were cut to 4.1 percent, for an all-in marginal tax rate of 35 percent, the annual pretax cost would drop nearly $10,000, to $38,462.

The same can be said for putting money away for retirement. In order to save an extra $10,000 or $20,000, an individual in the highest Federal income-tax bracket has to earn an extra $19,000 to $38,000.

A study commissioned by Merrill Lynch indicates that the boomer generation has yet to get serious about building the assets they will need to retire. For every wunderkind who has become a millionaire by working for and owning stock in a high-tech company, there are a thousand or more who have barely gotten started. Although the strong returns in the stock market beginning in 1995 have helped, surveys indicate that average boomers would have to nearly triple their rate of savings to achieve a comfortable retirement.[1]

Moreover, many individuals are probably underestimating the amount of money they will need when they retire. Study after study demonstrates that the Social Security system is unlikely to keep its promise to pay the boomers the level of benefits currently being paid their parents when it's time for them to retire. The Social Security system is at risk because the boomers did not have enough children to maintain the system at its current level. In 1950, there were 16.5 workers for every Social Security beneficiary. By 1997, that had declined to 3.4 workers for every beneficiary. And, by the year 2030, that number is expected to fall to only two workers for every person drawing on the Social Security system.

In addition, many individuals are probably overestimating the amount of money they can safely withdraw from their nest egg each year without risking running out of money during their golden years. A study done by a team that I led at J. & W. Seligman & Co. Incorporated, for example, used a statistical analysis to examine financial-market returns for the entire 1950-through-1997 period to answer this question: What is the highest fixed dollar amount of money that can be withdrawn each year and increased for the prior year's inflation that will not deplete that money after 20 years at least 90 percent of the time? The answer: only 6 percent. That is, from $1 million invested in a mix of stocks, bonds, and cash, $60,000 per year. The initial withdrawal rate could be increased to $80,000 by introducing a process to automatically reduce withdrawals somewhat during down markets and could still produce a 90-percent probability of not running out of money over 20 years. (We will examine this research and strategy in Chapter 13.)

Let's put some numbers on this for you. Table 6–1 summarizes the assets you will need to produce various levels of initial income. With an 8-percent withdrawal, to take $50,000 in year one, for example, would require $625,000 in assets, while a $100,000 draw implies a need for at least $1,250,000 in *investable* assets.

Now, let's look at the amount of money you would need to invest each year even if you put 100 percent of your assets into stocks, and your investments returned 13.5 percent a year, the average annual return for the S&P 500 for the 1950–1998 period. If you are 50 years old and plan to retire in 15 years with $1 million more in financial assets than you have today, that implies you need to save nearly $24,000 a year (Table 6–2). By contrast, if you have five years to accumulate $1 million

TABLE 6–1 Assets vs. Retirement Income

Required Assets at Different Withdrawal Rates

Income	6%	7%	8%	9%	10%
$ 50,000	$ 833,333	$ 714,286	$ 625,000	$ 555,556	$ 500,000
$ 100,000	$ 1,666,667	$ 1,428,571	$ 1,250,000	$ 1,111,111	$ 1,000,000
$ 250,000	$ 4,166,667	$ 3,571,429	$ 3,125,000	$ 2,777,778	$ 2,500,000
$ 500,000	$ 8,333,333	$ 7,142,857	$ 6,250,000	$ 5,555,556	$ 5,000,000
$ 750,000	$12,500,000	$10,714,286	$ 9,375,000	$ 8,333,333	$ 7,500,000
$1,000,000	$16,666,667	$14,285,714	$12,500,000	$11,111,111	$10,000,000

TABLE 6–2 Required Investment to Reach Wealth Goal

				Wealth Goal			
	$250,000	**$500,000**	**$750,000**	**$1,000,000**	**$1,250,000**	**$2,500,000**	**$5,000,000**
				(Required Annual Investment)*			
5	$38,198	$76,396	$114,593	$152,791	$190,989	$381,978	$763,955
10	$13,247	$26,493	$ 39,740	$ 52,987	$ 66,234	$132,467	$264,935
15	$ 5,939	$11,879	$ 17,818	$ 23,757	$ 29,697	$ 59,393	$118,786
20	$ 2,913	$ 5,826	$ 8,738	$ 11,651	$ 14,564	$ 29,128	$ 58,256
25	$ 1,486	$ 2,973	$ 4,459	$ 5,945	$ 7,431	$ 14,863	$ 29,725
30	$ 773	$ 1,546	$ 2,319	$ 3,092	$ 3,865	$ 7,731	$ 15,462

Years to Retirement

*Note: Calculations based upon a 13.5% annual rate of return.

(assuming a 13.5 percent-per-year return) you need to save more than $152,000 per year.

The baby-boom generation is about to turn its attention to accumulating assets in anticipation of the day in which it will no longer be generating a paycheck.

For many boomers, this will be more than a wake-up call. This will be an alarm clock.

Making alimony payments and paying for fancy vacations are all issues, but they pale by comparison to the challenges of providing a college education for children and accumulating the assets for retirement. Both financial challenges are made even more difficult by high marginal-tax rates, which virtually double the cost. As the alarm clock goes off, the boomers will be focused as never before on reforming Social Security and reducing income-tax rates.

Boomers and Social Security

President Clinton's call to "put Social Security first" before any personal income tax-rate reductions has put Social Security reform at the top of the political agenda. The President's rhetorical flourish may have started as a political maneuver to save the budget surplus for increased spending, but it uncovered the boomers' gnawing concern that the promise of Social Security would be broken before their retirement years were over. The consequence is a bipartisan agreement to use the Federal budget surplus to reform and bolster the Social Security system.

The evolving debate over Social Security reform signals the possibility of one of the largest tax cuts in American history. There is little downside. Any reform that makes Social Security more reliable for the baby boomers will be viewed as a positive; but real reform, including partial privatization, would signal another move up on the road to Dow 100,000.

Here's why I say that:

My father and his generation rightly considered their Social Security payments as *"contributions."* The money he has received in exchange for those payments represent one of the best investments he could have made. In his day, Social Security was a good deal. It was not a barrier to commerce; it was an enticement to work.

By contrast, payments to Social Security by the boomers, to say nothing of the younger Generation Xers, are considered a *tax* because so little is expected in return. Even if Social Security were maintained in its present form, by some estimates, it is promising only a 2-percent rate of return. That is far below what the individual could receive if he or she invested directly in risk-free long-term government bonds, to say nothing of the historical long-term average returns earned by investing in the stock market. What's more, surveys show that most individuals below the age of 50 do not expect Social Security will be able to keep even this modest promise. According to one recent poll, 55 percent of registered voters have little if any confidence in Social Security's long-term financial stability.[2]

Because of both the reality and these perceptions, Social Security constitutes a major tax or tariff on employment. For anyone at or below the wage cap ($72,600 in 1999), payments made to the Social Security system by themselves and their employer represent an additional marginal tax rate of 12.4 percent. For those in the 15-percent tax bracket, that increases the *effective* marginal-tax rate to 27.4 percent, and for those in the 28-percent tax bracket, to 40.4 percent.

One proposal that is likely to be part of any reform is to use the current surpluses being generated by the Social Security payroll tax to finance a partial privatization of Social Security. According to the 1996 "Equitable Nest Egg Study," fully 69 percent of baby boomers support the idea of directing how their Social Security contributions are invested,[3] and in a fall 1998 poll of registered voters by Mark Penn, 61 percent of all respondents and 60 percent of Democrats favored investing a portion of their payroll taxes in personal savings accounts.[4]

Not surprisingly, partial privatization of Social Security is gaining bipartisan support. The allocation of a portion of the payroll tax to individually controlled accounts could be financed by the current Social Security surplus, which is equal to nearly 20 percent of current Social Security payroll taxes and growing.

Here is how it might work.

- Today's workers would be given the option of investing 2.5 percentage points of their Social Security payroll tax in a self-directed IRA. This would require no reduction of any kind in the benefits currently being paid to Social Security recipients.

- Anyone who selected this option would be paying less into the Social Security system, and would therefore get proportionately less in future benefits.

This change would enhance the solvency of the system and make future benefits more secure.

This combination of a reduction in the payroll tax and an increase in the future return on Social Security taxes paid would make Social Security a better deal. As Social Security becomes a better deal, it becomes less of a tax, and more of a forced savings plan that offers competitive rates of return.

Partial privatization alone would directly reduce the effective tax rate by 2.5 percentage points. Moreover, with future benefits now more secure, we might be willing voluntarily to pay a 3-percent payroll deduction for those benefits. Because individuals would be willing to pay this much for the future benefits, they would treat this portion of their payroll deduction not as a tax, but as a contribution or payment for future benefits much as they would pay for a fixed annuity contract. That change in perception would reduce the *effective* tax-rate another 3 percentage points for a combined payroll tax rate reduction of 5.5 percentage points. A tax-rate reduction of that magnitude is important. The income + payroll-tax rate on lower incomes would fall 25 percent, to 21.9 percent, from 27.4 percent. And, the income + payroll-tax rate on higher incomes would fall 17 percent, to 34.9 percent, from 40.4 percent.

Any additional steps that increased the expected returns on today's payroll deductions to Social Security would constitute additional reductions in effective personal income-tax rates.

It would be easy to underestimate the positive effects on the U.S. economy of such reductions in the effective Social Security tax rate. Today, the Social Security tax applies to each additional dollar earned by more than 90 percent of the labor force and to virtually 100 percent of those who are unemployed but who are seeking employment. It is also a barrier to married women, who might otherwise choose to be in the work force. In each case, the Social Security tax acts like a tariff, increasing the price the employer must pay while reducing the income the employee receives. In the case of the unemployed, this added cost reduces the demand for their work and, given what they receive after tax, their desire to work. Reducing this barrier to commerce would therefore contribute directly to increased economic growth, higher incomes, and higher living standards in the years ahead. Such a broadening and deepening of the tax base would, in addition, further enhance the solvency of the Social Security system and would thereby reduce the threat of future tax increases as well. Corporate profits would also rise on a crest of increased economic activity, propelling the stock market higher as well.

Moreover, partial privatization of the Social Security system would mean that virtually every working man or woman in America would become a member of the investing class. Call it stockholder populism. We can expect people to vote for their interests. If stockholder populism were to spread, the apparent dichotomy between capital and labor would begin to disappear. All who labored would also become owners of the means of production. That would represent a significant shift in power away from those who believe in government toward those who see the private sector as the source of income and wealth. Pitting the more numerous workers against the less numerous owners would be impossible. The notion of class warfare between labor and capital would become moot. Reducing the risk of such a conflict would also contribute to a positive, longer-term outlook for economic policy.

The Boomers and the Personal Income-Tax System

Even if Social Security is "saved," Social Security benefits alone were never designed to be the sole source of retirement income. The maximum annual benefit that could be received by a worker retiring at age 65 in 1999 was $16,476, and for a married couple, $24,714. The rule of thumb is that retirement income equal to 70 percent of pre-retirement income is necessary to maintain someone's standard of living. That means that while Social Security may be a meaningful supplement, private savings also are required to meet most people's retirement goals.

The challenge to building the wealth needed to finance retirement was made more difficult by the tax increases enacted under Presidents Bush and Clinton. These tax increases raised the top personal-income and Medicare tax rate to 42.5 percent, from 28 percent. Supposedly, these taxes were targeted at the "rich." Of course, really rich people do not need to save for retirement, since, by definition, they have already accumulated significant assets. Shocking as it may seem, these tax increases were not targeted at the "rich," that is, people who were already wealthy, at all. Instead, the Bush and Clinton tax increases were targeted at *high incomes*, regardless of an individual's wealth.

This fact is particularly important to baby boomers because they are rapidly approaching the 45-to-64 age bracket, their peak earning years. In the four years since 1995, the number of Americans in this age group has increased 7 million to 58 million. In the year 2000, there will be 3 million more people in the 45-to-64 age group. And, by the year 2010, this number will soar to 79 million people (Figure 6–1). Today, 5,000 baby boomers turned age 50, and another 5,000 will celebrate their fiftieth birthday tomorrow, and the day after, and the day after.

Based on my personal experience, I can tell you that as they do, they will begin to think more seriously about what it will take to retire than they ever have before. In fact, a recent study sponsored by Merrill Lynch

FIGURE 6–1   The Boomers Hit Middle Age (Population Ages 45–64)

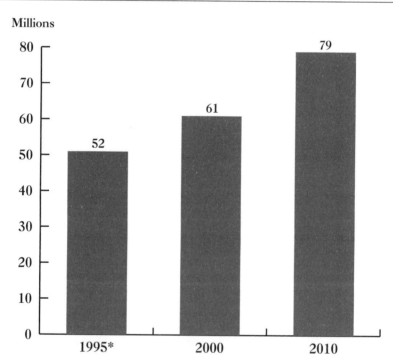

*Midpoint between July 1994 and July 1996.
Source: U.S. Census Bureau

indicates a significant pickup in the savings rate by the leading edge of the boomers who have just turned 50.[5]

As the boomers begin to confront the reality of what it takes to accumulate $500,000 or $1 million in the 10, 15, or 20 years they have before retiring, those high tax rates are going to breed a tax revolt. The slogan that today's high marginal tax rates are aimed at the rich will begin to ring hollow to the boomers. *From their vantage point, high tax rates on higher incomes will look more and more as if they are targeted right at them, just as they hit their peak earning years.*

This is a classical standoff between the boomers and the traditional political establishment, and it will only intensify in the years ahead.

Whom are you going to bet on?

I am betting that as soon as the Social Security reforms are complete, the baby boomers will begin to demand a reduction in today's high marginal-tax rates.

Those who will attempt to characterize this political impulse to lower the highest tax rate as greed will misinterpret the times. The fundamental force among the boomers will be self-defense, a primal desire to prepare for their retirement and for their financial security in a way that ensures their dignity and independence. The boomers' goal will be to accumulate capital now so that they will not have to rely on a promise made by government that has become subject to change. This desire will be a second, powerful social and political force that will reinforce the populist impulse toward lower tax rates.

In 1997, for example, the maximum capital-gains tax rate was reduced to 20 percent from 28 percent. And, a new tax-protected savings vehicle, the Roth IRA, was made available to those with less than $100,000 in income. Investments in the Roth IRA—up to $2,000 per year—are not tax deductible as they are in a traditional IRA. However, the returns on the investments inside the Roth IRA—capital gains, dividend-and-interest income—are free from all Federal income taxes. For someone in the 28-percent tax bracket, that increases the after-tax return on his or her investments from 72 percent to 100 percent of the pretax return, an increase of 39 percent.

Reduction in the capital-gains tax rate and creation of the Roth IRA in the 1997 tax bill are just the beginning of changes that will make it easier for the individuals to save money for their retirements. In the years ahead, watch for

- Increased deductions to 401(k)s, now limited to $10,000 a year

- Expansion of the Roth IRA to higher incomes
- Across-the-board tax-rate reductions and simplification of the tax code

Those who are saying that such tax cuts are not in the cards are ignoring the historical forces that underlie today's political debates. Polls, too, show the latent desire for tax relief. All that is missing is a political leader who can link such tax reductions to the longer-term concerns of the baby boomers, in particular, and the American people, in general.

A landmark poll by *Reader's Digest* in October 1995 points the way.[6] Although four years old, the poll of a cross-section of 1,015 Americans, conducted by the Roper Center for Public Opinion Research at the University of Connecticut, revealed a remarkable consensus among Americans across economic, racial, and political lines. When asked: "What is the highest percentage of income that would be fair for a family of four making $200,000 to pay in all taxes combined," the median answer was 25 percent. That includes Federal income and payroll taxes, as well as all other Federal, state, and local taxes!

Moreover, 25 percent was the median answer among conservatives, liberals, men, women, blacks, whites, singles and marrieds, young and old, and across all income levels (Figure 6–2). Democrats, where the median was 29 percent, were the only group that differed significantly from the 25-percent answer.

In reality, however, those who make $200,000 face a marginal Federal income and Medicare tax rate of 42.5 percent. All in all, the typical family of four with $200,000 in income pays an average of $78,000 in taxes, or 39 percent of their income. Moreover, a family of four with as little as $18,000 in income faces marginal tax rates inclusive of payroll taxes of 30 percent. Many families of four with less than $60,000 of earnings pay 25 percent of their total income in Federal income and payroll taxes alone. Add in state and local income, sales and property taxes, and that number quickly approaches 30 percent.

Not surprisingly, a growing number of Americans are unhappy with their tax bill. In the *Reader's Digest* poll, 68 percent felt their own total tax payments were "too high." That was up from 60 percent in 1982 and 46 percent in 1961.

FIGURE 6–2 A Consensus for Lower Tax Rates

Q: What is the highest percentage of income that would be fair for a family of four making $200,000 to pay in all taxes combined?

Answered by:		Fair:
Males	25%	
Females	25%	
Whites	25%	
Blacks	25%	
Those with high-school		The typical
degree or less	25%	answer is 25%
...some college	25%	
...college degree or more	25%	
Those under 35 yrs. of age	25%	
... 36–49 yrs. of age	25%	
... 50–64 yrs. of age	25%	Reality:
... 65 yrs. of age	25%	
Republicans	25%	
Independents	25%	
Conservatives	25%	
Moderates	25%	In reality
Liberals	25%	such a family
Democrats	29%	pays 39%

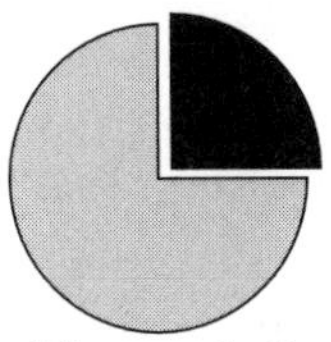

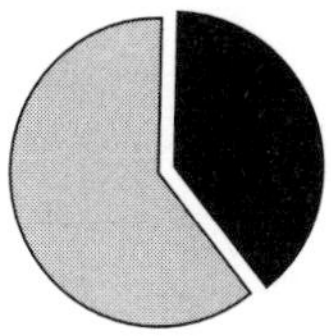

*Source: Roper Center for Public Opinion Research for *Reader's Digest*, October 21–29, 1995

That sets the stage for a radical reduction in tax rates and an overall reduction in the tax burden. In February 1998, a national poll conducted by Zogby International for political columnist Robert Novak found a small plurality (38.6 percent to 35.3 percent) in favor of a 23-percent national sales tax as a replacement for all federal taxes. Of those favoring the 23-percent sales tax, nearly half (49.4 percent) have a household income between $25,000 and $34,999. Support among other income groups was in the 30 percentile range.[7] According to the poll, the national sales tax was more heavily favored by younger than by older Americans, by blacks and Hispanics more than by whites, and by men more than by women.

A more recent poll by John McLaughlin & Associates for Steve Forbes's advocacy organization, Americans for Hope, Growth and Opportunity, found a majority of voters in favor of a flat 17-percent income tax. Fully 60 percent said they would approve a "new federal tax code which applies one low rate to all Americans." In addition, when asked to choose between the current tax code and a 23-percent national sales tax, Forbes's proposal for a 17-percent tax was preferred by half of the respondents.

You may be discounting the results of that poll because it was done for the proponent of a 17-percent flat tax. But, before you totally dismiss it, consider the results of a Harris poll conducted just before April 15 of 1999. Three-quarters of those polled by Lou Harris & Associates said they favored changing the income tax system. Moreover, 59 percent of those with income of more than $75,000, which would include many of the boomers as they hit their peak earning years, would prefer *a completely new system.*[8]

When taken together, these polls show that the American people are ready to consider a simpler tax system with far lower tax rates than the one that currently exists. Reforming and strengthening the Social Security system will come first, but broad-based tax reduction is coming to the Federal tax code as well.

Will we get all the way to a flat tax? Perhaps. More likely will be a return to a modified flat tax similar to that which was enacted in 1986. In any case, the more boomers who turn age 50, the more likely the top marginal-tax rate is headed lower, much lower. Returning the top marginal-tax rate below 30 percent is likely; reducing it to 25 percent or less is possible.

The aging of the boomers portends significant reductions in both the effective Social Security tax and personal-income tax rates in the years ahead. Such broad-based reductions in the barriers to domestic commerce will have a predictable, positive impact on economic growth and incomes. They will make a significant contribution to the Great Prosperity and the trip to Dow 100,000.

The Boomers and Price Stability

The boomers will also prove to be a powerful force in favor of price stability.

As the boomers increase their wealth and begin to reduce their home mortgages, their concerns will grow to include the safety of their savings. For most of the past 50 years, the biggest single threat to the value of our savings was nuclear war. Though that seems almost far-fetched today, many thoughtful people once believed we were perilously close to nuclear war. And recent disclosures from the internal files of the former Soviet Union show that their fears were well-grounded. Clearly, a nuclear war would have destroyed the factories and land and office buildings and infrastructure on which most of the value of our savings was based.

But now that the threat of all-out nuclear war has passed, the biggest single threat to the value of our savings is unanticipated inflation.

In fact, inflation can go back over 5 percent. There is no institutional structure in the United States today that can keep that from happening. We have to rely, just as we have since 1973, on the judgment and best efforts of the twelve voting members of the Federal Reserve's open-market committee and the leadership of its chairman.

Paul Volcker's appointment as chairman of the Federal Reserve Board in 1979 was the pivotal personnel change that ushered in the era of dis-inflation, and, under the extraordinarily capable leadership of Alan Greenspan, who has been chairman of the Federal Reserve since 1987, the U.S. economy has again achieved price stability.

But the Fed, and whoever its next chairman may be, can make mistakes. The Year 2000 issue that concerns me far more than the risk of some computer glitches causing widespread economic disruption is the possible retirement of Mr. Greenspan as chairman of the Federal Reserve. When his term expires in June 2000, he will be 74 years old. Moreover, the next President will likely want to appoint his own chairman to the all-powerful position of operating the country's monetary system.

Perhaps Mr. Greenspan will be asked to stay on. But sooner or later, a new Fed Chairman will take charge. And since Mr. Greenspan cannot explain how exactly he reaches the decisions he makes, his successor will be on his or her own to come up with a decision-making process. Monetary policy is based on the rule and judgment of individual men and women, not on the rule of law. That is one reason why interest rates remain at relatively high levels today, even though inflation is back below 2 percent.

For the sake of argument, let's say that inflation did go back up over 5 percent, or that prices began to fall by more than 2 percent a year. How long do you think such price instability would last? Probably not very long.

During the Great Inflation of the 1970s, the boomers were big users of debt. They were financing the purchase of their first homes, and first and second cars, and all of the other consumer durables that occur when establishing a family. High inflation did not look all bad to them, since they were anticipating paying off those loans in cheaper dollars.

While high inflation and rising housing prices benefited many boomers, they, and the rest of the American people, also learned that high inflation and monetary instability are bad for the economy, bad for jobs, bad for the stock market and, in the end, a threat to our standard of living.

Moreover, the boomers are becoming the lenders, the sources of capital. Today, high inflation is at odds with their financial concerns. Getting paid back in cheaper dollars means accepting a lower standard of living in retirement. Deflation, too, would put the boomers and nearly everyone else's financial and economic well-being at risk. A widespread decline in prices, deflation, inevitably leads to widespread bankruptcies. Once again, lenders and owners of equities, that is, the boomers, would be significantly worse off.

As a result, the aging of the boomers is a second, powerful force that is amplifying the populist forces unleashed by the end of the Cold War in favor of maintaining a stable price environment. When the inflation sign points to price stability, we can anticipate above-average stock-market returns as well.

Demographics and Destiny

As powerful as they are, demographics are not destiny, as some claim. The aging of the baby boomers does not make the Great Prosperity or reaching Dow 100,000 a sure thing.

There is an element of truth in tracking spending patterns by demographic group and in concluding that the next 10 years are likely to be marked by above-average economic growth. There is also an almost magical allure to the charts that show the major ups and downs of the

U.S. stock market tracking the rate of change in the population between the ages of 46 and 48.

Treating demographics as destiny has several potential pitfalls, however.

1. These charts suggest that economic policies do not matter, that tax rates could be increased, inflation or deflation could appear, that the United States could revert to protectionist trade policies, and all would still be okay. But history says that tax, monetary, and trade policies do matter, that the future of the economy and financial markets will be determined to a significant extent by the policies we support and the politicians we elect.

Therefore, the general direction of the economy and financial markets is in our hands. The course we chart for the nation will make a difference.

2. The experience of the past four years contradicts an important premise of the "demographics-are-destiny" approach to anticipating the future direction of the stock market. The baby boomers' demand for stock as they increase their savings for retirement is supposed to be key to the projected gains in the stock market.

There are two reasons to be skeptical of this claim. First, it assumes that the supply of equities (the number of new shares created) will not respond to higher prices. Yet, as stock prices have risen in recent years, the number of initial public offerings, or IPOs, as they are known on Wall Street, also have gone up

Second, during the record advances posted by the S&P 500 from 1995 through 1998, individual investors were net *sellers* of stocks.

That's right. The supposed great engine of the market's projected advance was actually going in reverse during one of the great stock-market advances of all time. Even as the financial media were reporting that purchases of equity mutual funds were rising from $107 billion in 1994 to $137 billion in 1998 (Figure 6–3a), they were ignoring the fact that individuals were selling even more stock that they owned directly (Figure 6–3b). In 1998, for example, individuals sold $454 billion of individual securities from their stock portfolios.

Some of this stock was inherited. Some came from the sale of stock earned through stock-option programs. Some came from stock sold by those who had created the businesses that were being taken public in initial public offerings. From whatever the sources, the net *sale* of individual stocks by households rose from $62 billion in 1994 to $317 billion in 1998

(Figure 6–3c). Even if we take into account indirect purchases through public and private pension plans, [including 401(k)s and the like] individuals were net sellers of equities, with total net sales rising from $34 billion in 1994 to $304 billion in 1998. Yet, these were the first four consecutive years in history in which the S&P 500 posted 20 percent-plus returns.

If the cash flow into or out of the market determined the direction of stock prices, the 1995–1998 period would have been one of the worst, instead of being one of the best on record. Stock prices are driven primarily by current profits and the current value placed on future expected profits. If cash flows cannot even explain the direction of past movements in the market, they are of little value in forecasting the future as well.

3. Finally, a sole focus on the demographic dynamic of the boomers points to an end to the Great Prosperity and the beginning of a significant market decline in the years just before 2010. Here, too, skepticism is warranted. As the world becomes a more integrated economy, the only relevant demographic trends will be those of the entire world. Moreover, it would have to be adjusted for the rapid rise in incomes in most of the developing world. In the same way, to the extent that boomers become net sellers of financial assets, there will be individuals and corporations all over the world that will be potential buyers of those stocks and bonds.

The first boomers will turn 65 in the year 2011. The direction of the stock market in the years to come may be influenced to some degree by the actions of the boomers, but, as the 1995–1998 period has shown, tax, monetary, and trade policies will be far more important than how much stock the baby boomers are selling or buying in any one year.

Case Study: Japan

Some believers in the demographics-are-destiny school point to Japan as a telling case in point to what happens when the population begins to age. Japan's baby-boom generation is seven to ten years older than America's, and its stock market peaked in 1989 at 38,915.9. At the end of 1998, it was at 13,706.7, down more than 60 percent from its peak. The fall in the Japanese market is all the more remarkable because it had been the world's leading economy. Between 1960 and 1990, the Japanese economy expanded five-fold. By contrast, since the end of 1991, the Japanese economy has failed to post any growth at all. Since 1991,

FIGURE 6–3   Households: Big Sellers of Stock

6.3a: Individuals have been big buyers of equity mutual funds . . .

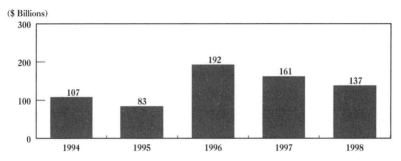

6.3b: But even bigger sellers of individual stocks . . .

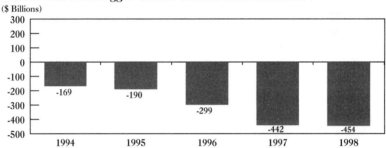

6.3c: Turning them into big net sellers of stocks . . .

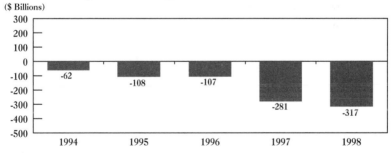

Source: Federal Reserve Board; Flow of Funds data

the U.S. economy has grown 24 percent, and even the German economy has grown 12 percent.

Blaming the Japanese economy's stall and its stock market's collapse on the aging of its boomers, however, misses the importance of a dramatic change in the direction of economic policies that began in 1989.

In my view, the shift toward higher tax rates and a deflationary monetary policy are far better explanations of the sudden change in the fortunes of the Japanese economy than the far more gradual aging of its population.

The Japanese economy in the last half of the 1980s had been in a boom. This surge in economic activity and its stock market had followed a reduction in Japan's highest marginal-tax rates by 15 to 20 percentage points. The top personal income-tax rate, for example, between 1986 and 1988 was cut to 50 percent from 70 percent, while the 45-percent rate was reduced to 30 percent. The rate of growth more than doubled to 6.2 percent in 1988. Capital spending boomed, and the stock market soared. The Japanese trade surplus with the United States, however, remained stubbornly high, and under increasing pressure from the United States, the Japanese government set out to pierce what became known as the "bubble economy."

According to their story, the stock market was too high, and land prices had gone up too much. Prosperity had created a "mania" that, according to Japanese officials, required forceful government action. What happened next in Japan was elitism run amok.

In 1989, the government imposed a new 3-percent value-added tax and a 6-percent levy on new-car purchases and new taxes on inheritances. A 2.5-percent surtax was levied on corporate profits.[9] These tax increases were followed by monetary instability. An inflationary monetary policy quickly led to an increase in land prices, which enjoyed preferential capital-gains tax treatment, making it an ideal inflation hedge. Equity values also rose to reflect the land holdings by major corporations, which enjoyed an even more favorable tax treatment.[10]

Those preferential tax treatments were rescinded, in part, when the holding period required to qualify for the lower capital-gains tax rates was increased to ten years from five years effective January 1, 1990. The Japanese stock market peaked in the closing days of 1989. During 1990, the market fell 39 percent, closing the year at 23,848.7.

More errors were on the way. Monetary policy switched from inflation to disinflation and then to outright deflation. Next came another series of tax increases, including a provision that drove the short-term capital-gains tax rate on land sales to 67.5 percent, a rate that eliminated virtually all liquidity in the Japanese property market.[11]

Falling property values dragged the stock market down, just as rising property values had buoyed it in 1989. Higher tax rates increased the barriers to domestic commerce. Less business was done. The Japanese stock market closed 1993 at 17,272.03, 56 percent below its high.

Tax and monetary policies do matter, not only to the performance of the economy, but also to the direction of equity and land values. Just as bad policies can destroy a good economic environment, good policies can resuscitate a poorly performing economy. In early 1999, there were signs that the Japanese economic policy was shifting back toward reducing the barriers to economic growth. An across-the-board reduction in income-tax rates took effect on April 1, and the Bank of Japan was shifting its policy toward stabilizing Japan's price level.

As lower tax rates and stable prices take effect, look for growth to return to the Japanese economy. A return to growth will stabilize and then improve Japanese corporate profits. At that point, anticipated confidence will begin to appear among Japanese business leaders and consumers. Those are the key ingredients to a higher stock market in Japan, just as they are in the United States and elsewhere in the world. In my view, the decade of poor economic and financial-market performance is coming to an end in Japan.

The Outlook

Demographic destiny does not dictate that the United States will replicate the errors of the Japanese. In the United States, the aging of the baby boomers has set the stage for the kind of grassroots capitalism not seen in the world since perhaps the closing of the frontier and the end of the Homestead Act. Already, more than 120 million Americans have invested in the stock market. Even though individuals have been net sellers of stock, the spread of 401(k)s and Roth IRAs, the rise in the stock market, the issuance of stock options, and the creation of new companies worth billions of dollars have pushed the value of equities up to 43 percent of household wealth, its highest level since the 1960s. As stock ownership spreads, so, too, will the benefits of the Great Prosperity and the risks to those who would destroy it with ill-conceived policies.

The boomers will be central players in the Great Prosperity. Their ingenuity and inventions have already made important contributions to today's economy. As they ascend to the leadership roles, their concerns more and more will be reflected in public policy and private activity.

Lower tax rates and price stability are central to the boomers' desire for strong economic growth, a higher standard of living, and a rising stock market that assure their ability to retire with a standard of living at least as high as that enjoyed by their parents. The leadership this generation provides their companies, the nation, and the world will prove to be far more important to reaching Dow 100,000 than the amount of money they spend at the mall. Their presence as a political and social force is a source of confidence that the Great Prosperity will persist for years to come.

NOTES

1. Dr. B. Douglas Bernheim, "The 1996 Merrill Lynch Baby Boom Retirement Index," Merrill Lynch, Pierce, Fenner & Smith Incorporated, May 1996.
2. Mark J. Penn poll for Bluepoint, Fall 1998.
3. Maureen Landers, Melissa Fox, Marcia Tierney, "The Equitable Nest Egg Study," Middleberg & Associates and The Equitable Companies, Inc., June 1996.
4. Penn, see endnote 2.
5. Bernheim, see endnote 1.
6. Rachel Wildavsky, "How Fair Are Our Taxes?" *Reader's Digest*, February 1996, pp. 57–61.
7. John Zogby, Zogby America Poll, February 15–17, 1998, submitted to Robert Novak.
8. Tom Herman, "Tax Report," *The Wall Street Journal*, April 14, 1999, p. A1.
9. William Kucewicz and Jude Wanniski, "Japan's Ailing Economy: A Critical Diagnosis," Polyconomics, Inc., August 31, 1995, pp. 3–4.
10. *Ibid.*
11. *Ibid.*

CHAPTER SEVEN

THE TECHNOLOGICAL REVOLUTION— THE SUPERCHARGER

The prospects of lower tax rates, stable prices, and freer trade created by the end of the Cold War and the aging of the baby boomers would be reason enough to be optimistic about the future direction of the economy and the stock market, but the forces that will produce the Great Prosperity and propel the stock market to Dow 100,000 go beyond even these fundamental shifts in economic policy.

This is why we can have an unusually high level of confidence in the shape of the future and the direction of financial markets in the years ahead.

The technological revolution is one of those forces. It is a pervasive, powerful, secular force that is increasing our capacity to take care of our concerns as well as the concerns of others, more efficiently, more cost effectively, and more creatively. Every day, new innovations are announced, most of which seem unimportant because few of us can identify precisely how they will change our business or our lives. Yet, each of these innovations is but another step in a revolution that is altering the contours of the global economic landscape, shaping the direction of the economy, and driving us toward the next tenfold increase in the Dow.

Why is the technological revolution so powerful?

1. Technology has given us new tools that increase our ability to take care of our concerns and the concerns of others. For example, advances

in medicine have produced treatments for an ever wider range of diseases and conditions. Microprocessors have made possible an abundance of home appliances and a level of comfort that could hardly be imagined 50 years ago.

2. Of even greater importance, the technological revolution is breaking down the natural barriers of time and distance that have kept us from trading with millions of human beings, most of whom we do not even know. And any time, ANY TIME, we reduce the barriers to trade, more trade takes place. When more trade takes place, economic growth and rising living standards appear. Inevitably, new businesses are formed, corporate profits rise, and stock markets move higher.

It is almost trite to say that the technological revolution is the biggest economic event since the industrial revolution, but that does not make it untrue. We can get a sense of the increase in living standards, the opportunities for economic growth, and the potential for wealth creation that lie ahead by taking a quick, retrospective tour of the industrial revolution. There was no stock-market index comparable to today's that we can use to quantify the implications of the technological revolution on the stock market, but we can trace the fundamental factors that today will lead to higher stock prices during this earlier revolution. Then, as now, increased trade was recorded as economic growth. Today, we know that economic growth leads to higher corporate profits and rising stock prices.

With that in mind, let's turn to the beginning of the industrial revolution that began 287 years ago, with the invention of the steam engine. We know now that this invention would change the face of the Earth and touch the lives of every man, woman, and child in Europe, North America, and ultimately the entire world. So, too, the invention of the transistor is transforming the world in our own time. And just as the industrial revolution over time produced an epochal increase in the average person's standard of living, so, too, the technological revolution will contribute to the Great Prosperity that lies ahead.

An Industrial Revolution at Electronic Speed

The invention of the steam engine first gave human beings the ability to better take care of their concerns and the concerns of others by breaking through the physical limitations of power that had bound the vast majority of humanity to a primitive life. Since the beginning of time, humans' ability to harvest their crops, move their goods to market, shape and mine the Earth had depended on the strength of their own bodies or on the muscle power of domesticated animals and on the power of wind and water. As noted historian William Manchester points out, the life of the average person at the end of the Middle Ages had not changed for 1,000 years. In the early 1500s, at the time of Magellan's voyage around the world, the day-to-day life of the average person was filled with toil and hardship. Between 80 percent and 90 percent of the population lived in small villages and maintained life by working the fields.[1] Life was not much different 200 years later at the dawn of the industrial revolution.

The advent of the steam engine changed all that. Like most innovations, it was first used to increase output by doing better what was already being done. Like most innovations, its first application was to reduce the toil of humans at routine tasks. The first use of the steam engine was to pump water out of coal mines. Over time, as the steam engine was refined, its applications widened. The use of steam power freed factories from their dependence on wind or moving water for power, allowing them to be located near customers in large cities. That dramatically reduced the time and cost of transportation of goods to market. Thousands of people were drawn into the cities to work in the factories and mills in what today looks like deplorable conditions. Since the vast majority of these people chose to leave their rural villages, however, we can only imagine that life working the land was an even harsher existence.

The production of goods and services began to rise. Cotton, a luxury fabric, became commonplace. Over time, public services improved and living standards began to rise. Soon steam engines would begin to change the scope of what was possible. Over the next two centuries, a gulf of wealth and comfort would appear that separated modern times from ages past. Steam-powered locomotives and ships, electricity, the Panama Canal, household appliances, the automobile, the telephone, central plumbing: All of the abundance and weapons of war that were known by the end of the 1940s were the fruit of the industrial revolution.

What makes the technological revolution even more stunning is the pace at which it is moving forward and sweeping us into a future as different from 1948 as 1948 was from 1700. The first practical steam engine

135

was developed in 1712 by Thomas Newcomen. Because of its size, weight, and consumption of fuel, it had to be very close to its fuel source.

The first major innovation to the steam engine occurred 57 years later, in 1769, when James Watt added a second condenser, which produced a *four-fold* increase in the fuel efficiency of the steam engine. Now it became practical to locate a steam engine anywhere, and steam power began to drive the industrial revolution.

Another 13 years passed before Watt produced his second major innovation, converting the up–down motion of the cylinders in the engine to a rotary motion that could control a shaft. That made steamships and railroads possible, but it would be another 25 years before the first steamship sailed up the Hudson River in New York in 1807. The first railroad based on the steam locomotive did not begin business until 1829.

Contrast these 117 years of history with the pace of the technological revolution.

- The first computer, the Eniac, was built in 1946 using thousands of vacuum tubes.
- The transistor was invented 1948.
- The first practical computer, built by Univac, was delivered to the U.S. Bureau of the Census in 1951. A year later, IBM introduced the first computer with an electronically stored program.
- During the next eight years, the integrated circuit, the method of placing more than one transistor on a single silicon wafer (1958), the first, all-transistor super computer (1958), and the minicomputer (1960), all were invented.

Twenty years after IBM introduced the first computer with an electronically stored program, Intel invented the microprocessor, a computer on a chip. The next year, the first hand-held calculators hit the market, at a cost, in today's dollars, of more than $400 each.

The power of the steam engine was quadrupled in 57 years. The power of computers has been quadrupling every three years ever since Intel produced that first microprocessor in 1971. IBM introduced the Intel-based PC in 1981. Its microprocessor had 29,000 transistors, the computer could perform 0.3 million instructions per second (MIPS), and it cost $10,000 in 1998 dollars. Today, you can buy a PC that has 7.5 *million* transistors that can perform 675 million instructions per second for one-tenth the price. In 1981, the cost per MIP was more than $3,000 (in 1998 dollars). Today, it is below $1. Less than 50 years after the first practical computer was built, and less than 20 years after IBM introduced the PC, people routinely carry in their briefcase a computer that weighs less than four pounds, has more power than a mainframe computer of 20 years ago, can be used anywhere from the beach to an airplane flying at 35,000 feet, and costs less than $2,000.

The dramatic reduction in the cost of the microprocessor has permitted computing power to proliferate to produce ever better and more efficient products. Technology today is so much a part of our everyday life that it is hard to imagine what life was like before integrated circuits controlled everything from dishwashers and car engines to our cellular phones and today's most powerful computers.

This abundance has lifted our standard of living in ways not fully captured by government statistics. Consider just 10 of the improvements since 1970. Since then, the number of homes or households with these improvements have increased as follows:

- Color TVs, to 98 percent from 34 percent
- Telephones, to 94 percent from 87 percent
- VCRs, to 89 percent from 0 percent
- Frost-free refrigerators, to 87 percent from less than 25 percent
- Clothes washers, to 83 percent from 62 percent
- Answering machines, to 65 percent from 0 percent
- Cable TV, to 63 percent from 6.3 percent
- Two or more vehicles, to 62 percent from 29 percent
- Dishwashers, to 55 percent from 27 percent
- Computers, to more than 41 percent from 0 percent[2]

Technology and Prosperity

Everywhere we look, we find technology increasing our capacity to take care of the concerns of our fellow human beings. Only this time, instead of increasing our muscle power, computers are being used to increase our brainpower. During the 1980s, for example, dedicated computer chips were used to increase the fuel economy of cars. The consequent reduction in oil consumption is an estimated 1.9 million barrels a day. That is equivalent to discovering another oilfield the size of the Alaskan North Slope, one of the largest single oil discoveries in North America.[3]

Even as technology was reducing the demand for oil, it was being used to increase its supply beyond what the conventional wisdom in the 1970s and even the early 1980s had deemed possible. Thanks in large measure to the direct and indirect use of technology, it takes less energy and less money to discover a barrel of oil in the United States than it did in 1981. The average well is deeper, but, more important, the success rate has improved nearly six-fold thanks to computer imaging and sophisticated sensing technology. As a consequence, the cost of finding a barrel of oil in the United States has fallen from $21 in 1981 to under $5 in 1998, to as low as fifty cents in the Middle East. And, the pretax price of a gallon of gasoline is less than the price of bottled water.

Virtually every industry can point to similar examples of how technology has changed what is possible. Off-the-shelf software programs help us to do everything from manage our personal finances to run a small- to medium-sized business. With spreadsheets, virtually anyone can create and modify sophisticated business reports that can be updated daily from data downloaded from thousands of sites around the country, or for that matter, around the world. On a larger scale, databases consisting of far more information than human beings could ever track manually are used by merchandisers to manage inventories and respond quickly to provide more of what is selling to provide better selections at lower prices. Wal-Mart, for example, used technology to reduce its administrative costs to 15 percent of sales in 1993 from 20 percent of sales in 1983, saving $3 billion in 1993 alone. That was key to its strategy of providing everyday low prices and winning market share. The company went public in 1970, joined the Dow Industrials in 1997, and, at the end of 1998 was the fourth largest company in the S&P 500.

Modern finance would not exist without computers. At the same time, everyday banking provides us 24-hour access to our accounts through automated teller machines. Breakthroughs in medicine and materials improve our health and add to the comfort of our lives. Farmers use global-positioning satellites and computers on board their tractors to precisely apply fertilizer and pest controls to their fields, and a grocery wholesaler in central Brazil uses a $2,000 computer that runs the same sophisticated software used by large U.S. distributors to route its trucks. Deliveries are up 30 percent, even as the fleet of trucks has been trimmed by 35 percent.[4]

Today, American car manufacturers are designing cars in half the time at less than half the cost. For the first time in a generation, automobile prices in nominal as well as in inflation-adjusted dollars are falling. Yet, few of these increases in our capacity to improve one another's lives shows up in traditional measures of productivity. During the industrial revolution, when a man who had used a hand shovel began to operate a steam shovel, it was easy to observe that he was 100 times more productive, but, with technology, you frequently eliminate the need to move the dirt.

For example, how can the government measure the increased productivity created by the cellular telephone that transforms travel time by a salesperson into office time in his or her car? You can't, and therefore, the government doesn't. But from firsthand experience, I have seen it save a day each week, producing a 25-percent increase in productivity, yet all our tools to measure productivity are calibrated to an industrial world and hence leave these kinds of gains unmeasured.

But just because they go unmeasured does not mean that they don't count. Measured or not, these kind of productivity gains add up to higher living standards, increased corporate profits, and, in the end, higher stock prices as well.

The Communications Revolution

As important as all these gains are, and they are very important, they pale by comparison to this single fact. *For the first time in history, the cost of communications is no longer correlated to the distance over which people are communicating.*

Think of it. When you place a telephone call and the signal goes to a satellite, it really doesn't matter whether it comes down in Chicago, or New York, or Los Angeles, or for that matter, Tokyo or London. The cost is essentially the same. At the beginning of 1999, you could call anywhere in the country for 10 cents a minute. And AT&T was offering cellular phone services that could be used anywhere in the country with no roaming charges and a flat rate of as little as 10 cents a minute.

The cost of communication is going lower still. Sprint, for example, announced in June 1998 that it had spent $2 billion to redesign its all-fiber network, already among the most modern in the world, in a way that would increase its call-handling capacity 17-fold while cutting the cost of long-distance calls 70 percent. The United States negotiated a free-trade pact in telecommunications equipment in February 1997. As a result, the cost of an international call will fall from 88 cents a minute or more to about 20 cents a minute by 2002. If you adjust for inflation, that is about what it had cost me to call across town and speak to my high-school friends in the early 1960s and far less than it had cost me to call home when I went away to college in the mid 1960s.

The communications revolution constitutes a radical reduction in a physical barrier to commerce. The reduction in the cost of communications makes it easier for people to talk to one another. When people find it easier to speak with one another, inevitably, they begin to do more business. What we know about human beings is that anytime you make it easier to do business, more business gets done.

Let me give you one example that illustrates the potential of the communication revolution. What makes this story remarkable is that it is about a young couple who live in a small town in Wyoming far from the high-tech silicon valleys of the West or East coasts. The variety store they were running failed, and they ended up with a garage full of inventory, including 144 Santa ornaments with tiny helicopter blades attached to their heads. All efforts to get rid of the Santas failed, including an attempt to give them away.

For the heck of it, they listed an ornament for auction on the Internet with a minimum price of $2.95. Soon, they received an e-mail from halfway around the world offering $8, and asking if more Santas were available. Today, this couple is running their variety shop on the Internet, reaching millions of people who visit auction sites—a cyberspace version of a variety store—from all over the world.

Just like that, a business is born. The Wyoming couple's income rises, a woman halfway around the world becomes a satisfied customer. The barriers to business—distance and convenience—fall. Suddenly, a trade among human beings that otherwise would never have happened occurs. Economic growth takes place. Multiply this times thousands and then millions of cases, and you can get a sense of how the Internet will be contributing to economic growth in the years ahead.

To give you a sense of the potential of the communications revolution for the economy as a whole, I thought we'd again look at the industrial revolution and how the communications revolution that was associated with it changed the shape of the economy and dramatically increased living standards. What we find is that the rapid increase in living standards that is associated with the industrial revolution began to accelerate in the 1820s, the moment when steam power began to be used to produce break-

140

throughs in communications in the form of the steamship and steam-powered locomotive. During the industrial revolution, the annual rate of increase in *world* living standards accelerated 13-fold to 1.17 percent beginning in the 1820s. In Western Europe and North America, where the industrial revolution had already begun to lift living standards, annual growth in per capita GDP registered a near five-fold increase.[5]

Steam power brought a radical increase in speed to business and travel. The first railroads in the United States spanned out from existing commercial centers such as Boston, New York City, and Philadelphia, and then connected these commercial centers. By 1830, travel time between Boston and New York had been cut from four days to a matter of hours.[6]

The invention of the telegraph in 1844 and its commercial deployment beginning in 1847 gave the railroads the communications tool they needed to manage a network that covered hundreds and then thousands of miles. With it, the communications revolution of the industrial age began to accelerate.

A railroad building boom commenced in the late 1840s and early 1850s. By 1860, the rail and telegraph network stretched up and down the East Coast and as far west as Chicago. In 1800, it took six weeks to travel from New York City to Chicago. By 1830, that had been reduced to three weeks. By 1857, the trip between these two cities had been reduced to a relatively comfortable and safe three days.[7]

It took six years and the work of 20,000 men to build the Transcontinental Railroad. The connection of Omaha, Nebraska and San Francisco with two continuous, parallel ribbons of steel in 1869 cut the travel time between New York City and San Francisco to ten days from four weeks. Before the building of the railroad, it had taken less time to travel from San Francisco to China than to New York City. After the Transcontinental Railroad was complete, California became a truly integral part of the U.S. economy.

We cannot measure what happened next in terms of the Dow Industrials, but we can report that in the next 30 years, the one quarter of the continent that stretched from Omaha, Nebraska to California was settled. In 1869, the only town of any size west of Omaha was Salt Lake City. During the next three decades, this vast frontier would be settled with a nearly six-fold increase in population to 1.7 million people. Vast stretches of arid land were put into production raising beef and growing wheat, which could be shipped to the East even as the industrial products and supplies were provided to the settlers in the West.

We can only imagine the increase in property values that were produced during those 30 years. Today, the frontier created by the Internet stretches into cyberspace. And the increased values will be reflected in the price of corporations that participate directly and indirectly in its development.

There would be financial panics in 1873 and again in 1893. The railroads would overbuild, consolidate, become overly leveraged. Some would go bankrupt and be reorganized. Through it all, they were a central factor in the expansion and remaking of the American economy. The combination of the railroad and telegraph made possible reliable, direct, incredibly fast, and less expensive transportation and communication.

This industrial communications network changed forevermore the velocity and complexity of business. Business and labor reorganized themselves around these new tools of commerce, which made possible huge organizations and demanded modern management and modern finance. Wall Street became the financial center of the country and one of the largest and most sophisticated financial centers of the world. During the 1850s, the volume of trading in the securities of railroads, banks, and municipalities increased to hundreds of thousands of shares per week. The use of speculative instruments such as puts and calls was perfected. And the modern call market was invented to permit trading on margin.[8] After the Civil War, the telegraph was used to provide a stock-market ticker to record and report the price of trades on the floor of the stock exchange.

The combination of the railroad and the telegraph gave rise to mass distribution. Chicago became the major distribution center for the Midwest. By 1866, there were 59 jobbers in Chicago with sales of over $1 million. Regional centers such as St. Louis and Cincinnati had 15 each.[9] Mass merchants followed with the great department stores including Macy's, Bloomingdales, and Lord & Taylor of New York; Marshall Field of Chicago; and Jordan Marsh of Boston. Chain stores such as Woolworth's and mail-order companies such as Sears Roebuck and Montgomery Ward were built by merchants who mastered these new tools of commerce. Montgomery Ward invented offering "Satisfaction guaranteed or your money back." Commercial empires were created by delivering quality merchandise to millions of people at ever lower prices.

The Internet, Prosperity, and the Stock Market

We are just beginning a similar transformation of our economy. Although the changes are occurring first in the United States, the communications revolution of the technological age embraces the entire world. Moreover, the technology of today is advancing at a speed that is at least triple that of the industrial revolution, which means that changes on the magnitude of those created by the deployment of the railroads and telegraph are likely to occur within the next 20 years. It may happen even faster than that.

The Internet was opened to commercial use in 1994. Within two years it had become the World Wide Web and was known as an "information highway." Within four years, 50 million people in the United States had been "on the Web." During 1999, the number of people using the Internet doubled to 102 million. That number is expected to double and then double again by 2002.

By 1998, it was clear that the Internet would become far more than a ready source of information. As the communications network of the technological age, it would become the world's major commercial thoroughfare. Prognosticators were forecasting that $2.3 billion of 1998 Christmas sales would be conducted over the Web. By the end of the season, that number had soared to more than $5 billion. For all of 1998, International Data Corp. estimated that U.S. online shoppers spent $2.8 billion in travel, $1.9 billion on computer hardware, and generated more than $1 billion in commissions as they bought and sold stock on line.[10] Schwab, one of the leaders in providing on-line brokerage services, for example, at year-end 1998 had 2.2 million active on-line accounts with $174 billion in assets. Schwab now has a higher market value than Merrill Lynch.

Just as the communications breakthrough created by the industrial revolution made possible mass merchandisers and department stores, the technological revolution is making possible a new kind of mass marketer. Amazon.com offers what amounts to one of the biggest bookstores in the world to the entire world. eBay™ offers an auction market where individuals from all over the world can meet without travel or virtually any other cost to buy and sell a range of collectibles from sports memorabilia to Santa ornaments to Beanie Babies.

For all of its glitz, on-line shopping by consumers is a pittance compared to what American business is doing. Business-to-business commerce on the Internet could top $300 billion within a year or two. Even so, it would represent only 3 percent of GDP. The gains from these advances stretch years into the future.

Just as the railroad and telegraph changed the definition of speed and distance in the industrial age, the Internet is providing incredibly fast, efficient, and reliable communications to the technological age. It is

143

eliminating the need for stores and reducing the need for inventories, freeing precious capital, reducing costs, and offering convenience all with the point and click of a mouse button. In just one example, Ford Motor Company is shifting the purchase of an estimated $15.5 billion of office supplies and other nonproduction goods and services to the Internet. It expects to cut its costs by 30 percent, generating annual savings approaching $5 billion. Part of that savings will come from getting more competitive prices, but most of the savings will come from eliminating administrative and accounting tasks (such as entering data on everything from cutting checks to the filling out of expense reports) that add little value to its customers.

Some of those cost savings will be passed onto car buyers in the form of lower prices. Making cars more affordable will increase sales. Some of the cost savings will be captured by Ford in the form of improved margins and higher profits. In a world of stable prices, the ability of companies to increase their profits by raising prices is limited. Instead, higher profits will be generated by cost-saving strategies that can lower prices through increased sales and cost savings.

As the Internet gets easier and cheaper to use, more of us will use it. And, as we get better at using the Internet, we will use it more. Bandwidth is the crucial variable for the Internet. It dictates the carrying capacity or a communications line and hence the speed with which you can transmit an image or information across the Internet. Bandwidth has begun to *triple* every year. If that pace were sustained, there would be a nine-fold increase in bandwidth every two years, and 59,000-fold increase over the next 10 years. Communications companies such as AT&T are already deploying systems using coaxial cable that will increase 100-fold the speed with which computers can send and receive not only e-mails, but data and pictures and drawings and live telecasts for video phones and whatever else humans can invent across this new medium of business.

The Outlook

The pieces that can produce a Great Prosperity are falling into place even as you read this book. Perhaps the best historical parallel to help us anticipate the prosperity that lies ahead is the decade of the twenties.

There are sure to be significant differences between the 1920s and what lies ahead. For starters, I do not expect the Great Prosperity to lead to a Great Depression. The prosperity of the 1920s did not have to end in 1929, nor was the end of that boom *caused* by the stock-market crash of 1929. Instead, there were a series of economic policy errors that began with passage of the Smoot–Hawley tariffs, which triggered a collapse in international capital markets and a sharp fall in the price level and a massive tax increase. This combination of monumental policy errors produced the collapse in stock prices in the early 1930s and the Depression that would stretch out to the end of the decade. (We will address the risks to the Great Prosperity and reaching Dow 100,000 in Chapter 10.)

Three events that coalesced before and during the 1920s remind us of the moment in which we are living. They are

1. The end of World War I and a "return to normalcy," which included tax cuts and restoration of price stability. The top tax rate was reduced to 24 percent in 1929 from 73 percent in 1921, and the consumer price index between 1921 and 1929 remained virtually unchanged, falling on average 0.5 percent a year.

2. A series of breakthroughs in manufacturing processes that created an abundance of consumer goods never before known in history. Ford Motor Company's invention of mass production in 1908 and the creation of the assembly line in 1913 permitted it to sell the Model T for less than half the price of its competitors even as it was doubling the minimum wage it was paying its workers. The creation of an affordable car reverberates to this day in the structure and customs of our society. Just as important, Ford began to sell tractors for less than the price of a team of horses. That revolutionized the farm economy in a way that would reduce the number of people working the soil to less than 5 percent of the population.

In addition, at the beginning of the 1920s, only about one-third of U.S. factories used electric power to drive their machinery. These were centralized motors called dynamos that were connected to every machine by a series of belts and drive shafts. Advances in electric-motor technology, however, made it possible to power each machine tool with its own electric motor. By 1929, more than half the factories in America used machine-top electric motors. That shift transformed manufacturing and elevated the wages of factory workers to unheard of levels.[11]

Similarly, the 1990s were preceded by the invention of a new approach to manufacturing known as "lean production" or "just-in-

145

time," which was invented by the Toyota Motor Company of Japan. Just as the mass-production techniques developed by Ford were adopted by one industry after another during the 1920s, the lean-production techniques are spreading across all of manufacturing. Moreover, just as the shift to "machine-top" electric motors amplified this production breakthrough, today's shift from mainframe computers to desktop PCs and microprocessors is making possible a new set of consumer products and services that will elevate the standard of living enjoyed by the middle class.

3. The deployment of the telephone, which had been invented in 1876, as a means of doing business. By 1920, there were 123 phones for every thousand people in America and an estimated 4.3 million business phones. During the 1920s, the number of total phones grew 51 percent, and business phones grew 61 percent to 6.8 million. Deals could now be struck or orders taken as easily from someone down the street as from across town, or even from across the country. As the speed of business increased, so did its volume. Today, the use of the computer as a communications tool is similarly adding to the speed of business and to its volume as well.

Here is what happened during those nine years known as the Roaring Twenties. Real GNP increased 45 percent, or an average of 4.2 percent a year. Productivity increased on average 2.7 percent per year. Real incomes rose 27 percent, housing starts doubled, and automobile registrations per year nearly tripled. The percent of dwellings with electricity jumped to 68 percent from 35 percent (Table 7–1).

The prospects of gains across the spectrum of our lives similar in magnitude lie ahead. The technological revolution is about to unleash historic increases in productivity while breaking down barriers to trade not only within the United States, but around the world. We have already seen economic growth accelerate to near 4 percent and productivity gains rise above 2 percent a year. Real incomes are on the rise, and the number of households with access to the Internet is growing rapidly.

What about the Dow? Between 1920 and 1929, the Dow Jones Industrial average increased 2.5 times, or at an average rate of 14.8 percent a year. If the Dow were to increase at a similar rate beginning in 1998, it would approach 50,000 by the end of the next decade and hit 100,000 by 2016.

FIGURE 7–1 The Roaring Twenties

	Real GNP (Billions of 1998 Dollars)	Output per Man-Hour	Real GNP per Capita (1998 Dollars)	Housing Starts (000)	Automobile Registrations (000)	U.S. Pop. (000)	Dow Industrials	Consumer Price Inflation
1920	$608	$38	$5,713	247	9,239	106,461	72	15.6
1921	555	41	5,113	449	10,494	108,538	81	(10.5)
1922	643	40	5,843	716	12,274	110,049	99	(6.2)
1923	721	43	6,438	871	15,102	111,947	96	1.8
1924	719	45	6,299	893	17,613	114,109	121	0.0
1925	779	45	6,729	937	20,069	115,829	157	2.3
1926	825	46	7,033	849	22,200	117,397	157	1.1
1927	825	47	6,925	810	23,303	119,035	202	(1.7)
1928	829	47	6,881	753	24,689	120,509	300	(1.7)
1929	884	49	7,259	509	26,705	121,767	248	0.0
Total Growth 1920–1929	45.4%	27.6%	27.1%	106.1%	189%	14.4%	245.4%	(14.5)%
Avg. Annual Growth 1920–1929	4.2%	2.7%	2.7%	8.4%	12.5%	1.5%	14.8%	(1.6)%

The impact of the technological revolution is also reducing, though not eliminating, the risk of the kind of policy errors that brought the prosperity of the 1920s to an untimely end.

- *The technological revolution will reinforce the populist impulse that is percolating through the U.S. political system.* The notion of centralized bureaucratic control will seem more and more out of step with a world in which individuals can have the power of a supercomputer in their homes and be connected directly to any business in the world.

- *The technological revolution also makes the notion of protectionism seem quaint.* Of course we can raise barriers to the goods of the industrial age, steel, autos, and the like. But how can governments stop free trade in the goods and services of the technological age, when they can be transmitted to anyone on the face of the Earth from satellites that are in stationary orbit 22,000 miles above the surface of the Earth.

The Internet is a decentralizing force in the American and world economy. Yes, there will be several giant corporations that assemble and manage global communications networks for all to use. On the other hand, the benefits of virtually free communications will accrue to all, creating new business, personal, social, and spiritual opportunities and challenges.

Finally, the technological revolution is making the world a smaller place, if not transforming it into a global village. In that light, its greatest legacy may be as a catalyst to the spread of freedom in the world, the next secular force to which we turn.

NOTES

1. William Manchester, *A World Lit Only By Fire. . .* Little, Brown and Company, Boston, 1992.

2. W. Michael Cox and Richard Alm, *Myths of Rich and Poor*, Basic Books, New York, NY, 1999, p. 7.

3. Victor A. Canto and Charles W. Kadlec, "The Shape of Energy Markets to Come," *Public Utilities Fortnightly*, January 9, 1986.

4. Scot McCartney and Jonathan Friedland, "Computer Sales Sizzle as Developing Nations Try to Shrink PC Gap," *The Wall Street Journal*, June 29, 1995, pp. A1, A8.

5. Angus Maddison, "Poor Until 1820," *The Wall Street Journal*, January 11, 1999, p. RS4.

6. Alfred D. Chandler, Jr., *The Visible Hand*, The Belknap Press of Harvard University Press, Cambridge, MA, 1977, pp. 83–85.

7. *Ibid.*

8. *Ibid*, p. 92.

9. Robert W. Twyman, *History of Marshall Field & Co.* (Philadelphia 1954), p. 31 as quoted in Chandler, p. 217.

10. Brian Tracey, "The Color of Money," *The Wall Street Journal*, November 16, 1998, p. R28.

11. Bob Davis and David Wessel, *Prosperity: The Coming 20-Year Boom*, Times Books/Random House, New York, 1998.

149

CHAPTER EIGHT

THE SPREAD
OF FREEDOM—
UNTAPPED POWER

Today, 15 percent of the world's people produce more than half of the world's output. They control but 21 percent of the land mass of the Earth, and 35 percent of the planet's natural resources. Yet, the equity markets where they live constitute 95 percent of the value of equity markets in the entire world.

Who are these people? Do you think they are scattered randomly about the world? Where do they live?

Well, you and your neighbors are among these people if you live in the United States, Canada, the Western rim of Europe, Australia, Japan, or in one of a few select Asian countries (Table 8–1).

What do all these countries have in common?

The common denominators include basic property rights, the right to trade with people throughout the world, tax and monetary systems that permit the accumulation of wealth, free speech, and political and legal systems that give individuals the wherewithal to check the power of government.

In a word, *freedom*.

Your success and the success of your friends, neighbors, and compatriots in taking care of your families and producing an abundance never before dreamed possible attests to this simple, sometimes taken-for-granted, but vital piece of the map of the road to Dow 100,000:

150

Freedom is the most powerful social organization ever devised by people for the creation of prosperity.

This historical fact is a wonderful endorsement of the ability of people to find ways to cooperate with one another by creating win–win situations—exchanges where both parties are better off. When combined with what we know about economic growth, we find that freedom is at the foundation of prosperity because it gives us and everyone else the right to

1. Enter into exchanges with whomever we choose. In every exchange, we contribute to the life of another, even as they contribute to our lives.
2. Decline entering into an exchange. It protects the individual from being forced to enter into one-sided exchanges. This right recognizes the autonomy and respects the dignity of every human being. It invites competition.

When these conditions are in place, people have proven themselves to be extraordinarily creative in finding ways to cooperate with other people through mutually beneficial exchanges. Each exchange holds the promise of contributing to the life of others even as they contribute to our own lives. If the promise is fulfilled and mutual satisfaction is produced, more exchanges take place.

As people respond to new opportunities to trade, they voluntarily form cooperative enterprises called businesses and corporations. To the extent that these businesses and corporations are successful in producing customer satisfaction, they grow, increasing their revenues. To the extent that they produce more than they consume, these revenues exceed their costs. That produces profits, and rising existing and future expected profits are the foundation of a rising stock market.

Remember, this is the basis of all economic activity. Mutually beneficial exchanges are called commerce or economic activity. As they multiply, economic growth ensues, living standards rise, a thousand flowers bloom.

Free societies are known by their institutions and practices. These include property rights, an impartial legal system, open trade, non-oppressive tax and regulatory systems, banking systems and credit markets that are not controlled by the state, minimal regulations on wages and labor markets, and money with a stable value. Each of these facilitates voluntary exchanges.

151

TABLE 8–1 Freedom Dominates the World Economy

	Population (000)	GDP Purchasing Power Parity (US$ Billions)	Land Mass (Sq. km)	Equity Markets Market Capitalization (US$ Billions)
Developed Countries				
North America				
Canada	29,964	658	9,976,140	311
U.S.	265,284	8,083	9,629,091	8,456
Total North America	**295,248**	**8,741**	**19,605,231**	**8,767**
Europe				
Austria	8,059	174	83,850	24
Belgium	10,159	236	30,510	126
Denmark	5,262	123	43,094	57
Finland	5,125	102	337,030	137
France	58,375	1,320	547,030	714
Germany	81,912	1,740	356,910	724
Ireland	3,626	60	70,280	37
Italy	57,380	1,240	301,230	378
Luxembourg	416	13	2,586	
Netherlands	15,517	344	37,330	445
Norway	4,381	121	324,220	31
Portugal	9,930	150	92,391	45
Spain	39,260	642	504,750	232
Sweden	8,843	176	449,964	207
Switzerland	7,074	172	41,290	559
UK	58,782	1,200	244,820	1,694
Total Europe	**374,101**	**7,813**	**3,467,285**	**5,410**

152

Pacific				
Australia	18,312	394	7,686,850	216
Hong Kong	6,311	175	1,092	164
Japan	125,761	3,080	377,835	1,782
Malaysia	20,565	227	329,750	38
New Zealand	3,635	63	268,680	15
Singapore — Free	3,044	85	648	56
Total Pacific	**177,628**	**4,024**	**8,664,855**	**2,271**
Total Developed Countries	**846,977**	**20,578**	**31,737,371**	**16,448**
Total Emerging Markets*	**5,079,489**	**17,422**	**117,202,630**	**839**
Total World	**5,926,466**	**38,000**	**148,940,000**	**17,287**
Developed as % of World	**14.3%**	**54.1%**	**21.3%**	**95.1%**

*Population, GDP, and land mass calculated as difference from world total.

Source: Equity Markets; MSCI; all other, *1998 CIA World Factbook* and Heritage Foundation, *Index of World Economic Freedom*

Without freedom, life, liberty, and the pursuit of happiness can be pursued only at the sufferance of the politically powerful. Inevitably, the politically powerful use the coercive power of the state to protect themselves, their favorite programs, or their friends with economic interests from competition. If this were not the case, the notion of political power would be meaningless. Too much success by an outsider or upstart brings unwanted attention from "the authorities." Opportunities to form a business, or to increase its size, become limited.

Stock markets seldom exist without freedom. Of what value is a company if, in the extreme, at any moment the state can seize it, take it away, without paying the stockholders? In the same vein, of what value is a company if the state can move against it the moment its success begins to reduce the profits or the power of the politically connected? State-run enterprises seldom permit competition. Politicians and bureaucrats prefer monopolies and have the power to enforce them.

By contrast, freedom permits competition. It allows for progress, which inevitably entails upending the existing entrenched order. It also facilitates cooperation through market exchanges so complex that we seldom know the names of those who benefit from our work, nor the names of those who provide life's necessities to us. Freedom and all of its institutions provide the nexus for the creation of prosperity.

The spread of freedom implies the spread of lower tax rates, stable money, and freer trade. Just as the direction of these key signposts point toward above-average economic growth and stock-market performance in the United States, they point to higher growth and above-average market returns internationally. That is why the spread of freedom will make the Great Prosperity a global prosperity. As prosperity spreads globally, the opportunities for commerce, profits, and exchanges will grow apace. That is why the spread of freedom, as much as any other historical force, will contribute to the Dow's reaching 100,000 by the year 2020.

The Power of Freedom

The benefits of the spread of freedom are difficult to quantify and easy to overlook when viewing the world or financial markets on a day-to-day basis. You probably will never hear a television announcer say, "The stock market closed at new highs today because of the increase in freedom in Korea or Thailand or Hungary or Brazil." In fact, the spread of freedom is probably of little consequence to the success of a speculator who is engaged only in day trading.

But our focus is on putting together a strategy for the next ten to twenty years or even longer. In this context, the spread of freedom is a historical force that increases our conviction of the general direction of not only the United States, but of international stock markets as well.

Unlike tax, monetary, and trade policy, there has been little work done to quantify the relationship between freedom, prosperity, and stock markets. One of the best studies was done by the Heritage Foundation. It examined the relationship between freedom and economic growth for the period 1980 through 1993. For this study, the authors developed 10 indicators of freedom, which they used to rank more than 100 countries around the world. These indicators included trade policy, taxation, government intervention in the economy, monetary policy, capital flows and foreign investment policy, banking, wage and price controls, property rights, regulation, and the presence and extent of black markets.[1]

Here's what they found: Over these entire 13 years, the per-capita GDP or living standards grew on average

- *minus* 1.44 percent in repressed economies
- *minus* 0.32 percent a year in mostly unfree countries
- 0.97 percent a year in mostly free countries
- 2.88 percent a year in free countries

In other words, living standards rose nearly three times faster in free societies than in mostly free societies; and actually declined in mostly unfree and repressed economies (Figure 8–1).[2]

The history of what is now the developed world also speaks to the power of freedom to produce a prosperity that was unimaginable even 200 years ago.

Prior to the American Revolution, intellectuals actually debated whether or not progress was even a possibility. For thousands of years, people had been struggling simply to maintain their existence on the face of the Earth. The majority of them had always been hungry. Famines and pestilence were "facts of life." Governments ruled. The people were subjects of the crown, or the emperor, the church, or some other authority that told them what could and could not be done. Freedom was the exception, not the rule.

Consider, for example, the political reaction to the creation of the steamboat. In 1807, Robert Fulton's *Clermont,* using a steam engine built

FIGURE 8–1 Spread of Freedom

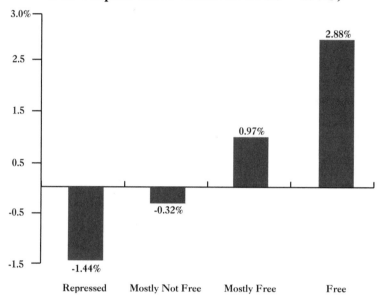

Freedom and Growth (Annual Real
Per Capita GDP Growth 1980 – 1993)

Source: Heritage Foundation

in England, traveled up the Hudson River from New York City to Albany at a remarkable four miles per hour. At the first sight of progress, the owners of sailing ships saw the competitive threat of the steamboat to their businesses and fortunes. They responded by using their political power to persuade the Connecticut and Rhode Island legislatures to protect their businesses and the jobs of their employees by restricting the rights of steamboats to operate in their waters and utilize their harbors. This reaction is not uncommon. Throughout history, the established order has used political power to resist, if not stop, economic progress.

In the United States, however, such laws were found to be unconstitutional. People who could provide a better service or product could not be stopped by government edicts or laws. Freedom reigned. Within 12 years, steamboats were sailing up and down the great rivers of the midwest, and a steam-powered ship built in America had crossed the Atlantic Ocean, connecting the new and old worlds as never before.[3] The established order had been overturned.

156

In the next 100 years, the modern world was created. Today, for the first time in history, in what is now the developed world, only a small minority of people are hungry. For 152 years, ever since the Irish famine, no whole villages of Western Europeans have starved to death.

By contrast, even during the post-World War II abundance, repressed peoples have sometimes failed to produce even enough food to sustain themselves. In the late 1950s, for example, Mao's "Great Leap Forward" in China triggered a famine in which tens of millions starved to death. With the goal of increased prosperity, the political cadres were given the power to seize control of the workings of the economy in every village. Farmers who had worked the land, taking care of their families while producing a small surplus of food, were mobilized, military style, into communes or work brigades. Commune-based light industry, including "backyard" steel furnaces, were created.

At first, output increased. But soon, the workers realized that all of this increased output, and, in some cases, more was taken by the government. Once it became clear that hard work was not rewarded, the human desire to participate in mutually beneficial exchanges was squelched, and as repression increased, agricultural and industrial output decreased. Famine, accentuated by a series of natural disasters, followed.

Freedom and the Computer Revolution

In our own time, freedom has provided the fertile soil for the creation of the technological revolution. The computer, the transistor, the microprocessor, and the Internet—all were invented in the United States. Each invention led to new companies and new industries that reduced the authority of those in power. Digital Equipment Company (DEC) invented the minicomputer, leading to the demise of mainframe computer makers whose names we no longer remember. Then, the creation of ever more powerful personal computers led to the demise of the makers of minicomputers. Compaq computer, one of the largest producers of PCs, bought DEC in part to acquire its skilled sales and support people. Today, minicomputers are a thing of the past. As we find new ways to use the Internet, whether it's e-trading or buying books, established brokerage firms and booksellers begin to lose market share. They will either respond, by offering comparable or better goods and services, or over time they, too, will go out of business.

It is true that some of us experience these innovations as jobs lost to downsizing or to the failures of the companies that had employed us. We are forced to adjust, to find new jobs and new careers. In some cases, the jobs are not so good as the ones that were lost. But, overall, we experience these innovations as rising living standards and witness them in the form of rising stock prices.

The Discovery of Freedom

To fully appreciate the untapped power the spread of freedom can unleash, it is important to see freedom in its full, historical context. Freedom was not preordained. Freedom is a human discovery. Freedom, as we know it today, as a structure for the organization of society, is the product of humanity's ageless struggle to reconcile the autonomy of the individual and the need for cooperative action without resorting to coercion and force.

Human beings are social beings. More than any other animal, we are dependent upon one another for our existence. Yet, we are autonomous beings in the sense that no one can control our thoughts, or, for that matter, control our actions. As anyone who has dealt with children knows, only we, through our own volition, can walk by putting one foot in front of another.

The challenge facing humans ever since the beginning of history has been to find ways to coordinate their respective actions with those of other autonomous, but dependent human beings to achieve a common good.

Coercion is one alternative. Central authority can make the trains run on time. It offers the lure of efficiency, and for most of history, societies have sought a central authority to provide order and to dictate the role of each human being in the society as a whole. Such authorities have always resorted to coercion to force the action of other human beings.

Freedom is a second alternative. It permits individuals to maintain their autonomy and enter into voluntary cooperation with other people. The result is what Frederich Hayek calls a "spontaneous order."[4] Free people have invented and contributed to the institutions of the marketplace. A reliable monetary system, property rights, double-entry bookkeeping, contracts, insurance, banks, limited-liability corporations, bond and stock markets, mutual funds, and money-market accounts are but a few of these institutions that enable us to increase the scope and complexity of this spontaneous order.

158

Each of these institutions has been invented by human beings to increase the range and scope of free exchanges. Freedom does not produce the carefully managed order envisioned by bureaucrats, all neat and tidy. Free people do produce a dynamic order that facilitates innovation, adapts to change, and permits people to trade with one another in complex patterns that no one person can plan or control. Mistakes are made, but they tend to be self-correcting. The net result is what historians call economic progress.

The Victory of Freedom

The defeat of communism in the Cold War has made freedom the unchallenged principle for organizing the social systems of the world. In one, admittedly limited sense, you can think of the Cold War as a great experiment in which Europe was divided to test which form of government and social organization could better meet, satisfy, and care for the economic and social concerns of its inhabitants.

Communism promised to move toward a utopian goal, in which all could share in near-equal proportion in the fruits of everyone's output. Communists and socialists embraced the word *freedom*, but changed its meaning. Freedom had meant free from coercion and the arbitrary power of other people, freedom from feudal ties to the land or to a person of superior rank. In its stead, the authoritarians of the left promised freedom from economic necessity or wants.[5] Central control, replete with five-year plans, promised significantly increased material wealth. The waste and mistakes inherent in a market economy would be eliminated. Instead, government officials would allocate the capital and direct labor toward producing the most desirable mix of products as determined by "the plan."

On the eastern side of the Iron Curtain, central planners were energized by the conviction that as leaders of the Communist Party they were in the vanguard of history. They were given and took all of the power and resources of the state to forge a better future for their people. The spontaneous human search for exchanges was replaced with central control and five-year plans. The premise was that an elite cadre of government officials could do a better job of allocating capital and directing labor than could individuals left to their own devices. In exchange for the loss of individual liberty, people were promised freedom from economic necessity and the uncertainty of competing in

159

a market economy. All would be secure in the protective care and guidance of government.

On the western side of the Iron Curtain, the perceived sharp edges of capitalism were smoothed with a socialism whose excesses were checked by democratic processes. The spontaneous human search for mutually beneficial exchanges was heavily regulated and taxed, but nonetheless allowed to continue as the basic organizing principle of society. Individuals and companies could have five-year plans, but they would be forced to face the test of the marketplace. The economies of Western Europe were integrated with the United States through the Bretton Woods international monetary system of fixed exchange rates, reductions in tariffs, and were given the military protection of U.S. troops through the creation of the North Atlantic Treaty Organization.

After 43 years, the results of the experiment were in. The disparities in average living standards were so great that it was inevitable that the Iron Curtain would fall. Certainly, if the use of central planning had outperformed spontaneous human action by the same magnitude, the people in the West would have torn down the wall. The same experiment was run in Asia between Mainland China on the one side and Hong Kong and Taiwan on the other; and between North and South Korea. In all cases, the freedom afforded by democratic capitalism proved superior to authoritarian rule. At the same time, Japan demonstrated that the political and economic institutions of the West could be adapted to the culture and traditions of an Asian society.

Why did capitalism win the Cold War?

Not through might of arms, Capitalism won because it demonstrated beyond a reasonable doubt that it was the superior organizing principle around which human beings could create a community that enabled them to coordinate their actions with those of other human beings for mutual advantage while living in dignity.

In a real sense, the ageless struggle to find a political and economic structure that is coherent with the autonomous nature of human beings and their dependence on one another for survival has been settled.[6] The paradox of the need to recognize the dignity of individual human beings and yet provide a structure for the cooperative behavior necessary for survival has found its resolution in political institutions of democracy and the commercial institutions of the marketplace.

The resolution of this paradox is one of the great watershed events of the twentieth century. For all practical purposes, the need for democracy and the marketplace have become the accepted starting points for the creation of prosperity. The consequence will be more prosperity in the years ahead.

Freedom and the Great Prosperity

The history of the world, the history of the United States, and the experience of the twentieth century all attest to the power of freedom to create prosperity. *Wherever freedom goes, prosperity follows*. This lesson is being learned anew in our own time.

What we find over and over again is that in societies that provide for freedom of action and property rights, people spontaneously create an extended order of cooperative action with other people in which mutually beneficial exchanges are rewarded and one-sided exchanges are, over time, rooted out.[7] The location of this spontaneous order for cooperative action is called the marketplace, which is, itself, an incredible human invention where cooperation and competition coexist. We call the result of this grand human endeavor *progress*.

What we can observe is that as societies become more free, prosperity begins to appear. In Russia, democracy has replaced authoritarian rule, but repressive tax rates, a series of devaluations that have made the ruble virtually worthless, the lack of property rights, and a lawless society have kept economic freedom at bay. The result: economic collapse.

In Eastern Europe and China, however, the spread of freedom is beginning to bring improved living standards. In China, for example, in the now famous plenum of the Tenth Central Committee in 1978, the Communist Party increased the freedom of that country's 800 million peasants. Each would owe the government the same amount of grain they had grown the year before. After that, all additional output was theirs to keep or trade. In just five years, grain output in China doubled. The results were so incredible that the political leadership has gradually increased economic freedom in the industrial and commercial sectors as well.

There is still much to deplore in China, but that should not blind us to freedom's progress within its borders. Elections have now been held in 500,000 rural villages, and the government continues to bring a sense of law and legal rights to the financial sector. Direct elections are also being

161

extended from villages into more urban townships. Moreover, at the Communist Party Congress in 1997, Chinese President Jiang Zemin announced that the ownership of the majority of China's state-owned enterprises will be transferred to individual shareholders in a program that is expected to last between five and ten years. In addition, China announced plans to unilaterally reduce its tariffs an average of 26 percent.

As China has become more free, the Chinese people have become more prosperous. Since the shift toward freedom began in 1978, the Chinese people have increased economic activity at a near 10-percent rate every year. Per-capita GDP in China today is near $3,000, up from virtually nothing in just 20 years.

But the spread of freedom is not just about China. The movement toward market-based economic principles and increased freedom elsewhere in Asia has corresponded to a historic decrease in poverty throughout the region. According to the World Bank, the number of people classified as poor in East and Southeast Asia was reduced to 345.7 million people from 716.8 million in the 20 years ending 1995, a feat that is unprecedented in human history. Think of it: 371 million people lifted from poverty in 20 years, an average of 18.5 million a year, or more than 50,000 each and every day for 20 years. What government program would even dare to promise such an outcome? South Korea, Taiwan, Hong Kong, and Singapore have essentially eliminated absolute poverty as a national concern.[8]

The benefits of increased freedom are also being experienced in the United States. Welfare reform has freed people from a system that promised freedom from economic wants, but penalized all market-based economic activity by dramatically reducing benefits and, hence, the individual's standard of living. For many, a compassionate safety net had become a snare, trapping them in poverty. Going to work meant being worse off because of the loss of welfare benefits. In other words, for those on welfare, taking a job meant getting a bill from the government that exceeded the value of their paycheck.

At its heart, welfare reform is an important step toward increasing the opportunities of those who are poor to contribute to the lives of others and thereby to improve their own lives as well. This increase in freedom in America's inner cities recognizes the dignity of the individual. Hope and ambition are being reborn in these communities. Commercial life will spring out of the natural human desire to enter into cooperative exchanges with other people that improve the lives of both parties to the exchange. The revitalization of our inner cities may prove to be one of the great marvels of the Great Prosperity.

Increased freedom brings with it increased opportunities for trade. As skills and living standards rise in the developing world, our opportunities to increase our living standards will rise as well. A more prosperous world means more customers for the goods and services we make, everything from Coca-Cola, detergents, Pampers, toothbrushes, and razor blades to Caterpillar tractors, apples, wheat, corn and other agricultural products, movies, music, computers, telephone-equipment networks, and all of the software and organizational skills required to give them their power. A more prosperous world also means a greater assortment of goods and services in our own stores and markets. Today, those goods and services include raw materials, textiles, footwear, machine tools, and semi-conductors. Tomorrow, it will include the more sophisticated goods and services that will be produced by a more prosperous world population free to participate in the creation and invention of the goods and services of the future.

Think of it as the flip side of 1998, when the economic collapse in Asia and the Russian default threatened U.S. economic growth and triggered a 20-percent correction in U.S. markets. In the same way, an increase in economic growth in the rest of the world will contribute to U.S. growth and advances in the U.S. stock market.

As prosperity follows the spread of freedom, it means that people in what had been the developing world will now be in a better position to contribute to our lives by making more powerful offers in the marketplace. The more people who can contribute to our lives, the more opportunities we will have to trade. The more opportunities we have to trade, the greater the opportunity to increase our living standards.

Yes, in many ways, it is this simple. Economists can and do make it appear more complex with their formulas and mathematical models. But, underneath it all, are these four facts:

- The foundation of what is called "the economy" is trade among human beings.
- An increase in trade is recorded as economic growth.
- An expanding economy implies rising incomes and increasing corporate profits.
- Generally speaking, higher current and future profits are the fundamental driver behind higher stock prices.

The Outlook

The currency crisis of 1998 was a setback to the spread of freedom. Devaluations and tax increases that spread from Thailand to Indonesia and then throughout Southeast Asia, Korea, Eastern Europe and Russia, and finally Brazil, initially brought high inflation and increased government intervention in the economy. Trade restrictions were also imposed by the U.S. and other countries that feared a flood of exports from these countries. Stock markets in the developing world fell 50 percent and more in dollar terms.

However, in the aftermath of the crisis, government control of the banking system and credit markets in the developing world is receding. The "fall of crony capitalism" (Chapter 5) also portends less government control over the economy in general and access to capital in particular. Tax rates in some countries have begun to be reduced. As we go to press, the crisis appears to be fading, Brazil has stabilized its currency, and signs of rapid economic recovery in Korea and Southeast Asia were apparent. Not least among these signs were stable to strong currencies, lower inflation, and lower interest rates. Stock markets were on the rise once again.

In monitoring the spread of freedom, watch for the following positive signs:

1. Reductions in oppressive tax rates, wherever they may exist.
2. Increased efforts to provide the institutions and mechanisms that the developing world needs to stabilize its currencies and provide a stable price environment to its citizens. In particular, watch for the International Monetary Fund to become a supporter, instead of an opponent, of stable exchange rates.
3. The reduction in the power of government officials to allocate capital through political control of the banking system or manipulation of capital markets, and increased independence of each country's banking system.
4. The spread of free trade from the Common Market in Europe and the free-trade area that now includes Mexico, the United States, and Canada in North America to the rest of the world.

And be aware of the following risks:

1. Currency devaluations. China contributed to containing the Asian currency crisis by maintaining a fixed rate of exchange between its currency and the U.S. dollar during the crisis. A devaluation of the Chinese *yuan*, however, could signal a new round of global monetary instability.

2. An attempt to assert government controls over the flows of foreign capital into or out of developing country economies. The use of capital controls inevitably discriminates against small domestic firms that do not have access to international capital markets and favors large domestic and multinational corporations that can effectively avoid capital controls through internal means. Capital controls reduce freedom, interfere with economic progress, and usually fail to stabilize a country's currency.

Absent a global catastrophe, any future setbacks to freedom's spread are likely to become more and more isolated and less and less consequential. Here, too, the technological revolution is playing a pivotal role in two important ways.

First, the technological revolution is embedding the tenets of freedom in the structure of societies everywhere in the world. The power of the personal computer makes manifest, tangible, and concrete one of the central claims of freedom: the creative power and the spirit of the individual human being. Rather than the Orwellian nightmare of central control and mainframe computers, the PC has liberated its users from the tyranny of the central computer. Moreover, today's PC, with 7.5 million transistors on a single microprocessor, puts in the hands of its user the power of a super computer of just 20 years ago. That has shifted economic power from control of the raw-material resources that come out of the Earth to the ability to attract, inspire, and liberate individual minds.

That shift radically reduces the power of government over the freedom of the individual. In the industrial age, wealth and the production of income were tied to the physical world of steel mills, copper mines, railroad tracks, and the like. Governments can tax, regulate, expropriate, and therefore control the physical world.

But in the information age, wealth and the production of income are tied to knowledge and thought processes. The value of Microsoft's computer programs is not in the physical medium anymore than the value of

165

this book can be quantified by the value of the paper upon which it is printed. Imagine a government attempting to control the development of technology by nationalizing a software or semi-conductor company. The absurdity of the idea illustrates the gain in freedom wrought by the technological age.[9]

This shift in power from government to the private sector decreases the advantages of political connections and inevitably will force big business, big labor, and all other special-interest groups that rely on the power of government to shift their attention to competing in the marketplace. That implies increased competition to each of us as producers and increased power to each of us as consumers to obtain what we want at a price we are willing to pay.

Second, the Internet allows millions of people to experience what Hayek called the "extended order" that spontaneous human action generates every day in cyberspace, a place that has no physical location, that exists only in its use, and is therefore out of the reach of government. Government initially created the infrastructure of the Internet. But there is no authority that controls or plans or even regulates its use or its growth. Yet, in less than a decade, people acting in freedom have produced the richness, diversity, and commercial and business opportunities that we now know as the Internet.

Third, the Internet has made it all but impossible for governments to isolate their people from the ideas and ideals of freedom. The mere existence of the Internet in China, for example, has made it much more difficult for the government to control speech than when Chinese citizens had recourse only to a single wall in Beijing on which to post their political tracts. Today, more than three million mainland Chinese have access to the Internet. The Ministry of Information Industry controls the infrastructure of the Internet and can attempt control of its content, but with virtually free sources of information and the contact with people all over the world it facilitates, any attempt to control the thoughts of the Chinese people, or what they know or don't know, are doomed to fail. This is even more true when you consider the communication satellites overhead beaming news and entertainment to rooftops everywhere.

What is true for China is true for all governments. At the end of World War I, for example, President Woodrow Wilson was able to control the flow of information to the American people during the negotiations of the Treaty of Versailles. Under his orders, the postmaster general

166

assumed control over all transatlantic cable lines in order to censor the news from Europe.[10] By contrast, during the 1991 Gulf War, millions of people all over the world tuned in live to witness the bombing of Baghdad on CNN.

The creation of the personal computer and the Internet has replaced the metaphor of the production line or a powerful mainframe computer governing all of our lives with the metaphor of individual humans linked to one another across a vast, complex, and ever changing network. The personal computer validates our notion of autonomy. It empowers our creativity and, when connected to the Internet, reveals that the full potential of our humanity is realized as part of a vast network of human beings that can span the globe, available for idle talk, collaboration, and commerce.

Here is the good news. The Great Prosperity does not rely on a single great ruler, or on an all-powerful, all-knowing government that will devise exactly the right plan for the next 10 or 20 years. If that were the case, then the shape of the future, and the direction of the stock market, would rest on the judgment of only a handful of men and women, who, no matter how intelligent or how well-intentioned, have failings like all the rest of us. We would all be at risk. In some sense, if all of our fortunes and futures were tied exclusively to decisions of a few people with the absolute power of government, then none of us would be free.

And here is the best news of all: The Great Prosperity will be created by the free expression of the spirit and talents of our fellow human beings meeting to compete and cooperate in a marketplace that spans the globe. Through trade, these millions of people living in every corner of the globe will increase their capacity to contribute to our lives, and in the process, increase their living standards as well. This untapped power of freedom will produce an increase in living standards that will be part and parcel of the Great Prosperity. It will contribute to the increase in corporate profits that will provide the fundamental strength for reaching Dow 100,000. But, even as the importance of achieving that milestone fades, the increase in human rights and dignity that the spread of freedom implies will be celebrated for generations to come.

NOTES

1. Bryan T. Johnson, Kim R. Holmes, and Melanie Kirkpatrick, *1998 Index of Economic Freedom*, The Heritage Foundation, and *The Wall Street Journal*, 1998.

2. *Ibid.*

3. Rose Wilder Lane, *The Discovery of Freedom*, Fox & Wilkes, San Francisco, 1993, pp. 229–234.

4. Friedrich A. Hayek, *The Fatal Conceit*, The University of Chicago Press, Chicago, 1988.

5. ——, *The Road to Serfdom*, The University of Chicago Press, Chicago, 1944, p. 25.

6. Francis Fukuyama, "The End of History?" *The National Interest*, Summer 1989, pp. 3–18.

7. For a discussion of the "extended order," see Hayek.

8. Eduardo Lachica, "East, Southeast Asia Make Huge Strides in Reducing Poverty, World Bank Says," *The Wall Street Journal*, August 27, 1997, p. A8.

9. George Gilder, *Microcosm*, Simon & Shuster, New York, pp. 353–356.

10. Walter B. Wriston, "Bits, Bytes and Diplomacy," *Foreign Affairs*, September/October 1997, p. 174.

CHAPTER NINE

GLOBAL COMPETITION— THE CREATIVE SPARK

Global competition constitutes the fifth historical force that is shaping the future of the economy and the direction of financial markets. It, too, is pointing toward above-average economic growth and financial market returns.

Global competition has long existed among *companies*. What is new is competition among *countries* for the location of economic activity. The implicit reduction in the power of government will be a pervasive force for long-term growth and prosperity throughout the world. As politicians and bureaucrats are forced to compete, political forces will guide them toward policies that produce growth and prosperity and away from policies that reduce growth and prosperity.

Consider just a few events in the global marketplace that are symptomatic of this new reality.

- Sweden's largest labor union calls for a government commission to investigate a sharp increase in the number of leading companies moving management functions and even their headquarters out of Sweden.
- The ministers of Organization of Economic Cooperation and Development (OECD) issue a communiqué on "Harmful Tax Competition."[1]

- Thailand's legislature considers censuring the government for embracing International Monetary Fund policies that contributed to that country's economic collapse.
- State-owned telecommunications companies throughout Europe and Latin America are privatized.
- The "euro" becomes a single currency for 11 nations in Europe.
- Adopting the U.S. dollar as their currency gains popularity in Mexico.
- Daimler Benz and Chrysler merge; Ford buys Volvo.
- The finance minister of Germany's newly elected left-of-center government and head of the Socialist Party is forced to resign after pushing through a tax increase on business.

Each of these events points to a growing fact of life for politicians, special interests, and government officials and citizens of every political persuasion: Government policies are increasingly being subjected to the scrutiny of the marketplace. Corporations and, to a lesser extent, individuals, are gaining flexibility on where in the world they choose to locate their economic activity. As a consequence, onerous taxes, monetary instability, or counterproductive regulatory policies are ever more quickly leading to increased unemployment, a shrinking tax base, and lost elections. By contrast, lower tax rates, monetary stability, and productive regulatory policies are leading to higher employment, faster economic growth, an expanding tax base, and winning elections.

Global competition helps us map the road to Dow 100,000 for four reasons.

1. It points toward lower tax rates, stable prices, and freer trade, not only in the United States and other industrial countries, but in the developing world as well.

2. It points to an acceleration in economic growth outside the United States. Higher economic growth rates in Europe, Japan, Latin America, and elsewhere in the world will increase opportunities for U.S. companies to increase their international sales and profits. More than 40 percent of the profits of companies that make up the S&P 500, for example, come from outside the United States. An acceleration in the growth of profits from non-U.S. operations will contribute to the fundamentals underlying the road to Dow 100,000.

170

3. Better economic policies in Japan and Europe will also tend to reduce the U.S. trade deficit. A lower trade deficit has political importance because it will reduce pressures to impose restrictions on U.S. imports.

4. Success begets success. It invites imitation. For example, to the extent the European and Japanese governments in particular are successful in producing a stable price environment, the lower the risk of the Federal Reserve committing a monetary error. Such a mistake would become immediately evident in the movement of the dollar against the euro and yen. An inflationary policy would be signaled by a weakening dollar, and a deflationary policy would be signaled by a strengthening dollar.

The Role of Competition

As consumers, all of us adore competition. If Nike fails to make the best shoe, Reebok is right behind. When U.S. automakers stopped producing good cars, Japanese automakers stepped into the breach, forcing the auto companies, and the autoworkers, to make better cars. Who among us has not sought at least two bids when shopping for a car or remodeling a kitchen? Indeed, the foundation of the stock market is competitive bids in an open marketplace.

But as producers, we often wish that we did not have to contend with competition. Management and unions alike seek protection from competitive forces. The financial-services industry was far simpler, if also far less dynamic and efficient, when fixed commissions were legal and enforced by the New York Stock Exchange. Today, E*Trade and other on-line brokerage services have reduced the cost and increased the ease of trading so much that thousands of individuals actively trade their own accounts, something that once was reserved to those professionals who sat at a brokerage-company's trading desk.

In competitive markets, a misstep in the marketplace shows up in lost sales and market share, a shortfall in profits, a lower stock price, and less income. Jobs are lost or must be eliminated to stay in business. Our best-laid plans and good ideas sometimes just don't "pass go" with the consumer. What company does not have an "Edsel" in its history?

Competition is a positive force. It winnows the 10 percent of the good ideas that consumers are willing to pay for from the other 90 percent that

171

are, well, just good ideas. By so doing, competition forces us to abandon what does not work in favor of what does. In the same way, competition invites innovation, not only the breakthroughs, but also the small advances that, at the margin, save pennies, but over time and rising volumes save thousands if not millions of dollars of precious economic resources.

Finally, competition creates the opportunity to learn through trial and error. The test of the marketplace provides powerful feedback that distinguishes what works from what doesn't, and spreads the benefits of learning as we imitate and innovate on top of what works, and stop doing what does not work. In so doing, competition causes us to adapt to change and, in the process, abandon the past in favor of the future.

Government and Competition

Government plays a vital role in all this, much as the officials of any sport play a vital role in governing the play of the game. Many of the laws that govern a free society assure competition by prohibiting actions that interfere with the right of either party to choose not to enter into an exchange. Theft and extortion, for example, are not free exchanges, nor are they mutually satisfactory. They are outlawed. Fraud means that one party to the exchange knowingly misled or lied to the other party for the purpose of gaining a one-sided advantage. Antitrust laws are meant to protect competition by prohibiting collusion among sellers or outright monopoly practices.

Contracts codify the actions required by two parties over extended periods of time. Government and corporate bonds, for example, commit the borrower of the money to a variety of promises, which are stated in the bond's covenants. These include the amount of interest to be paid, the frequency of payments, and a date on which the money will be repaid to the lender. Additional clauses may specify other obligations of the borrower, including paying a premium if the bonds are retired earlier than promised. These promises can be enforced in a court of law. If the borrower does not have the financial resources to repay the loan, then the bankruptcy law provides a legal mechanism for the lenders to recoup as much of their money as possible, including the possibility of liquidating the business. Contracts, then, are an invention that increase the ability of individuals to coordinate their actions by agreeing in a legally enforceable way to a statement of conditions that both assess will be mutually satisfactory.

The one sector of our economy that has been relatively immune to competition, that is not compelled to meet the test of mutual satisfaction, has been the government itself. Politicians and government use the coercive power of the state to deny their citizens the right to say "no" to the "good ideas" embodied in government programs, regulations, and the tax code. In 1997, for example, the Medicare bureaucracy in the United States won a reprieve from impending private-sector competition by prohibiting any doctor who sees even *one* senior citizen on a private-pay (non-Medicare paid) basis from seeing *any* Medicare patient for two years. As the *Wall Street Journal* points out, if Social Security were regulated in this manner, a retiree collecting Social Security could not see a registered investment adviser.[2]

But now, market forces are coming into play to check the power of government. In the United States, we have already witnessed and have benefited from competition among state governments. For example, under liberal democratic Governor Mario Cuomo, New York State reduced personal income-tax rates roughly in half even though he and the liberal wing of the Democratic Party opposed tax-rate reductions on those with high incomes.

Why did these tax cuts take place?

Because more and more people were saying "no" to the state's fiscal policies by moving their families, companies, and jobs to more hospitable economic climes. As Governor Cuomo explained, the tax-rate reductions were necessary for New York to remain "competitive." New York's monopoly power over its citizens was effectively broken.

These competitive pressures on the monopoly power of government are beginning to build on an international scale. The illustrative case in point concerns the extension of the Value Added Tax to auctions held in London. European governments agreed to harmonize their tax policies as a way of minimizing competition, forcing the British government in 1995 to impose a 2.5-percent VAT on the previously untaxed sale of antiques, works of art, and collectibles. Largely as a consequence, imports of these items into Britain the following year fell 40 percent, to $600 million. A growing share of the antique business shifted to New York City, whose 8.5-percent sales tax is not imposed on any goods shipped out of the city.

Global competition at work. Effectively, Britain raised the price of doing business in London, but, while it can use all of its powers to collect the tax, it cannot force anyone to transact in London. With modern communications, it turned out to be relatively easy to shift the economic activity to New York City. The vast majority of sellers and buyers do not reside in Britain and participate in the auctions through their agents by telephone. It matters not whether the person at the other end of the line is on the Eastern or Western rim of the Atlantic. What attracts this economic activity to New York is the narrower spread between the price paid by the buyer and the price received by the seller. *Both buyer and seller have a chance of being better off.*

That's the key. High tax rates increase the spread between buyer and seller relative to low tax rates. What is true for the auction market in the world of art is just as true for all other economic activity everywhere in the world. People everywhere are driven to find ways to enter into mutually beneficial exchanges with other people. Just as high tariffs make it difficult for trade to occur between countries, high tax rates make domestic trade more difficult. Low tax rates make it easier. High tax-rate economies tend to repel economic activity. A low tax-rate environment attracts transactions, including employment and investment.

The Global Economy

Companies have more freedom to choose where to locate economic activity than ever before. Today, we can communicate by fax and phone to virtually every major city in the world, all of which can be reached by commercial airliner with no more than one stop from New York. As a result, it has become easier and easier for economic activity to shift to where tax and regulatory policies are most conducive to employment and the production of wealth. The low-cost airline Virgin Express, for example, has moved its headquarters to Ireland from Belgium to avoid what the company considered Belgium's high labor costs and excessive government and union interference. The move was expected to increase the airline's profitability by more than 30 percent and position it to compete against other low-cost airlines invading the European market.[3]

As companies increase their ability to operate globally, they gain the ability to shift profits to subsidiaries in lower-tax countries from operations in higher-tax countries. For example, foreign subsidiaries of American companies report higher profit margins in low-tax than in high-tax countries.[4]

174

These competitive forces are likely to intensify in the years ahead. The plummeting cost of communications and the growing ease of use of the Internet alone are homogenizing the world economy.

One symptom of this globalization of the world economy is the increasingly dominant use of English as the language of business everywhere in the world. On the Internet, the language of choice is English. Virtually all computer programming is done in English, and CNN beams its *Headline News* from Atlanta and London in English to TVs throughout the world.

The European Union has 15 official languages, one for each of its 15 members. When the new European Central Bank meets, it uses English as its common language, even though Britain is not a part of the euro and is not at the meeting. European companies with managers from various countries such as Merloni S.p.A. of Italy and LVMH, the French conglomerate, have similarly adopted English as the company's official language. Even at Insead, the prestigious business school outside Paris, the official language for teaching and research is English.[5]

Until now, the movement of individuals to avoid high tax rates has been limited, for the most part to international stars in sports and entertainment. Swedish tennis star Mat Wilander and German tennis star Boris Becker, for example, have left high-tax Sweden and Germany and now live in Monaco, where they are exempt from income and capital-gains taxes. And Sweden's Stefan Edberg has chosen the lower-tax clime of London over the high-tax-rate environment of his home country.

As Swedish firms are discovering, their most talented employees are also starting to move to lower-tax countries, including the United States. In France—where the top personal income tax rate is 54 percent, social taxes add 50 percent to the cost of employment, and the Value Added Tax takes another 20.6 percent—1.7 million French, or 7 percent of the work force, were employed outside the country in 1997. The government estimates that one-quarter of graduates from the nation's universities now exit the country after graduation.[6]

As English becomes the common language of the business world, workers and managers at all levels will find it easier to challenge the monopoly power of government by moving. For example, a citizen of Germany or France or any of the other countries in the European Community could live and work in any other member country. In the past, the need to learn another language acted as a barrier to such movement. Thus, a common language for business represents a dramatic reduction in the barriers to people relocating to another country to seek better economic opportunities.

The Creation of the Euro

The creation of the euro as a common currency in 11 European countries can only intensify competitive forces among governments as well as companies (Figure 9–1). In one sense, the creation of the euro, which effectively extends German monetary policy to most of Europe, can itself be seen as the result of competitive forces. The German central bank, with its constitutional responsibility to stabilize the price level, has consistently produced lower inflation and lower interest rates than the other central banks of Europe. Moreover, all past attempts to stabilize European cur-

FIGURE 9–1   The Euro Member Countries

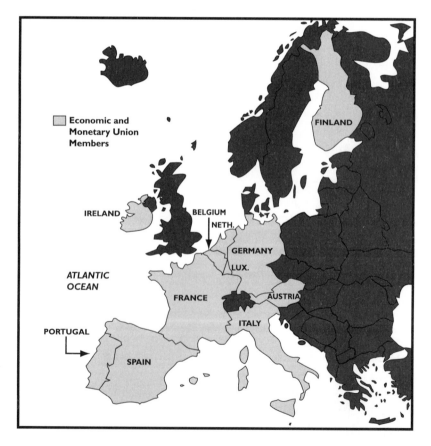

rencies ultimately succumbed to central-bank error, speculative forces, or a combination of the two. As a result, Europeans in one referendum after another voted to forgo monetary sovereignty in favor of a single currency whose central bank would effectively adopt the operating procedures of the German Bundesbank. The benefits go beyond eliminating the complexities of coping with 11 different currencies to achieving low inflation and stable prices for virtually all of Continental Europe.

Now that the common currency is in place, the ability of governments and bureaucrats to disguise poor tax and regulatory policies is disappearing. Unlike stars of sports and entertainment, people do not relocate their families in search of a better job or economic environment in Europe the way they do the United States, so the impact of disparate tax policies and regulatory policies will not be so immediately apparent. But all incremental economic activity and investment will seek the most advantageous economic environment, and their cumulative effects will be every bit as great as they are in the United States.

Companies will choose to locate their most profitable operations in those countries with the lowest tax rates. They will experience higher after-tax profits. But the underlying phenomenon is increased trade—in this case between the providers and users of capital. Increased trade between the suppliers and users of capital will, in turn, produce increased employment and production. Economic growth in the low-tax countries will increase.

At the same time, marginally profitable operations will be left to operate in high-tax-rate countries. No profits, no tax. Growth in these countries will slow. Factories will age. Where losses occur, government subsidies may be provided in the name of saving jobs, all the while covering up the corrosive effects of the high tax rates. Governments can set the rules, but they cannot determine the outcomes. Unemployment will inevitably rise. The equally inevitable consequence will be political upheaval and, just as happened in New York, lower tax rates.

We can already see the cutting edge of the coming wave of global competition in Europe. As the barriers to competition fall, businesses are acquiring or merging with other companies to become pan European, if not global in their operations. In 1989, the year before agreement was reached to form a single European currency in the Dutch city of Maastrich, mergers-and-acquisition activity in Europe totaled $186 billion. Since 1996, M&A activity in Europe has exceeded $335 billion a year, and it totaled $845 billion in 1998.

177

In 1998, the German auto giant Daimler merged with American Chrysler Corporation. In 1999, Ford bought Volvo of Sweden. Operations over time will be consolidated. New factories will be located in the best economic environment. As DaimlerChrysler Cochairman Jurgen Schrempp explained to *Forbes* magazine in early 1999, "You will have companies making decisions on a neutral basis, not a German or U.S. basis."[7]

Global Competition and the Signposts to Dow 100,000

Increasing competition among governments is a historical force that politicians and societies cannot control, but must respond to. By anticipating their response, we can gain confidence in the direction of the economy and financial markets that lie ahead.

Global Competition and Taxes

The first reaction among European Community bureaucrats to the pressure of increased competition has been to call for "tax harmonization." Sensing the loss of power, they sought increased power on the part of the European Community's government to impose minimum tax rates throughout the EC.

But hopes of blunting competitive pressures were dashed, first by Ireland and then by political pressures within Britain, Germany, and Sweden. Just before the euro formally came into existence on January 1, 1999, for example, the European Commission ordered Ireland to stop "subsidizing" its exporters with a corporate income-tax rate of only 10 percent compared to the 32-percent rate applied to nonexporters. Ireland's response, however, was to announce it would normalize the two tax rates at 12.5 percent by the year 2003, creating the lowest corporate income-tax rate by far in Europe.[8]

Even before the creation of the euro, voters in Britain, France, and Germany voted for left-of-center governments, perhaps in part hoping to soften the brute impact of global competitive pressures. However, to get elected, the leaders of these parties had to eschew their socialist policies of the past. The political realities of the present are forcing a pragmatism that is symptomatic of a competitive environment. The leader of France's left-wing coalition government, Prime Minister Lionel Jospin, for example, sold more state assets in his first 18 months of governing than the prior right-wing government had sold in its two years in power. At the end of 1998, his budget called for cutting government spending to 51 percent from 54 percent of GDP. Echoing a guiding sentiment of Britain's Tony Blair, the leading political sage of the so-called "Third Way" between socialism and capitalism, Jospin explained his policies by saying, "What counts is what works."[9]

What works, of course, are lower tax rates, stable prices, and less burdensome government. In this regard, Ireland is leading the way. Beginning in 1987, it embarked upon an economic liberalization program that has turned its economy into the most competitive in Europe. Government spending was cut to one-third of total economic output from more than half. The corporate tax rate was reduced to 32 percent from 40 percent. Other tax abatements and targeted incentives, which are allowed under European rules, were offered multinational corporations to locate in Ireland.

Since 1993, Irish economy has been growing 8 percent a year. At the end of 1998, the unemployment rate had fallen to 7.8 percent, half its former level and well below the double-digit unemployment rates common to most of the rest of Europe. For the first time since the Irish famine, the country has experienced a net immigration of people, many of whom are of Irish descent and are moving back to Ireland from America. Joining the euro will only improve Ireland's competitive position, removing the risk of currency instability while giving its businesses access to a much broader and deeper capital market.

Tax-rate reductions will be spreading in Europe, as governments are forced, one after the other, to respond to unemployment rates that average more than 10 percent for the entire work force and exceed 20 percent for those under 25. Spain in 1999, for example, reduced its top personal income-tax rate to 48 percent from 56 percent. That will only increase the competitive pressure on Portugal, Italy, France, and Germany to follow suit.

A new round of across-the-board tax-rate reductions in the United States will increase competitive pressures on the rest of the world to reduce the tax barriers to commerce as well. Between 1980 and 1988, the United States reduced its top personal income-tax rate to 28 percent from 70 percent. One consequence was a renaissance in the competitiveness of U.S. corporations. A second consequence was that tax rates

179

fell all over the world. During those eight years, the top personal income tax rate was reduced to

- 40 percent from 83 percent in Britain
- 53 percent from 60 percent in France
- 50 percent from 75 percent in Japan

Among developing countries, the top tax rate was reduced to

- 48 percent from 89 percent in South Korea
- 28 percent from 55 percent in Singapore
- 30 percent from 45 percent in Argentina
- 10 percent from 48 percent in Bolivia

Totaled, more than 25 nations reduced their personal income-tax rates during the 1980s (Table 9–1).

Competitive pressures are pointing toward lower tax rates throughout the world. Lower tax rates in Europe, Japan, and the rest of Asia will reduce the barriers to domestic trade within these countries. More domestic trade will produce higher economic growth and lower unemployment. As employment and incomes rise, so will demand, just as it has in the United States in recent years. These expanding markets will also attract investment, especially in technology equipment where the United States leads. Thus, more rapid economic growth outside the United States will increase opportunities for U.S. businesses. Some of those increased opportunities will be realized through increased exports. Other opportunities will be realized through the foreign operations of U.S. companies. Both activities will lead to increased corporate profits and higher stock prices.

Global Competition and Monetary Policy

The International Monetary Fund (IMF) was originally created as part of the post-World War II Bretton Woods international monetary system to provide short-term loans to governments for the purpose of stabilizing their exchange rates. With the collapse of fixed exchange rates that began in 1971, however, the IMF changed its role, and became a source of capital to governments that were running out of money, usually because of bad domestic economic policies. Because it is the "lender of last resort" to incumbent governments and bureaucrats, it wields enormous power to impose economic policies on the recipients of its largesse.

Unfortunately, the IMF's standard prescription is to raise tax rates and devalue the currency. The increased barriers to domestic trade and

TABLE 9–1 Global Competition and Tax Rates in the 1980s

Highest Tax Rates

	1979	1984	1989	1996
G-7 Countries:				
United States	**70**	**50**	**28**	**40**
Canada (Ontario)	58	50	47	53
France	60	53	53	52
Germany	56	56	53	58
Italy	72	65	50	51
Japan	75	70	50	50
United Kingdom	83	60	40	40
Average	68	58	46	49
Argentina	45	62	30	30
Bolivia	48	30	10	13
Botswana	75	60	40	35
Brazil	55	60	25	25
Chile	60	57	50	45
Colombia	56	49	30	30
Costa Rica	50	50	30	25
El Salvador	60	48	30	30
Hong Kong	15	17	20	15
India	60	62	53	40
Indonesia	50	35	35	30
Malayasia	60	45	45	30
Mauritius	60	35	35	30
New Zealand	66	66	33	33
Pakistan	50	60	35	39
Peru	65	50	37	30
Singapore	55	40	33	28
South Korea	89	55	48	40
Thailand	60	65	55	37
Average	57	50	35	31

Note: Some countries that sharply reduced top tax rates to 25–35% in recent years such as Uganda, Ghana, Sri Lanka, Tunisia, and the Dominican Republic are excluded due to lack of detailed historical information. State and local taxes are not included for Japan, where they can add up to 15 percentage points, or for the U.S.

Source: *The International Importance of Low Tax Rates;* The Hudson Institute

monetary instability have proven lethal to economic activity. As a result, wherever the IMF has gone, poverty has followed.

This became evident after the government of Thailand followed the IMF's advice in the spring of 1997 and devalued its currency by 10 percent. What resulted became known as the Asian flu, which of course, was not a disease, but a policy error. As businesspeople all over Asia realized that the system of pegged exchange rates that had provided a stable currency, low inflation, and low interest rates were at risk, they began a rush out of their local currencies into the dollar. The ensuing currency crisis leaped from Thailand to Indonesia, Singapore, Malaysia, and then to Korea. In 1998, it crushed Russia. And, in early 1999, in spite of a $41 billion standby line of credit and the full support of the U.S. government, it toppled the Brazilian currency, the *real*.

Currency devaluations do not improve a country's competitiveness. They reduce a country's ability to compete. Currency instability undermines a country's financial system, destroys private capital, and creates political instability. Devaluations are followed by inflation to reflect that the currency is now worth less. Indonesia exports oil. Nonetheless, the price of oil in *rupiah* increased 10-fold after the rupiah was devalued because it took 10 times as many rupiah to buy a dollar, and oil is priced in dollars. The same is true for every other commodity, as well as all imports of goods and services. Consequently, the price level in Indonesia increased at a 122-percent annual rate during the first three months after it devalued. In Jakarta, the nation's capital, traffic jams were replaced by food riots.

People everywhere, throughout time, are engaged in an effort to make a better future for themselves and their children. By its nature, this process is one of trial and error. In the case of the Asian currency crisis, the error was of such a magnitude that the theoretical arguments in favor of currency devaluations have fallen to the practical reality of the preeminent need to provide a stable currency.

As a result, the currency crisis that began in Asia in 1997 has put international monetary reform back on the political agenda for the first time since the final collapse of the Bretton Woods system of fixed exchange rates in 1973. Instead of stabilizing trade flows, floating exchange rates have proven to be a source of incredibly destabilizing capital flows. Quasi-pegged systems that were used in Thailand, Indonesia, Korea, Mexico, and Brazil also invite speculative attack.

The success of the euro acts as a guiding light to people everywhere who are searching for an alternative to the monetary systems that have failed them. By being part of the formation of a continent-wide currency, the people of Spain, Portugal, and Italy, and perhaps France and other European countries, avoided runs on their currencies and the high interest rates and economic upheaval created by the Asian currency crisis. Currency boards, which guarantee convertibility by backing up each dollar's worth of local currency with a dollar's worth of U.S. Treasury securities held at the currency board, also survived the crisis in Argentina and Hong Kong.

Restoration of an international monetary system is the last piece of unfinished business from the Great Inflation of the 1970s. The return of price stability and fiscal balance in the United States provides a solid foundation for the United States to lead this effort. The creation of the euro, which has brought currency stability and low rates of inflation to Western Europe, gives the United States a strong partner in this effort. A world of instant communications, sophisticated financial instruments, hedge funds, and the ability to move billions of dollars in capital with the push of a button demands such a system.

Those who say that a new international monetary system cannot be created will be proven wrong. On December 14, 1941, one week after the Japanese attack on Pearl Harbor, then Treasury Secretary Henry Morgenthau asked his assistant, Harry Dexter White, to begin work on a global system that would provide a stable monetary system to the entire world once the war was won.[10] All that is lacking for a similar undertaking today is the same kind of leadership.

Competitive pressures point to the creation of an international monetary system that will provide stable prices and low interest rates to all the people of the world. If the United States and Europe fail to provide a stable monetary system to Latin America, Asia, and Africa, then we can expect that the people of these regions will find their own alternative to the dollar and euro. In either case, restoration of a stable international monetary system will be one of the great achievements in the decade that lies ahead. The architects of the system will have their rightful place in history. Their legacy will be a dramatic increase in freedom and prosperity and rising equity prices throughout the developing world. The subsequent increase in incomes and corporate profits in the United States will contribute to the fundamental underpinnings for the Dow Jones Industrial's 21-year climb to 100,000.

Global Competition and Trade Policy

The ascendancy of the global market can also be seen in the increasing number of countries seeking to be part of larger free-trade zones. As the power of governments recedes, the natural desire of people to extend their boundaries of trade is becoming manifest throughout the world.

President Ronald Reagan declared the possibility of a free-trade zone that embraced the entire Western Hemisphere. He achieved a free-trade pact with Canada and initiated the negotiations that extended free trade to Mexico. At the same time, virtually all of Eastern Europe aspires to be admitted to the European Union, as does Turkey in the Middle East.

The free-trade movement has since stalled in the United States, but the world is not standing still. A free-trade pact among Argentina, Brazil, Uruguay, and Paraguay, called Mercorsur, shows that the vision of free trade continues to live in Latin America. Moreover, Chile, rebuffed by the United States, has negotiated free-trade pacts with Mexico and Canada, and Mexico is exploring a free-trade agreement with the European Union. If policies don't change, the United States could, one day, find that it is at risk of losing its natural competitive advantage in trade with a Latin America that has formed a closer free-trade association with the European Continent.

Here, too, global competition shows itself to be a positive force on the road to Dow 100,000.

The Changing Role of Government

Global competition extends well beyond tax, monetary, and trade policies to the role of government in societies. Some bemoan the loss of power of government to the global economic forces, but governments are not disinterested parties; they serve powerful constituencies. Competitive forces not only check the power these constituencies have over the rest of society, but also encourage government to improve its own functions and thereby increase its contributions to the society as a whole.

Global competition not only means less government, it means better government. Governments that effectively provide public services, sound infrastructure from harbors to highways, good schools, and otherwise spend wisely the monies their societies entrust in their care will gain share of global economic activity. Those that fail will inevitably lose share of global economic activity and power.

184

During the past 20 years, global competitive forces have already led to widespread privatization of state-owned enterprises, especially telecommunications companies, throughout the world. Although governments do not normally give up so much patronage and power, in today's fast-moving world economy, if a country does not have a modern telecommunications system, it cannot hope to be fully competitive, and government bureaucracies have demonstrated that they are incapable of competing in this fast-changing arena.

Crony Capitalism

One of the unexpected lessons of the 1997–1998 Asian economic crisis was the failure of the Japanese model of state-directed capitalism to provide for sustained economic growth. Instead, it showed itself to be inherently unstable, structurally inflexible, and all too often corrupt.

Crony capitalism, as the Japanese economic model has become known, increases the economic risks faced by the people of an entire nation. Bureaucrats, like all human beings, make mistakes. However, sheltered from the day-to-day rigors of the market place, they have the power to perpetuate their mistakes longer than most through the power of government. Therefore, when the mistake is finally revealed, the consequences can be catastrophic.

In Korea, for example, the government used the banking system to direct subsidized capital to a few giant family conglomerates known as *chaebol*. These industrial conglomerates pursued expansion and capital investment with little regard to returns on capital or profitability. These policies produced jobs and cash flow in government-favored industries including steel, autos, and semi-conductors, but, according to a study by Merrill Lynch, the top 10 companies in Korea earned only 4 percent on their capital. Moreover, their balance sheets were highly leveraged, with debt exceeding capital by ratios of four and even eight to one.

When the Asian currency crisis hit, the Korean currency, stock market, and economy all collapsed, with the currency and stock market each falling by more than 50 percent in dollar terms. By contrast, in Taiwan, where small- and medium-sized companies were allowed to compete for capital and market share, the currency fell less than 20 percent, the economy continued to grow, and the stock market actually rose in dollar terms.

The lesson has been learned all across East Asia. Foreign investors, who had once been forbidden or discouraged, are now being welcomed,

185

if with some mixed emotions, in Korea and Japan. The power of markets is growing; the power of governments, shrinking.

The Outlook

As you read the road signs that lie ahead, be on the lookout for

1. The spread of lower tax rates
2. An increasing number of countries that commit to a stable exchange rate
3. A shift in policy at the IMF toward supporting stable exchange rates and lower tax rates
4. A major Latin American country negotiating a free-trade pact with the European Community
5. Privatization of government-run monopolies wherever they exist
6. A leading U.S. politician arguing that global competitive pressures should be taken into account in the design of U.S. economic, regulatory, and trade policies

The spread of lower tax rates, stable prices, and freer trade will produce increased economic activity and better financial-market returns throughout the world. U.S. companies will share in those benefits, both directly and indirectly. U.S. economic policy, too, will become somewhat more responsive to global competitive forces. For all these reasons, global competition will act as a spark to the creation of those policies that will contribute to the Great Prosperity and reaching Dow 100,000 by 2020.

NOTES

1. "Harmful Tax Competition: An Emerging Global Issue," Extract from the Communiqué OECD Council Meeting at Ministerial Level, Paris, 27–28 April 1998.

2. "Medicare Showstopper," *The Wall Street Journal*, August 22, 1997.

3. Jonathan Ford, "Virgin Express plans move to Ireland," *Financial Times*, July 8, 1998, p. 17.

4. *The Economist*, May 31, 1997.

5. Jon Tagliabue, "In Europe, Steps Toward a Common Language," *The New York Times*, July 19, 1998, Section 4, pp. 1, 4.

6. Richard C. Morais, "Even the chefs are leaving France," *Forbes*, November 30, 1998, pp. 84–94.

7. Justin Doebele, "No more barriers," *Forbes*, January 11, 1999, p. 65.

8. Therese Raphael, "Irish Economy Creates a Pot of Gold," *The Wall Street Journal*, December 30, 1998, p. A10.

9. "The French left begins to falter," *The Economist*, January 9, 1999, p. 45.

10. Judy Shelton, "Time for a New Bretton Woods," *The Wall Street Journal*, October 15, 1998.

CHAPTER TEN

POSSIBLE DETOURS— THE THREATS TO DOW 100,000

The Great Prosperity should last at least 20 years. For one thing, it has just gotten underway. For another, the historical forces behind this prosperity are powerful. And, finally, our memories of the Great Depression of the 1930s and the Great Inflation of the 1970s are still so strong that they limit the risk of a policy error of such magnitude that it could bring an abrupt end to this prosperity.

But there are always risks—we know that there are no sure things. No map would be complete without noting the dangers that may lie ahead. The Great Prosperity cannot be guaranteed, nor can reaching 100,000 on the Dow over the next 21 years. This chapter explores the threats to the Great Prosperity and the risks to reaching that centurion milestone.

We can be sure of one thing: The road to 100,000 on the Dow will not be straight. A Great Prosperity does not rule out short-term economic shocks or stock-market corrections. Moreover, there will be doubters and naysayers all along the way, encouraging people to sell their stocks when markets are down, only to miss out on the subsequent rises to new highs. Distinguishing between such short-term shocks and era-threatening changes is therefore essential to preparing for and building wealth during the Great Prosperity.

The Roaring Twenties, for all of their promise, came to a crashing end that was signaled by the collapse in equity prices in October 1929. The policy errors: a dramatic increase in trade restrictions followed by a more than doubling of tax rates, and the deflationary collapse of price stability.

The last era of growth with price stability, the 1950s and 1960s, ended in fits and starts. Once again, policy errors were at the heart of prosperity's end. Taxes were raised to fight the Vietnam War in Southeast Asia and the "War on Poverty" at home. The rapid increase in government spending ultimately led to a devaluation of the dollar and then the collapse of the international monetary system. The combination of tax increases, monetary instability, and increased trade restrictions brought that era of growth with price stability to an end with an economy mired in high inflation, rising unemployment, and falling living standards. *Adjusted for inflation, the Dow Jones Industrials between 1966 and 1982 fell 73 percent, nearly equaling the 87-percent decline experienced during the 1930s.*

What are the detours and roadblocks that may lie ahead?

One risk that always deserves our attention is that markets can get ahead of themselves; prices can rise in the short term more than may be warranted by the underlying fundamentals of corporate profits, interest rates, and inflation. A reversal in such a situation, however, is just that, an adjustment to the current economic fundamentals. As we go to press, for example, the value of many Internet stocks have been bid up to extremely high valuations. Any downward adjustment to the prospects for these companies could lead to significant price declines in the technology sector of the market in particular and the broader market in general.

Another near-term risk is that Robert Rubin is no longer Treasury Secretary and Alan Greenspan's term as chairman of the Federal Reserve ends in June 2000. These two people, more than any other, worked to support a strong dollar and restore stable prices to the U.S. economy. Because their policies are not codified in any law or process, their departure inevitably adds some risk of a loss of price stability to the near-term outlook.

While important, these potential disruptions to the market's upward climb can be characterized as likely detours or short-term setbacks on the road to 100,000 on the Dow because they do not threaten to end the Great Prosperity. In short, markets do not go straight up. Corrections—declines of at least 10 percent—periodically occur. In fact, the S&P 500 has declined

189

in 10 of the 48 years between 1950 and 1997, though the last calendar decline occurred in 1990. Moreover, twice during 1997, the S&P 500 declined at least 10 percent from a peak to a trough. For the year as a whole, though, this broad measure of the U.S. equity market produced a total return of 33.36 percent. In the last half of 1998, the market fell within a fraction of 20 percent, but recovered before year-end, finishing the year with a total return of 28.6 percent. Periodic market declines are part and parcel of the ebb and flow of markets and emotions. They are sure to mark the road ahead just as they have marked the road behind.

Disaster and the Dow

A strategic approach requires a different focus, a search for changes so powerful that they can end the Great Prosperity and block the road to 100,000 on the Dow. There are at least five events that have the capacity to interrupt at least one of the five positive historical forces and trigger an increase in taxes, monetary instability, or massive trade restrictions. They include the outbreak of war, a terrorist attack in the United States, a trade war with China, an international monetary crisis, and the looming crisis of Medicare.

War

The past century was one of the bloodiest in history, a hundred years punctuated by two world wars, a series of regional conflicts, and a 45-year standoff between two nuclear powers. The Cold War may be over, but the risk of war has not been banished from the face of the Earth.

The risk is not of a conventional war among regional antagonists. During the Gulf War of 1991, the United States demonstrated to the entire world its unchallenged military superiority if it deemed its own national interests to be at stake.

The risk is that in such a war a nation would use a weapon of mass destruction. Within the past two years, the United States has bombed Iraq out of concerns that it was rearming itself with chemical and biological weapons of mass destruction. India and Pakistan each detonated nuclear bombs of their own. North Korea fired a ballistic missile that flew over Japan. Soon, it will have the capability of firing on Alaska or perhaps Seattle. China, too, is deploying missiles along its southeast coast that are capable of carrying nuclear weapons and that are targeted at Taiwan.

During the next 20 years, the weapons of mass destruction are likely to spread. Starving Russian scientists are selling their nuclear know-how to Iran and perhaps Libya and Syria as well.[1] The technological revolution is putting the kind of super-computing power necessary to design nuclear weapons on sale at the local computer store. Today, PCs that cost less than $2,000 run 40 times faster than the computers that required export licenses as late as 1993.[2] In addition, at least 17 nations are suspected of having or trying to acquire germ weapons.

The United States stands defenseless against the consequences of a missile attack. If a nation were to use a weapon of mass destruction, especially in the Middle East, the Great Prosperity would be at risk. At a minimum, such a war would disrupt international trade, especially in oil, and threaten a new global emergency. Talk of tax reductions would cease in the face of a rapid increase in defense expenditures. Inflation could once again threaten the outlook. The spread of freedom, too, could be put at risk.

It is not possible to quantify the threat of war, but we must be aware that the possibility of war has faded from market valuations. If this risk were to reappear, we could anticipate a contraction in price earnings ratios as the future suddenly became less certain and more dangerous. The Dow Industrials, for example, fell 28 percent between the end of 1938 and the end of 1941 and did not return to its 1938 close until 1945, well after it was clear that the Allies would win World War II. The War in Vietnam, too, coincided with below-average stock-market performance.

Terrorism

Perhaps a risk that is greater than war is a terrorist attack in which germ warfare or a biological weapon were used, especially if it occurred in the United States. Such a horrifying event would create a new "state of emergency" and would cut to the heart of the populist impulse that, with the Cold War fading into memory, is just now beginning to fully assert itself.

America's military superiority may not be enough to ward off a terrorist attack. In 1998, the attacks were on U.S. embassies in Africa. In the next 20 years, they may be on public places in a major U.S. city such as New York or even Washington DC. These are not pleasant thoughts, but they must be considered. *The New York Times*, after a yearlong inquiry in 1998, identified the following trends that "suggest the threat of germ tranquility may indeed be ending:

- Uprooted weapon scientists from Iraq, Russia, and South Africa are hunting for new jobs and spreading germ secrets.
- Radical states with reputations for supporting terror, such as Iran and Libya, are seeking germ weapons.
- Terrorists, such as Osama bin Laden, are increasingly interested in pestilential germs. Some boast openly of being able to kill foes with deadly plagues."[3]

In an interview with *The New York Times*, former Director of the Central Intelligence Agency R. James Woolsey said, "Germ terrorism is 'the single most dangerous threat to our national security in the foreseeable future.'"[4]

The United States has begun to commit billions of dollars to defend against such an attack. Vaccinations are given American troops in the Persian Gulf and to some FBI and White House officials.[5] All U.S. troops now routinely are vaccinated against anthrax, and the military has begun to stockpile 18 other vaccines, including one against smallpox. The Federal government has also started to build precautionary supplies of medicines and antibiotics that could be used in an emergency to protect police, fire, and health workers. Perhaps one day all of use will have to be similarly protected. The risk today is low, most agree, but it is growing.[6]

A terrorist attack would signal a new emergency. Town meetings would once again look quaint and irrelevant in a devilishly dangerous world. There would be an automatic and perfectly understandable turn to government and an acceptance of increased intrusions in our lives. For example, *just the speculation* that terrorists were responsible for the explosion that ended TWA Flight 800 shortly after it took off from New York's Kennedy Airport led the Clinton Administration and many in Congress to advocate passage of a law that would have added an hour or more to every airline trip taken each day by tens of thousands of people. Think of the waste of human resources and the loss of productivity that implies. The law also called for increases in police powers and reductions in civil liberties that were so vast that, at the last minute, several Senators resisted the emotion to "do something" and successfully opposed the bill.

We can only imagine what freedoms we might be willing to forgo in the event of an actual terrorist attack. If freedom were at risk in the United States, it would be at risk everywhere in the world. A shrinkage of freedom inevitably reduces the opportunities for trade just as surely as the spread of freedom is expanding them.

Economic Backlash Against China

China today is the third largest economy in the world. Over the next decade, the Chinese government, businesses, and people will be buying tens of billions of dollars worth of goods and services, ranging from sophisticated machinery, power-generating equipment and telecommunications systems, to consumer durables such as televisions and automobiles and consumer staples, including toothpaste and razor blades.

To purchase these tens of billions of dollars worth of goods and services, the Chinese will have to sell an equal amount of goods and services to the rest of the world. Trade is a two-way street.

In just a dozen years—from 1983 to 1995—for example, China nearly tripled its share of manufactured exports to 3.4 percent of the world's total. So far, it has taken market share in light manufactured products such as footwear, textiles, and toys. China is the world's top exporter of textiles and clothing.

As the Chinese become bigger players in the world economy, their activities will change relative prices of goods and services. We are talking about freeing the energies of one-fifth of the world's population that lives in one of the oldest cultures in the world. The price of goods and services that China seeks in world markets will tend to rise versus those goods and services it seeks to sell to the rest of the world. In addition, just the sheer number of the Chinese people will tend to depress wages for unskilled workers the world around, from Shanghai to Harlem.

When you change relative prices, you also change relative fortunes of individual workers and businesses. Some companies and businesses will be positively affected, discovering and developing vast new markets for their products. But others will be negatively affected by our trade with China. Their economic fortunes will be hurt through no fault of their own. Moreover, the source of their misfortune will be a foreign entity that can easily bring forth our residual prejudice and perhaps latent fear.

The natural human response to something that can have a negative impact on our lives, but over which we have no control, is to seek protection for ourselves and our families. This impulse will add political support to those who want to restrict trade with China for ideological reasons as well as for self-centered economic reasons. (Goodness knows, there are a lot of things not to like about the Chinese government and its policies.)

193

There are also concerns about the increase in China's economic power relative to the United States and the rest of the world. For the past two decades, the Chinese economy has grown at near double-digit rates. Even in the midst of the Asian currency crisis, it managed to post an 8-percent increase in its GDP, producing approximately $1 trillion in Gross Domestic Product during the year. China now accounts for one-third of the region's economic activity, excluding Japan. China's stature and influence throughout Asia also increased as it maintained a stable value of its currency relative to the dollar during the region's currency crisis. The maintenance of the fixed exchange rate between Hong Kong's dollar and the U.S. dollar also has contributed to China's stature and economic power.

Though the Chinese economy is still only one-eighth the size of the United States, people are highly sensitive to shifts in relative power. We have all seen individuals who have had difficulty in adjusting to having a smaller piece of a larger pie even though they are better off in absolute terms, but worse off in relative terms.

This natural response to a shift in relative power is accentuated by a growing concern over China's ongoing military buildup. In early 1999, for example, the Pentagon reported Chinese plans to increase to 650 the number of missiles it has deployed along its southeast coast and targeted at Taiwan. This aggressive act invites a military confrontation with the United States, which, under its own Taiwan Relations Act, is obliged to provide the weapons necessary for Taiwan's defense.

Thus, we can see the outlines of a possible coalition to block renewal of the so-called "Most Favored Nation" treatment of Chinese trade with the United States. Left-wing liberals and right-wing Christians can join ranks under the banner of human rights. The isolationists of the left can join hands with the military hawks of the right to oppose trade with the Chinese, and all parties will be fed by business and labor interests that will be seeking protection from Chinese competition.

It was just this sort of confluence of political factors that led to the unexpected agreement to pass the Smoot–Hawley tariffs in October of 1929, which increased by one-third the tariffs on virtually all commodities imported into the United States.[7] *We can reproduce the economic depression of the 1930s. All we have to do is replicate the policies.*

If China were denied MFN status, then tariffs on Chinese imports would revert to the high, Smoot–Hawley rates. Imposition of Smoot–Hawley-like tariffs today on trade between America and China would lead directly to large increases in unemployment among

194

American workers. The rest of the world would be unlikely to join in the United States's initial effort to isolate the Chinese. More likely, competitors of American companies would rush in to take advantage of the loss of competitiveness of U.S. exporters and producers caused by the tariffs. Chinese trade would be diverted to Europe and the rest of the world.

However, faced with a flood of imports, Europeans, too, might react by trying to restrict trade with the Chinese. At that moment, the world-trading system would be disrupted, capital flows would be in disarray, and the world economy would be at risk. Moreover, China would have little choice but to treat the United States as an economic adversary and, most likely, a military adversary as well.

For those who want to increase the freedom of the Chinese people, the best way is to increase trade with them. Likewise, those who desire to decrease the power of the Chinese government should seek to increase trade with the Chinese private sector. The more trade, the greater the size of the Chinese private sector, the greater the attraction of freedom, the less the power of the Chinese government. Of course, we should take seriously the possibility of China becoming a military adversary, but that requires an appropriate increase in our defense capabilities, not a self-destructive trade war.

Yes, the increase in the Chinese economy will cause us some discomfort, but to resist it risks our prosperity. To engage the Chinese, to stand for human rights and the spread of freedom, to be willing to provide the American people the education and skills and management necessary to compete with the Chinese, offers the opportunity to enrich the material and cultural lives of the people of both countries. Such has always been the end result of a spread of freedom.

International Monetary Crisis

A currency crisis among developing nations can trigger a correction, as it did in 1998. A currency crisis among the key world currencies—the dollar, the euro, and the yen—could end the Great Prosperity. Both the Great Depression and the Great Inflation included a breakdown in the international monetary system. A breakdown of the world monetary system today would almost assuredly bring with it a contraction in economic activity, falling living standards, and a severe downward adjustment in the prices of equities.

Why is the global monetary system so important? Because it is at the heart of not only price stability, but also of our capacity to trade with

195

people everywhere. Just as price instability makes it more difficult to do business domestically, currency instability makes it more difficult to do business internationally. When the value of currencies become volatile, the ability to agree upon a price becomes impossible. Without money to facilitate exchanges, we are forced into spot-market transactions and barter. The intricate webs of communications and suppliers, which are required just to get groceries to our food stores and the vast variety of goods to all of the stores at the mall, seize up in confusion and disarray. When it becomes more difficult to do business, less business gets done. That's what we experience as fewer sales, more unemployment, lower corporate profits, and lower equity prices.

This kind of seizure on a global scale brings with it distrust and acrimony. People turn away from finding mutually satisfactory exchanges and instead look to grab an increased share of a shrinking pie in order to maintain their income. Trade restrictions gain favor, as workers desperate to keep their jobs, and owners, committed to maintaining the value of their investments, try to shift the burden of adjustment to foreigners. But any increase in trade restrictions further undermines our capacity to enter into other trades. When there is less trade, there is less opportunity to coordinate our actions with other people to take care of our respective concerns. Living standards fall.

The flip side of the communications revolution is that the world economy is more integrated than ever before. Hence, it is more susceptible to a disruption in the global monetary system than ever before. As we have seen, restoring price stability to the U.S. economy alone has contributed to stability among the key currencies of the world. Perhaps that will be enough to avoid an international monetary crisis in the future. While there is no immediate threat of a breakdown of the international monetary system, the consequences of its failure are so catastrophic that we must always remain watchful of this potential risk to our prosperity.

Medicare

The preceding threats are vexing, but resolving the issues surrounding Medicare are the most serious threat to the Great Prosperity and to reaching Dow 100,000. Compared to Medicare, even saving Social Security is easy.

Many Americans below the age of 50 already believe that the promise of Social Security will be broken and have made the adjustment to a system that offers among the poorest expected returns of any investment.

196

As a result, Social Security reform represents a huge potential positive. Social Security is a mathematical problem. Increasing the expected return on our Social Security payments would transform what is now widely considered a burdensome payroll tax into a compulsory purchase of an annuity that is somewhat overpriced. Giving people the option of investing their share of the Social Security surplus in a self-directed account could achieve this result while increasing the system's future solvency (see Chapter 6).

The key to the future of Social Security, however, is continued growth with price stability. The better-than-expected growth in 1997 and 1998 *alone* pushed back the "go-broke" year for Social Security by five years to 2036. This forecast assumes an economy that grows at an average rate of *less than* 2.0 percent a year after 2008 with unemployment rates averaging 5.5 percent a year. Through all the ups and downs, depressions, recessions, and wars, the U.S. economy between 1926 and 1998 grew at an average rate of 3.4 percent a year, which is more than twice as fast as the "most likely" growth rate the Social Security Administration projects for the next 75 years.

Slightly more realistic growth rates alone can "save Social Security." If the economy merely grows on average between 2.3 percent and 2.5 percent a year, with inflation averaging 2.3 percent and the unemployment rate settling at 4.5 percent, the Social Security Administration estimates that the Trust Fund will *never* run out of money. In fact, under these modest economic assumptions, the Trust Fund would total $1.5 trillion in 2004, a level triple that year's benefits. Moreover, the Trust Fund would remain more than three times the projected current benefits of the future for more than the next 75 years with a projected $8 TRILLION Trust Fund balance in 2075.[8]

By contrast, resolving the issues of Medicare reach beyond purely financial considerations into the kind of ethical issues that can define a society. Providing unlimited medical care to those 65 years and older is the act of a compassionate and caring society. It appeals to our best instincts. Medicare's opponent, the notion of scarcity, of not being able to afford all the care modern medicine can provide, fosters the deepest kind of resentment against the vigilance of economic forces.

One hundred years ago, the medical care you received had little to do with the amount of money you had. People's ability to recover from a disease was a function of the strength of their immune system and, for all practical purposes, was in the hands of God or fate, depending on your point of view. In either case, if you had kidney failure, you died. But today, access to the miracles of modern medicine can determine whether or not an individual recovers from a disease or survives kidney failure. And that costs money.

To maintain the current Medicare system, however, may require significant tax increases, but here, too, the combination of economic growth and reforms enacted in recent years have dramatically improved the outlook for Medicare and reduced this risk. Better-than-expected growth and rising incomes have produced more revenue than projected, while the reforms passed in the 1997 Balanced Budget Act and efforts to reduce fraud have reduced expenditures. As a consequence, the hospital insurance component of Medicare, which only two years ago was expected to go broke in 2001, is now expected to reach a $155 billion peak surplus in its Trust Account in 2006 and not be exhausted until 2015.[9]

These projections are based on the Social Security Administration's intermediate economic assumptions and the 2.9-percent payroll tax on all wages without limit.[10] Although these economic assumptions are modest, they also assume that the rate of increase in medical expenses declines to the rate of real wage gains over the next 25 years. To keep this portion of Medicare solvent implies an increase in the payroll tax to 3.33 percent by the year 2010, and more than 4.5 percent in 2025.[11]

Moreover, by 2008, the costs of providing the Supplemental Medical Insurance (Part B) component of Medicare will be running more than $130 billion above the premiums collected under the Medicare system. This shortfall must be met through income and other general tax revenues. By 2015, projected Medicare spending will exceed payroll-tax collections by more than $200 billion a year.

Economic growth will help close this deficit by increasing the overall payroll and income-tax base. Like Social Security, growth alone may be sufficient to close the gap. Under the more optimistic economic assumptions, which produce surpluses in the Social Security system for as far as the eye can see, Medicare, too, never goes broke. However, this projection requires the rate of advance in medical costs to slow dramatically and fall below the increase in real wages. It also assumes that the increase in life expectancy will slow dramatically over the next 75 years.

The assumptions regarding the slowdown in the rate of advance in medical costs may prove difficult to achieve. Cost controls appear to have gone as far as they can go in reducing the growth in Medicare expenditures. The 1997 Medicare reforms, for example, realized most of their projected savings by reducing the amount the government will pay doctors and hospitals to take care of Medicare patients. Government payments now cover only about 70 percent of the cost of providing care and services to those on Medicare.[12] The squeeze being imposed on medical-care providers was evident in 1998 when 96 Medicare HMOs—nearly one-fourth of the total—reduced their service area or withdrew completely from the Medicare system.[13]

Increased regulations have also proven to be counterproductive. According to a Galen Institute study, the 16 states with the strictest rules for small-group and individual coverage experienced a growth rate in their uninsured population significantly higher than that of the rest of the states between 1990 and 1996.[14]

Private alternatives have also been eliminated. The 1997 Act effectively prohibits any Medicare-eligible person from paying for any health service provided by Medicare. It accomplishes this by banning any doctor or hospital that accepts a private payment from a Medicare beneficiary for Medicare-covered services from receiving Medicare payments from any other patient for two years.

That may assure solidarity among the baby boomers as they turn 65 years old and demand tax increases on the rest of the population to pay for their medical care. However, significant tax increases for even as noble a function as providing medical care to the aged could threaten the Great Prosperity. It is hard to imagine that the economy will be robust enough or produce the jobs and wealth necessary to support all of the boomers in their old age if payroll taxes climb above 20 percent. A prolonged economic slowdown would produce a financial collapse in both the Social Security and Medicare systems. Under the government's pessimistic assumptions, for example, Social Security goes broke in 2022, and Medicare deficits grow to $194 billion in 2010 and exceed $500 billion a year by 2025.

In the end, we are going to be forced to answer a question that few of us even want to ask: "How are we going to ration medical care provided at public expense?" Should someone who is 100 receive open-heart surgery at public expense? If not, what if the person is 99? 89? What if it is your parent or spouse? Who decides? What criteria are used?

If we insist on making medical care "free" to all, we risk destroying our medical-care system. Early attempts to ration medical care by either the private or public sector, or to pay for the higher cost of the latest medical procedures, have failed to maintain public support. Individuals are angry

199

at attempts by HMOs to reduce the cost of medical insurance by providing managed care. At the same time, doctors have begun to refuse to participate in managed-care plans because of the lower payments and added administrative burdens they impose.

The rationing of medical care by government, too, has no political support. In fact, today's retirees are demanding an increase in Medicare coverage while resisting any efforts to increase deductibles or copayments above existing laws.

The direction we take in resolving the question of Medicare will have a lot to say about the future of the economy and the direction of financial markets in the years ahead. For better or for worse, how the baby boomers resolve the issue of Medicare may prove to be their most important legacy.

Other Threats

There will be other threats as well. During periods of rapid increases in prosperity, old power structures give way to the new. Prosperous eras are periods in which people remake the world in which they live. Politicians and those who believe in government stand to lose power relative to the private sector. The "buggy-whip" manufacturers of our time will face extinction, just as they did when Henry Ford invented the assembly line, which made cars affordable to the vast majority of Americans. Some of those who are threatened will have considerable financial and political power, and we can expect them to use that power to try to hold back change, to attack the prosperity that is creating change.

They will invariably call for new taxes, or new regulations, or subsidies, or protection from competition, all in the name of protecting jobs, or otherwise maintaining the status quo. Or they may reach for a new emergency that requires increased regulation of our lives and reductions in our freedoms. Global warming may be such a political vehicle.

The biggest risk to the Great Prosperity, to reaching 100,000 on the Dow by the year 2020, however, may be taking for granted our prosperity and freedom. Those of us who can remember the difficulties of the Great Inflation of the 1970s, or who can imagine what it was like to have lost everything during the Great Depression of the 1930s, will have a far greater appreciation of the Great Prosperity than those who know only the economic gains that began in the recovery of the 1980s.

The political debates of our time, the direction of economic and social policies, will have consequences for our futures, just as they have shaped the future of past generations. If we fail to pay attention to these debates, to be an active participant in the creation of our future, we put that future at risk. Hubris, an exaggerated sense that we deserve or are guaranteed our good fortune, would inevitably lead to a shift in power to those who would take it away.

Avoiding a Crash

There is no magic formula that will tell you when the market has reached a top. In Chapters 12 and 13, we will discuss strategies to manage the risks of short-term corrections, especially for those who are retired or who are about to retire and need to generate income from a pool of assets.

Right now, I want to focus on the bigger question. What actions can you take to minimize the risk of being fully invested in stocks during a protracted period of poor financial-market performance, such as the one that began in 1929, or in 1969? Here are some important rules of thumb to keep in mind to avoid such an outcome.

1. *You do not have to sell at the high.* Inevitably, such a goal will cause you to attempt to time the market and has little prospect of being successful. Moreover, even in the worst historical cases, there has been time to shift an investment strategy well before the worst part of the market's decline has occurred. For example, at the end of 1929, the Dow Industrials stood at 248. That was 35 percent below its earlier high, but still more than four times above the low it would hit three years later.

2. *Beware of a new trend toward higher tax rates, increased monetary instability, or significant increases in trade restrictions.* The Bush and Clinton tax increases, for example, were associated with below-average stock-market performance. Both occurred against a backdrop of public resistance, and the Republican victory in the 1994 election made clear that tax increases were coming to an end.

By contrast, when the devaluation in Thailand began to generate a currency crisis throughout Asia, it became clear that a dramatic increase in monetary instability and inflation would produce severe economic contraction and sharp decline in the regional stock markets.

201

3. *Continue to monitor the five historical forces that we discussed earlier.* In the case of a tax increase or a trade spat between the United States and one of its trading partners, examine whether or not it is changing the overall direction of policy. To the best of your ability, answer the question whether or not new historical forces in play are likely to lead to a series of policy errors.

4. *Never forget that one of the greatest risks is taking a short-term view and thereby failing to take advantage of the investment opportunities that lie ahead.*

In the end, managing your wealth requires your active participation and attention to the events of the world. By being aware of the potential bumps, detours, and roadblocks that may lie ahead, you can increase your ability to design, implement, and successfully stick to a strategic approach to managing risk as you seek your financial goals.

NOTES

1. Carla Anne Robbins and Andrew Higgins, "Money Hungry, Russia Finds a Foreign Market for Nuclear Knowledge," *The Wall Street Journal,* December 15, 1998, p. A1.

2. Carla Anne Robbins, "Why Nuclear Threat Today Can Be Found at the Electronics Store," *The Wall Street Journal,* December 14, 1998, p. A1.

3. William J. Broad and Judith Miller, "The Threat of Germ Weapons Is Rising. Fear, Too," *The New York Times,* December 27, 1998, Section 4, p. 1.

4. *Ibid.*

5. *Ibid.*

6. *Ibid.,* p. 5.

7. Jude Wanniski, *The Way the World Works.*

8. 1999 OASDI Trustees Report, Section D (Principal Economic and Demographic Assumptions) and Section G (Long Range Actuarial Assumptions).

9. 1999 HI Trustees Report, p. 37.

10. *Ibid.,* p. 8.

11. *Ibid.,* p. 44.

12. Medicare Payment Advisory Commission, *Report to the Congress: Medicare Payment Policy* (Washington: Government Printing Office, 1998), p. 2.

13. Nancy Ann Jeffrey, "The Elderly Agonize as HMOs Abandon Medicare," *The New York Times,* October 16, 1998.

14. Laura M. Litvan, "Getting It Wrong in the States," *Investor's Business Daily,* September 28, 1998.

THE ROAD AHEAD

Is Dow 100,000 fact or fiction? As long as the five historical forces hold sway, as long as the three key signposts are not pointing toward higher taxes, monetary instability, or increased trade restrictions, the answer is— fact. The road ahead, with all of its curves, bumps, and perhaps an occasional detour, is headed to 100,000 on the Dow.

We turn now to examine more closely how we will arrive at this destination, and will end with two investment strategies that will help you make the most of the journey. The first strategy is for those of you who are building wealth; the second is for those who are harvesting wealth, those who are retired, or sit as a trustee on a foundation, or for a variety of other reasons look to a pool of financial assets to provide a steady flow of income over time.

Each of these strategies goes beyond simple asset allocation based on your risk tolerance or some other psychological profile and lays out an investment process that can be used during the Great Prosperity that lies ahead. Both of these strategies were developed as part of my work as the chief investment strategist of Seligman Advisors, Inc., and have been used successfully by thousands of financial advisers who design customized strategies for individual investers that are consistent with each person's unique financial situation and his or her financial goals.

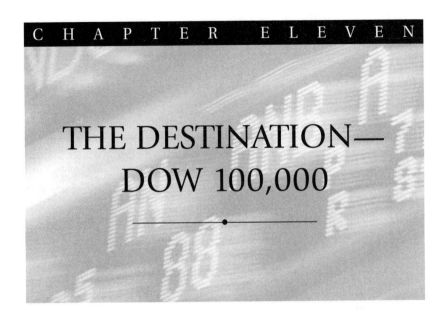

THE DESTINATION—
DOW 100,000

Bull markets—extended periods of rising stock prices—never die of old age. Bull markets are always killed by a policy error. The bull market of the 1920s was killed by the passage of the Smoot–Hawley Tariff and the personal income-tax increases and deflation that followed. The bull market of the 1960s was killed by the tax increases, inflation, and trade restrictions that marked the late 1960s.

The threats to Dow 100,000, to the Great Prosperity, must be kept in mind. They, and perhaps others that may loom ahead, will challenge the political and business leadership of the next 20 years. Each of us, too, will face challenges in our personal lives, business careers, and investment strategies.

However, the biggest risk facing individuals today is failing to grasp the power and implications of the historical forces shaping the direction of the economy and financial markets. The end of the Cold War, the political implications of the aging of the baby boomers, the incredible technological advances that have and are about to occur, the spread of freedom into the developing world, and competition among governments to provide the best mix of fiscal, monetary, and social policies for their respective societies, each of these historical forces points to lower tax rates, price stability, and increased trade.

Any one of these historical forces alone would bode well for the future. The combination of all five will make for a Great Prosperity and the continuation of the bull market. They provide the grounds for unusual confidence that Dow 100,000 will become a fact over the next 21 years.

Think of it. Never before in the history of Western civilization have the prospects of a sustained peace been so high. The United States has no military equal, and it has no ambition for expansion through war.

Never before have the people of the world reached such a consensus on the political and economic institutions to which they aspire. People everywhere want what the American middle class has, the freedom and abundance provided by democratic capitalism. To achieve that, they are imitating and adapting the institutions of democracy, embracing technological change, and seeking to trade freely with other people in their villages and towns, across their nations, and around the world. At the same time, the American middle class is creating a more abundant future. Today we are witnessing an increase in living standards and a stirring of a spiritual awakening and renewal that will further enrich our lives. All these factors are just now beginning to be incorporated into the valuations that have driven the Dow Jones Industrial Average to record highs.

We are just beginning to get a sense of the potential of the Great Prosperity. So much of our thinking is still shaped by the experience of the past 30 years that what lies ahead may seem less than possible. The era of "disinflation," which began with the marginal tax-rate reductions in 1983 and ran through 1997, has been spent repairing the damage of the Great Inflation of the 1970s. The average annual income of the median household in 1997 was $37,005. Once we take inflation into account, that was about where it stood in 1989, the last year of the 1980's expansion, and only $1,260 above its level in 1973.

Living standards haven't increased much since the 1960s. Surprisingly, neither has the Dow Jones Industrial Index. The Dow closed 1965 at 969. Since then, the Consumer Price Index has risen more than five-fold. If you adjust for the increase in the price level through 1998, the Dow closed 1965 at 5014, a level it did not see again until 1995 (Figure 11–1).

But 1998, the first year of the Great Prosperity, began to show the promise of what lies ahead. Economists, pundits, and politicians were all surprised by its effects.

- The economy grew 3.9 percent in spite of a near depression in Asia and continued recession in Japan.

FIGURE 11-1 The Dow Industrials Expressed in 1998 Dollars*

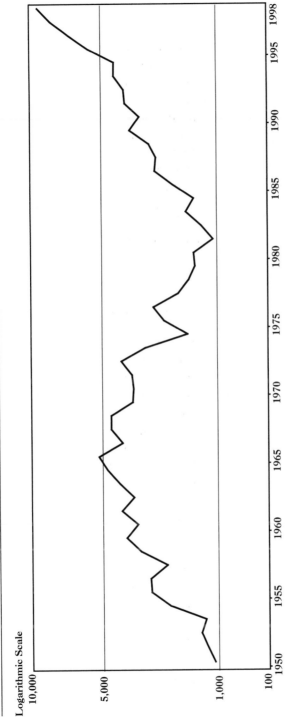

*The Dow Jones Industrial Average in 1998 dollars adjusted by the Consumer Price Index.

Note: An investor cannot invest directly in an unmanaged index, such as the Dow Jones Industrial Average. Past performance is no indication of future results.

Source: Dow Jones; Compustat; Stock Val

- The unemployment rate fell to 4.3 percent, its lowest level since 1970.
- Employment grew by 3.9 million new jobs.
- The Federal budget went from a $22 billion deficit in fiscal 1997 to a $69 billion surplus in fiscal 1998.
- Living standards rose 3.4 percent.
- Inflation, as measured by the Consumer Price Index, rose only 1.6 percent.
- Corporate profits rose 2.2 percent.
- The Dow Jones Industrial Index rose 16.1 percent to 9181.43.

The results of 1998 challenged many economic assumptions, including the belief that low unemployment *causes* inflation. More jobs mean more output, more supply, higher incomes, increased productivity, and rising living standards. Workers do not *cause* inflation. Rising prices in the form of higher wages or food prices do not *cause* inflation. Rising prices *are* inflation. Bad monetary policy is the source of monetary and price instability.

The results of 1998 also challenged the belief that growth *causes* inflation. Instead, 1998 shows that stable prices permit high growth. When prices are stable, it is easier to do business. When the government makes it easier to do business by providing a stable price environment with lower interest rates, we should expect continued better-than-average growth. Make it easier for people to commit commerce, you can bet they will.

Here is how they do it. Investment in new tools and equipment lead the way. For 1998 as a whole, business spending on equipment rose 16.5 percent, the sharpest rise since 1983. Underneath that number, spending on computers during the year in constant dollars rose an astounding 63.8 percent. The technological revolution is alive and well.

Workers do their share by investing in their human capital. They increase their skills and ability to use all of this new equipment. Nonfarm-business productivity in the fourth quarter rose at a 4.6 percent annual rate. That put fourth-quarter output per manhour 2.7 percent above its year-earlier level, the biggest gain since 1992. Manufacturing productivity rose at a blistering 5.2-percent rate during the fourth quarter and ended the year 3.9 percent above its year-earlier level. For the past five years, individuals working in manufacturing have increased their

208

productivity an average of 4 percent per year. Unit-labor costs in the manufacturing sector are *falling* at a near 1 percent annual rate even as wages rise at a better than 3-percent rate.

While most economists are quibbling over whether or not these productivity increases are believable or sustainable, they miss the fact that today's measuring devices were designed for an industrial economy. As a consequence, it is a fair bet that the government statisticians are missing many of the productivity improvements being produced by today's technology. For example, how do you measure the boost to output made possible by today's cellular phones in the hands of traveling salespeople? The Bureau of Labor Statistics can't. So it doesn't.

Whether it is measured or not, however, the result is some of the biggest advances in living standards since the 1960s. Personal-consumption expenditures in constant dollars rose 5.2 percent, while residential investment climbed 12.6 percent. By contrast, government spending on goods and services rose just 1.8 percent.

We are just now getting a sense of what the increase in wealth that will be produced during the Great Prosperity will be like. Ownership of single-family homes is on the rise—first-time buyers represented 46 percent of home purchases in 1998. During 1998, the value of stock portfolios owned by U.S. households increased 20 percent to $10.8 trillion. In the city where I live in New Jersey, we have just built a new town hall and a new library, in part with private contributions. A dramatic increase in school-age children is leading to an expansion of the grammar schools in my community and all the surrounding communities as well. A new tunnel to carry increased train traffic from New Jersey to New York City under the Hudson River is being planned. That will be the first new tunnel under the Hudson since 1937.

Wherever I travel—Boston, Atlanta, Detroit, Chicago, Los Angeles—the symptoms of a dramatic increase in prosperity are beginning to show, like leaf buds in the spring. This kind of prosperity takes some getting used to. It can make us feel uncomfortable. We have not experienced anything like it since the 1960s. But it is good.

A $5 Trillion Surplus

One implication of better-than-expected growth is bigger-than-expected Federal budget surpluses. The total dollars here get very big, very fast, even by the standards of Washington politicians. Consider that in

209

January 1993, the cumulative Federal budget *deficit* for the 1993-through-1998 period was projected to be $1.8 trillion. Instead, revenues totaled $620 billion more than projected, while spending totaled $548 billion less, a saving of $1.2 trillion in just six years (Figure 11–2).

Better-than-expected growth and lower-than-expected inflation and interest rates in 1998 produced an even larger impact on the projected deficit.

- In January 1997, the Administration projected a $5 billion deficit for fiscal 1998 and a $655 billion surplus over the following 10 years. Instead, the Federal government chalked up a $69 billion surplus in 1998 after spending more than $20 billion in "emergency" appropriations.

- By January 1998, the projected 10-year surplus had increased to $2.4 trillion, a $1.7 trillion gain in a single year (Figure 11–3). Less than four weeks later, the Congressional Budget Office, with slightly higher growth projections, found another $300 billion, putting the 10-year projected surplus at $2.7 trillion.

But the surplus, which in January 1999 was projected to reach $200 billion a year by 2002 and $300 billion a year by 2006, will be going higher still. In estimating those surpluses, the Congressional Budget Office (CBO) assumed economic growth of well below-average 2.3 percent a year, annual revenue growth of 4.2 percent, and annual expenditure growth of 3.2 percent.

The CBO's revenue-growth projections are incredibly low. Since 1981, Federal revenues have grown an average of 6.4 percent a year. That includes not only the 1982 recession, but, of course, the 25-percent across-the-board Reagan tax cuts. Using this more realistic growth rate in revenues and accepting the CBO's projected growth in spending produces

- a $209 billion surplus in the year 2000;
- a $741 billion surplus in 2006;
- a cumulative surplus of $5.3 trillion for the 10 years ending 2008 (Figure 11–3).

When the Federal government is running $100 billion plus surpluses over and above what is needed to save Social Security and all of the other spending called for by President Clinton in his 1999 State of the Union Speech, tax relief cannot be far behind.

210

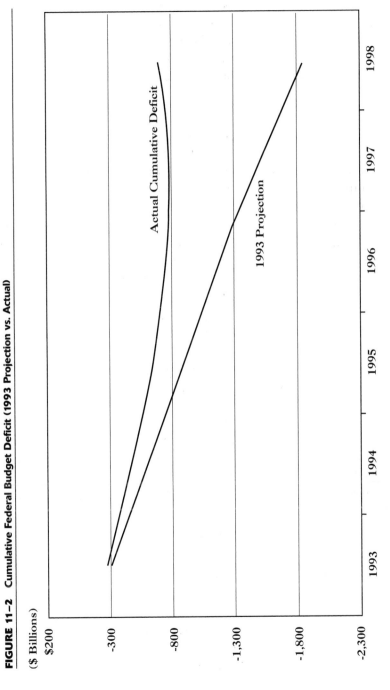

FIGURE 11–2 Cumulative Federal Budget Deficit (1993 Projection vs. Actual)

($ Billions)

Source: Congressional Budget Office, *The Economic and Budget Outlook*

FIGURE 11–3   A $5 Trillion Federal Budget Surplus*

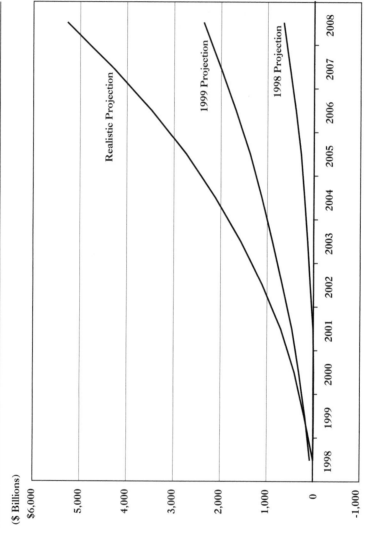

($ Billions)

*Cumulative Federal Budget Surplus.

Note: Realistic deficit projections are calculated with a 6.4% average annual growth in federal receipts.

Source: Congressional Budget Office, *The Economic and Budget Outlook*

These results are not flukes. They are each in their own way manifestations of the historical forces that are now shaping the direction of the economy and financial markets for the next 10 or 20 years. The reduction in defense spending made possible by the end of the Cold War has made an important contribution to the creation of budget surpluses. Sustained peace and burgeoning governmental surpluses provide the American people enormous resources and flexibility in meeting the challenges that lie ahead.

The boomers will demand that a good portion of that money be used to "save Social Security." To the extent "saving Social Security" gives individuals the option to invest a portion of their payroll tax into a self-directed IRA account, that portion of the payroll "tax" would disappear. It would be transformed into a compulsory savings plan. In this way, projected Social Security surpluses could finance a 2.5 percentage-point reduction in the payroll tax.

In addition, to the extent Social Security reforms make the future benefits more secure, the Social Security system will seem a better deal. As perceptions change, the money we pay into the system would be viewed less as a tax and more as a payment for a future benefit. The higher the expected return on our Social Security payments, the more they will be viewed as a way to buy an annuity, and the less they will be viewed as a tax with no direct benefit (see Chapter 6).

Restoring the promise of Social Security alone will constitute one of the largest effective tax-rate reductions in American history. It will reduce the effective tax rate or barrier to trade on the more than 90 percent of the American workers whose wages fall below the Social Security threshold. With this barrier to commerce removed, we can imagine people going to work to get into the Social Security system, instead of moving in the underground economy to avoid its exactions.

Income-tax rates in America will also be coming down. The top personal income-tax rate is probably headed back below 30 percent. As the barriers to domestic trade are pulled down, the amount of domestic trade will be going up. Supply will increase along with demand. Unemployment rates will edge down as businesses find ways to employ and train those with low skills. And those with low skills will be drawn to the opportunities to build a new life in trade with their fellow Americans. Imagine what life will be like in an America where Harlem, the South Side of Chicago, and East Los Angeles are prosperous.

Better than expected growth will also reduce the risk of a massive tax increase to sustain Medicare. The combination of Medicare reforms, which slowed the growth in spending and reduced fraud, and higher-than-projected employment and total payrolls during 1997 and 1998 alone added 14 years to Medicare's projected solvency. Continued better-than-expected growth will continue to reduce the threat an insolvent Medicare would pose to the Great Prosperity.

Agitation for a global monetary system also is on the rise. Government officials in Europe and Japan are calling for greater cooperation to stabilize the exchange rate among the dollar, the euro, and the yen. Dollarization is being explored throughout Latin America. So far, the United States is taking a "hands-off" approach, resisting calls for it to assume its global responsibility to provide an international monetary system. Although we can only speculate on the details of how such a system would work, we can know the direction of policy. *Price stability, lower interest rates, and more stable exchange rates will spread to the rest of the world.* This is a primordial demand by people everywhere seeking to do business with other people in a world made small by virtually free communications, the free flow of private capital, liberalized trade, and the absence of war.

Further trade liberalization is in the works. China is offering new concessions to gain admission to the World Trade Organization. Mexico is considering negotiating a free-trade pact with Europe. The integration of Eastern Europe into the EC lies ahead. The free-trade pacts in technology and telecommunications will be phased in between now and 2002. E-Commerce will continue to make obsolete old-fashioned trade barriers.

The trend toward lower interest rates in the United States also will continue. Today's interest rates are low only by comparison to the past 30 years. For 88 of the 90 years ending in 1968, for example, long government bond yields were never above 5 percent. In the early 1960s, before fears of inflation began to rise, 10-year government bonds yielded around 4 percent, 90-day treasury bills yielded around 3 percent, and business loans and home mortgages were all under 5 percent. There is no reason we cannot move toward a similar yield curve in the years ahead.

As tax, monetary, and international barriers to trade come down, we will find new ways to do business with one another. Corporate profits will rise, driven by increased sales to an expanding and more prosperous world economy and lower costs made possible by advances in technology. Living standards will rise throughout the world, and most especially in the United States. We are just at the beginning of a surge in productivity that will lift real wages in the United States as they haven't been lifted since the 1960s. In 20 years, we will marvel at the new abundance, the speed of commerce, and the manner in which we have remade the world.

The Road to Dow 100,000

These developments will also provide a positive environment for equity investing. To get a sense of what lies ahead, let's review briefly the key economic variables and relate them to the performance of the Dow Jones Industrial Average. Once again, we will go back to 1926 and take out the wartime decade of the 1940s.

In doing this review, it is important to keep in mind that the Dow is a price index and does not include the returns generated by dividends, which are part of the "total return" generated when investing in equities. From 1926 through 1998 (excluding the 1940s), for example, the Dow Jones Industrials advanced at an average annual rate of 6.2 percent, while the total return for the S&P 500, which includes the reinvestment of dividends, averaged 11.5 percent for the same period.

With this in mind, let's look at the historical results during periods when the key "signposts" have been pointed in a positive direction. The average annual advance in the Dow Jones Industrials Index has been

- 6.2 percent for the entire 1926-through-1998 period excluding the decade of the 1940s
- 11.2 percent during periods of falling tax rates
- 11.7 percent during periods of stable prices
- 10.3 percent during periods of freer trade policies

In 30 of the 63 years in our study, at least two of the three signposts were pointed in a positive direction (for example, lower tax rates, stable prices, or freer trade). Linking these 30 years, the Dow posted an average annual advance of 11.1 percent. In only three of the 63 years (1964, 1965, and 1985) were all three signposts pointing in a positive direction. During these years, the Dow advanced at a 15.9 percent average annual rate (Figure 11–4).

Are we headed to 100,000 on the Dow? Yes. As long as the five historical forces are in place and economic policy remains on track.

215

FIGURE 11–4   The Key Signposts vs. The Dow Industrials*

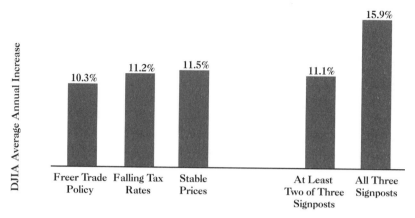

*DJIA price return excludes 1940–1949 because of distortions caused by World War II.
Average annual increase for entire period (excluding the 1940s) was 6.2%.
Note: An investor cannot invest directly in an unmanaged index, such as the Dow Jones Industrial Average. Past performance is no indication of future results.
Source: Dow Jones; Compustat; Federal Tax Policy, the Brookings Institution, 1987; Price Waterhouse

When will we arrive at this milestone? If we trace a line from the end of 1949 to the end of 1998, the Dow increases at an average annual rate of 8.1 percent, but that includes 17 years—from 1965 to 1982—when the Dow was unchanged. Even so, if we just project that line into the future, the Dow will double on average every nine years, reaching 50,000 by 2020 and 100,000 by 2029 (Figure 11–5).

However, if we take into account the economic and political forces that lie ahead, we would expect the Dow to advance at an annual rate better than that. Between the end of 1982 and the end of 1998, the Dow advanced at a 14.5 percent annual rate, the same as during the Roaring Twenties. At that rate, the Dow would post the next ten-fold increase in the next 17 years, just as it did in the past 17 years. Though possible, such a rate of advance from today's market valuations seems unduly optimistic.

Instead, to calculate when Dow 100,000 is likely to be fact, let's use the 11.1 percent rate at which the Dow has advanced during the 30 years since 1926 that at least two of the three key signposts have been pointed in a positive direction. At that rate, the Dow will double approximately every 7 years. The Dow reached 10,000 on March 29,

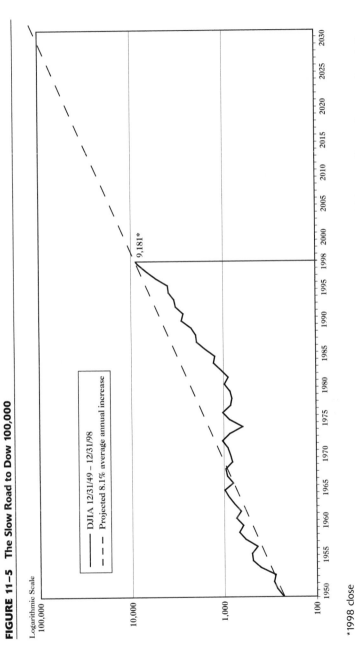

FIGURE 11–5   The Slow Road to Dow 100,000

Logarithmic Scale

——— DJIA 12/31/49 – 12/31/98
– – – Projected 8.1% average annual increase

9,181*

*1998 close

Note: An investor cannot invest directly in an unmanaged index, such as the Dow Jones Industrial Average. Past performance is no indication of future results.

Source: Compustat; Dow Jones

1999, and closed at 11,014 on May 3. If we assume that the Dow does not advance for the rest of the year, and use a year-end close of 11,000 as our starting point, the Dow would cross 20,000 in the year 2005, 35,000 in 2010, approach 60,000 in 2015, and achieve the 100,000 milestone in 2020 (Figure 11-6).

If we assume that the Dow's earnings grow at 6 percent a year, roughly their advance from 1949 through 1965, and a Dow at 100,000 in 2020, that implies a price-earnings multiple of 68 times trailing 2020 earnings. Now 68 times earnings is admittedly a high multiple. However, the Dow's earnings are likely to grow faster than 6 percent a year. The communications revolution and the spread of freedom will make it possible to expand business rapidly abroad. International growth could enable the companies in the Dow index to increase their earnings at a rate faster than the growth in the U.S. economy alone. An 8-percent annual growth in earnings would imply a price-earnings multiple of 44 times earnings in 2020, a level that is quite conceivable 21 years into a Great Prosperity.

You can use Table 11-1 to track the Dow relative to this path in the years ahead. Do not expect the line to 100,000 on the Dow to be so perfectly straight as the one in Figure 11-6 or in the table. There are likely to be corrections ahead, just as there were in the past. The business cycle has not been repealed. But in periods of price stability, the cycle hits different industries at different moments, allowing the overall economy to continue to grow. Certainly not all investments will prove successful. During 1998 and early 1999, the stock prices of Internet companies soared even though many of these companies had no earnings, and some of them may have only limited futures. Rapid change can shift the prospects of a company's strategy or its market position sometimes faster than management can respond. When that happens, what may have been a good investment can become a loser.

Still, the greatest risk in approaching the next 20 years is to fail to take a strategic approach to building your business or investing your money. Tactics are always important, but in the early stages of great prosperities, having a strategy that is coherent with the future is especially important. In building your own business or career, you should anticipate that the economy will be growing in real, inflation-adjusted terms at an average annual rate of above 3 percent per year, that technology will play an ever more important role in defining the competitive landscape, and that new competitors will appear, not only from

FIGURE 11-6 The Road to Dow 100,000

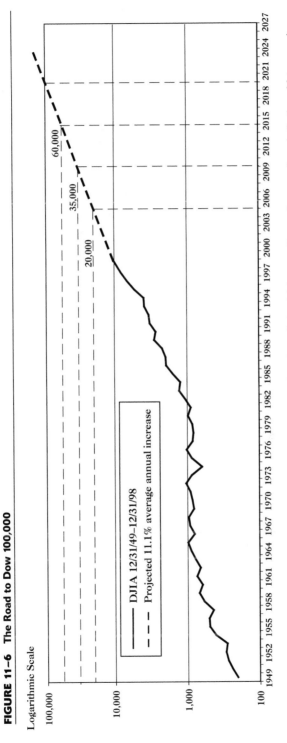

Logarithmic Scale

— DJIA 12/31/49–12/31/98
- - - Projected 11.1% average annual increase

Note: An investor cannot invest directly in an unmanaged index, such as the Dow Jones Industrial Average. Past performance is no indication of future results.

Source: Dow Jones

TABLE 11-1   The Road to Dow 100,000

	Projected	Actual	Difference
1998 (actual)	9,181	9,181	0
1999	11,000		
2000	12,221		
2001	13,578		
2002	15,085		
2003	16,759		
2004	18,619		
2005	20,686		
2006	22,982		
2007	25,533		
2008	28,367		
2009	31,516		
2010	35,014		
2011	38,901		
2012	43,219		
2013	48,016		
2014	53,346		
2015	59,268		
2016	65,846		
2017	73,155		
2018	81,276		
2019	90,297		
2020	100,320		

Note: The projected series is calculated with a 11.1% average annual increase from projected year-end 1999.

Source: Compustat; Dow Jones

across town, but from anywhere in the world. Continuous learning and development of new skills will be part and parcel of participating in the Great Prosperity. The years ahead will be challenging times, but unlike the last 30 years in which rising living standards seemed to be at someone else's expense, the next 10 or 20 years will see all rewarded for their efforts and contributions.

Now is also the moment to develop an investment strategy that is coherent with the Great Prosperity and that can increase your ability to invest wisely and prudently on the road to Dow 100,000. At the least, having a strategy can keep you from selling during uncertain times— when prices are low—only to rush back into the market when prices are high. A strategy helps to inoculate you against the fear, greed, and envy that are implicit in so much of what we hear and read on the markets on a day-to-day basis. These emotions are the enemies of building wealth and income over time.

At Seligman, I have led the teams that have developed investment strategies that are appropriate for the Great Prosperity, that are designed to take advantage of the opportunities that lie ahead. It is to those strategies that we now turn.

CHAPTER TWELVE

THE JOURNEY AHEAD— INVESTING IN THE GREAT PROSPERITY

Now is a moment in history when a strategic, long-term approach to investing is coherent with the world in which we live. Yet, you may find taking a long-term approach to investing extraordinarily difficult.

You are not alone.

- The record advances and increasing interest in financial markets has spawned an entire industry of instant analysis and seemingly even faster communications.

- Every day the media must fill hundreds of column inches with commentary and advice regarding personal investments.

- The multiplication of cable television channels, too, has created a whole new cadre of talking heads and instant analysis of events financial. CNBC alone hosts some 50 guests each day, each with his or her own, sometimes conflicting, point of view.

The rhythm of financial news flies in the face of creating—far less than executing—an investment strategy. The pulse of the reports is riveting. To be successful, TV, after all, must first and foremost be entertaining. And entertaining it is, the latest announcements of a corporation's earnings reported even as the company's chart is flashed up on the screen. The whole milieu has the mood and feeling of a sporting event. Every day is replete with its own winners and losers.

Every day, reporters provide all the statistics they can muster. One-on-one interviews with economists, strategists, and an occasional money manager add color. In the process, hundreds of points are made, as many opinions are given, and over a week, thousands of potential investments are mentioned.

Investing in financial markets, however, is not a game. Whether or not you will reach your investment goal in ten years will not be known at the end of the day. In fact, if investing were a game, its length would depend on the length of time you have to meet each of your financial goals. For speculators and news reporters, that may be a day-to-day event. But for the vast majority of investors and, most likely, for the most significant portion of your investments, the time horizon stretches out years into the future.

I have heard too many examples of people who have lost sight of this fact. Usually, they have fallen behind in achieving their financial goals because they were swayed by the emotions of the moment or the guru of the day. That is why I believe it is so important for you, as an investor, to have a firm understanding of the factors driving the Dow. Only then will you be able to decide whether or not Dow 100,000 is fact or fiction. Once you decide, you will be in a position to develop and stick to a strategy that is coherent with your answer.

The strategies that follow should be considered based in light of my assessment that the signposts on the road ahead are pointing toward the Great Prosperity and Dow 100,000. However, in reviewing these strategies for your own use, you should also keep in mind your specific financial situation. Moreover, it is important to remember that there are no guarantees about the future. That is why the standard disclaimer, "past performance is not indicative of future results," appears at the bottom of many of the figures in this section.

Yet, past results are the only ones that we have to work with as we develop a strategy for the future. To be helpful, past results should be used with a sense of modesty. As a practical matter, it is prudent to assume that the best-case scenario will not necessarily hold for the next 20 years. Even if the years ahead provide better-than-average returns, I expect there will be bumps in the road, challenges to policy makers, and moments of uncertainty. I am sure that the price of stocks in general, and the Dow Industrial index in particular, will not go only in one direction—up. Rather, as in the past, there will be short-term volatility and even corrections of 10 percent and more along the way.

223

Therefore, the strategies I have developed for investing in the Great Prosperity are not based solely on the extraordinarily good times of the last 17 years. Instead, I included what happened during the years of poor market performance that ran from 1965 to 1982, as well as the periods of above-average returns, including the period 1950 through 1965, and 1982 through 1998. Together, they take into account not only the market's short-term volatility, but also the possibility of a down year. For these strategies to work, the next 20 years generally have to be as good as the last 48 years have been on average. If, as I expect, the next 20 years are well above average, the investment results produced by these strategies are likely to be above average as well.

Finally, the strategies are coherent with the longer time frames over which you are likely to be investing as you try to reach your most important goals. As such, they are designed to help you avoid the temptations or side trips that can lead any one of us away from our long-term financial goals.

Three Temptations

All of us will be tempted to invest in hopes of becoming rich quickly by playing what I call "long-ball football"—going for that one stock, mutual fund, or limited partnership we hope will go up "a lot" in a short amount of time. This temptation will be fed by reports of those who got "rich" by buying one or two hot stocks, or by trading successfully in their own personal account. Some of these individuals may be skilled, but most are simply lucky, their good fortune the equivalent of winning the lottery. Notice that they never feature the same "great individual investor" any two years in a row on all of those do-it-yourself investment publications and columns.

A second temptation is to attempt to time markets: selling when the price is high and then buying back at the low. The potential gains for executing such a strategy, to realize only the upside of the market and avoid all of the downs, is extraordinary. Timing the market can look easy in retrospect, but, as a matter of fact, timing markets is extraordinarily difficult to do as markets are actually rising and falling.

For example, in 1995, the portfolio manager of one of the largest equity funds in the world thought that stock prices were too high. So, he sold billions of dollars worth of stock and invested in bonds and cash. The plan was to avoid what he thought would be a stock-market correction and then to reestablish his investments in stocks when the prices were much lower. However, the market headed higher. Those who invested in this mutual fund did not participate in those gains, and, by the end of the year, the portfolio manager was no longer managing that mutual fund.

Why is timing so difficult?

For one thing, timing markets requires you to act against every emotional instinct that you have—to sell when prices are high and euphoria reigns and then to buy back when prices have fallen and fear and bad news dominate the market and the financial news.

Second, to time markets successfully takes near-perfect execution. This point is so important that I am going to repeat the figure from Chapter 1 (Penalty of Missing the Market), but this time, I am going to label the bars with dollar values.

Let's assume an initial investment of $10,000 in the S&P 500 on December 31, 1981, and reinvesting all your dividends through December 31, 1998. (If you want to know the results with a $50,000 investment, simply multiply the following numbers by 5; a $100,000 initial investment, multiply by 10.)

Here are the results: At the end of 1998, your initial investment of $10,000 would have grown to

- $255,836 if you had held your investment the entire time and had never tried to time the market
- $129,893 if you had missed the 10 best days out of those 17 years
- $82,794 if you had missed the 20 best days out of those 17 years
- $45,488 if you had not been invested on the 30 best days out of the nearly 4,400 trading days between year-end 1981 and 1998 (Figure 12–1a)

Even during a single year such as 1998, attempting to time the market can prove to be a highly risky strategy. The S&P 500 produced a total return of 28.6 percent that year. But those who missed the best 10 days out of the entire year would have seen the value of their portfolios fall by 6.5 percent (Figure 12–1b).

As long as the signposts are pointing toward continuation of the Great Prosperity and 100,000 on the Dow, attempting to time markets could increase the risk of you not achieving your long-term financial goals.

A third strategy fraught with risk is chasing last year's winners. Last year's best performing funds typically attract a lot of new investors, as if

FIGURE 12–1 Penalty for Missing the Market: Hypothetical Return for a $10,000 Lump Sum Investment in the S&P 500

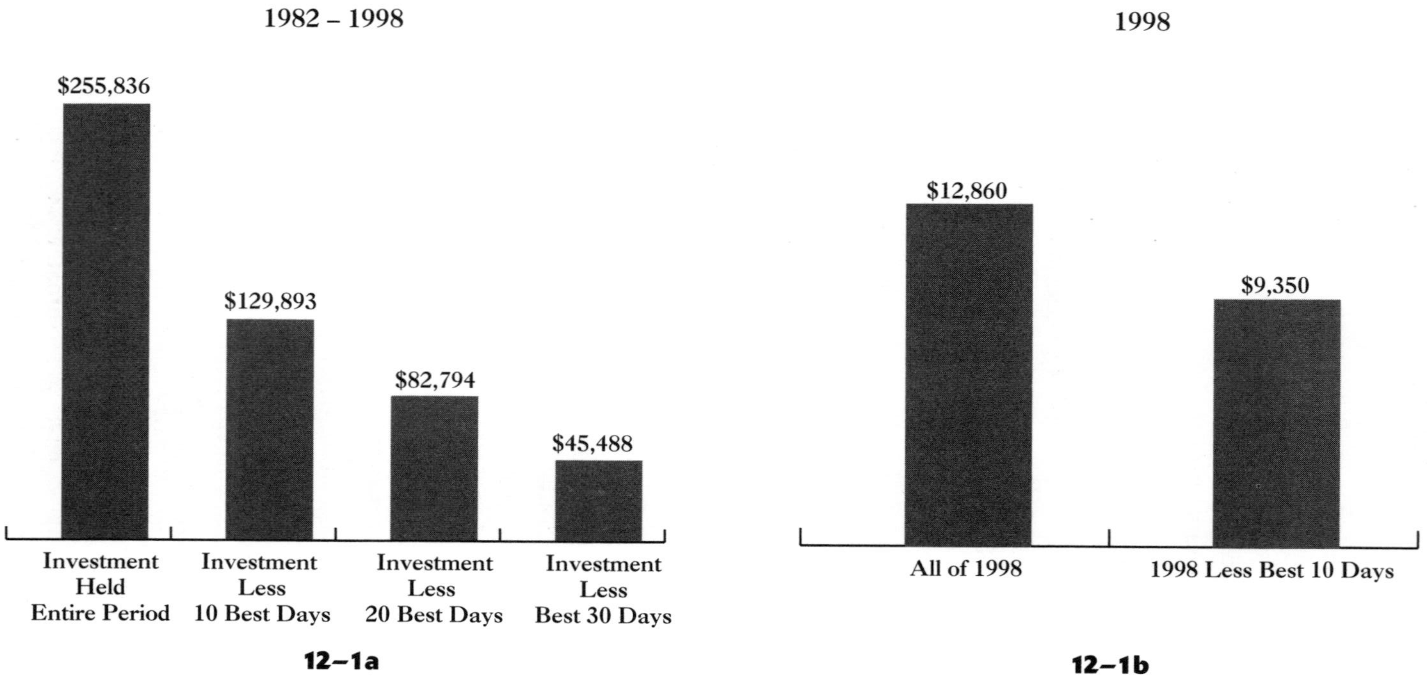

1982 – 1998

$255,836

$129,893

$82,794

$45,488

Investment
Held
Entire Period

Investment
Less
10 Best Days

Investment
Less
20 Best Days

Investment
Less
Best 30 Days

12–1a

1998

$12,860

$9,350

All of 1998

1998 Less Best 10 Days

12–1b

Note: An investor cannot invest directly in an unmanaged index, such as the S&P 500. Past performance is no indication of future results.

that past performance could be bought today. Chasing last year's winners is a self-deceiving strategy that more often than not reduces your chances of reaching your financial goals.

I propose a different approach, an approach that begins by your defining your investment goals, and then puts a strategy in place that is consistent with seeking those goals. Your first decision is to determine whether the purpose of the investment is to build wealth over time or to take an existing pool of assets to generate current as well as future income, what I call "harvesting" a lifetime of savings.

We turn first to a strategy for building wealth over time.

Wealth-Building Strategy

There is an old adage that says: "When you don't know where you are going, any road can take you there."

As a wealth builder, step one in designing a strategy is to decide where you are going, your goals, and how long you have to reach your financial destination. This is the essential step, because without it, you are like a rudderless dingy afloat on the sea, blown this way and that by the latest fad, captured by both fear and greed, and left with uncertainty and more than likely being far short of your goals.

So, I invite you to take out a piece of paper and a pencil right now, this minute, and write down

1. Two or three financial goals. Write each goal on a different line of the paper.
2. Next to each goal, right down the amount of time you have to reach that goal.
3. Then, write down the amount of money you anticipate you will need.

For example, a college education for your children today can cost $30,000 or $40,000 in a public university, and can range to more than $100,000 at a private college. These amounts are likely to increase with inflation, but then again, your child may qualify for financial assistance, including a scholarship.

For your retirement goal, a generally accepted rule of thumb is that you should strive to generate approximately 70 percent of what you anticipate will be your income during the final 5 years of employment from a combination of Social Security, pension plans, 401(k) plans, and other savings. In the next chapter, we will look at the risks and strategies involved in generating that income from your investments. For the purpose of this initial exercise, please write down a nice round number that looks like a reasonable goal for retirement. This will help you think about how to use the investment strategies that we will be discussing, and then you can go back and begin to refine your goals and strategies.

Right now, however, we are going to focus on the time you have to reach each of your goals. This is one of the most critical variables in the design of your strategies for investing in the Great Prosperity.

If, for example, you will need the money for your goal within the next year, investing in small-company stocks or even the large-company stocks of the S&P 500 would be quite risky. As Figure 12–2 shows, since 1950, stocks and long-term bonds have significant downside risk over periods of one year. As a consequence, the investment of choice for a one-year goal would be a cash account or money-market fund.

Time/Risk Relationship

As time horizons begin to lengthen, the relative risk among stocks, bonds, and cash begins to change. Figure 12–3, for example, adds a second set of bars that show the best and worst five-year average annual returns. Let's continue to look at the worst-case results since 1950, which include the steep decline in equity prices that occurred during the seventies. Although small-company stocks still have significant downside risk, the potential negative returns from an investment in the S&P 500 is not very different from the risk of investing in long-term government bonds.

If the time to reach one of your goals stretches out to 10 years, then the relationship between small- and large-cap stocks, and stocks, bonds, and cash begins to change rather dramatically. Now, on a worst-case basis, the small-company stock index actually produces a higher return than the large-company stock index, and both do better than bonds (Figure 12–4).

Finally, for goals that have a 20-year time frame, the picture of risk is totally different. In the *worst* 20 years since 1950 for small-cap stocks, the 20 years ending in the market sell-off of 1974, small-company stocks provided an average annual rate of return of 8.21 percent. That return was better than the *best* ever 20 years for Treasury bills, the 20-year high-interest rate period ending 1991 (Figure 12–5).

228

FIGURE 12–2 Different Time Horizons—Different Risks: Stocks, Bonds, and Treasury Bills

High/Low Average Annual Returns (1950–1998)

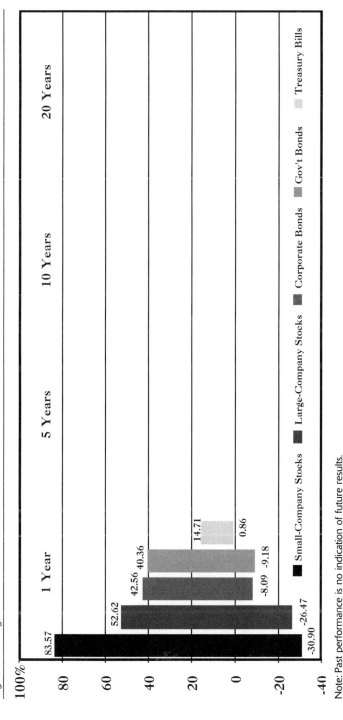

Note: Past performance is no indication of future results.

Source: Calculated by J. & W. Seligman & Co. Inc. using data presented in *Stocks, Bonds, Bills and Inflation*® *1999 Yearbook*, © 1999 Ibbotson Associates, Inc. Based on copyrighted works by Ibbotson and Sinquefield. All rights reserved. Used with permission.

FIGURE 12–3 Different Time Horizons—Different Risks: Stocks, Bonds, and Treasury Bills

High/Low Average Annual Returns (1950–1998)

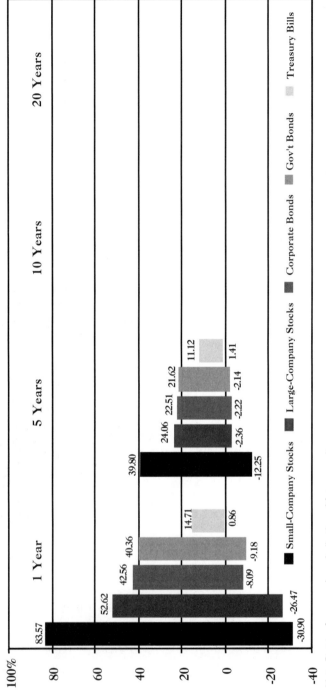

Note: Past performance is no indication of future results.

Source: Calculated by J. & W. Seligman & Co. Inc. using data presented in *Stocks, Bonds, Bills and Inflation®* *1999 Yearbook,* © 1999 Ibbotson Associates, Inc. Based on copyrighted works by Ibbotson and Sinquefield. All rights reserved. Used with permission.

FIGURE 12–4 Different Time Horizons—Different Risks: Stocks, Bonds, and Treasury Bills

High/Low Average Annual Returns (1950–1998)

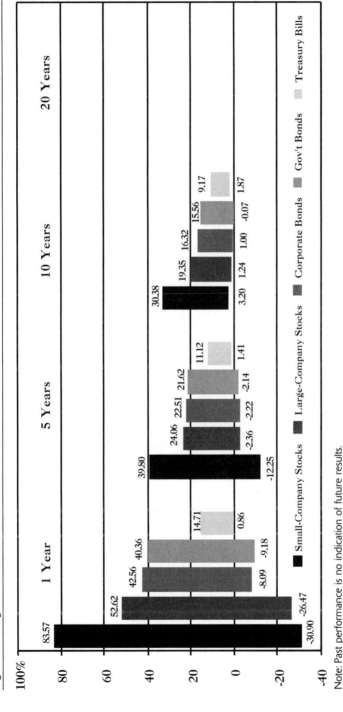

Note: Past performance is no indication of future results.

Source: Calculated by J. & W. Seligman & Co. Inc. using data presented in *Stocks, Bonds, Bills and Inflation® 1999 Yearbook*, © 1999 Ibbotson Associates, Inc. Based on copyrighted works by Ibbotson and Sinquefield. All rights reserved. Used with permission.

FIGURE 12-5 Different Time Horizons—Different Risks: Stocks, Bonds, and Treasury Bills

High/Low Average Annual Returns (1950–1998)

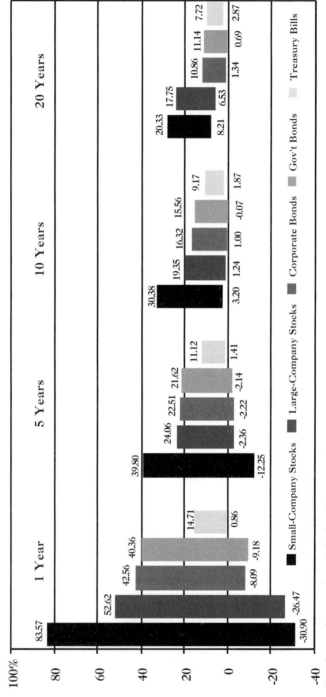

Note: Past performance is no indication of future results.

Source: Calculated by J. & W. Seligman & Co. Inc. using data presented in *Stocks, Bonds, Bills and Inflation*® *1999 Yearbook,* © 1999 Ibbotson Associates, Inc. Based on copyrighted works by Ibbotson and Sinquefield. All rights reserved. Used with permission.

The relative risk of stocks and bonds, and small- and large-cap stocks change as we change investment horizons. Once you see this, you are well on the way to designing an investment strategy to build wealth over time. It is so important, that I am going to say it again:

What constitutes risk over a one-year holding period
is not the same thing as what constitutes risk over
investment horizons of 10 or 20 years.

The question we need to be asking in developing a long-term strategy is not just whether you are a conservative or aggressive investor. In addition, you must ask:

What is the prudent way to invest my assets given
the amount of time I have to reach each of my specific goals?

The allocation you have for a long-term goal, such as the money you may be investing in your 401(k) for retirement 10 or 20 years from now, should be very different from the allocation you may have for a goal that is five years away, say buying a second home, or saving for a special occasion such as a daughter's wedding, or a twenty-fifth wedding anniversary.

For these longer-term goals, one of the greatest risks is not reaching your goal because you failed to invest in equities out of a concern about short-term market movements. Investing only to avoid short-term volatility creates other risks.

One of the greatest impediments to building wealth over time is inflation. Although inflation is likely to be low over the next 10 to 20 years, interest rates are also likely to move lower. Historically, the returns on Treasury bills and bonds have done little more than keep up with inflation. By contrast, equity investing is the equivalent of taking a stake in the future of the American and world economy, and the higher average returns provided by equities over 20-year periods have generated significant increases in wealth even after adjusting for inflation (Figure 12–6).

Let's put it in more practical terms. Imagine that you want to achieve a $1 million nest egg in 20 years. To realize this goal using the average returns from 1950 through 1998, Treasury bills would require a lump sum investment of $365,585 or estimated annual contributions of $28,276. The use of corporate bonds would have reduced this cost to an annual contribution of about $25,000. By contrast, investing in large-company stocks as illustrated by the S&P 500 would have reduced this cost to an estimated annual contribution of just over $10,000, while

234

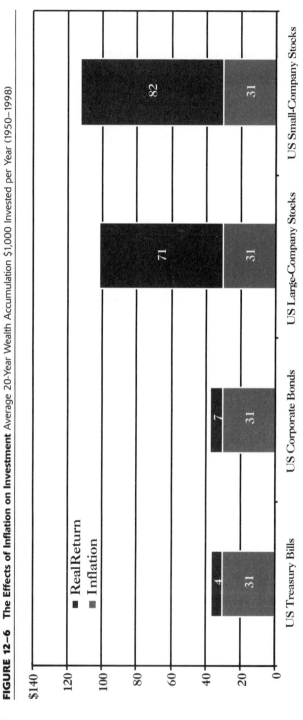

FIGURE 12–6 **The Effects of Inflation on Investment** Average 20-Year Wealth Accumulation $1,000 Invested per Year (1950–1998)

Note: Past performance is no indication of future results.

Source: Calculated by J. & W. Seligman & Co. Inc. using data presented in *Stocks, Bonds, Bills and Inflation*® *1999 Yearbook*, © 1999 Ibbotson Associates, Inc. Based on copyrighted works by Ibbotson and Sinquefield. All rights reserved. Used with permission.

investing in small-company stocks would have decreased the annual contribution to less than $10,000. Although equity investing experiences much greater yearly fluctuations than do Treasury bills, an overreliance on Treasury bills or fixed-income investments increases the risk of not reaching your long-term financial goals (Table 12–1).

However, just as investing in bonds or Treasury bills is not prudent in reaching a 20-year goal, neither is an exclusive reliance on equities. As you draw closer to your goal, time horizons shrink. Consequently, the risk of a portfolio invested exclusively in equities rises.

Seligman Time Horizon Matrix[sm]

As the chief investment strategist at Seligman Advisors, Inc., I led a team that developed Seligman Time Horizon Matrix[sm], an investment process that is designed to bridge that gap by providing a prudent investment strategy that extends out from 5 to 10 or 20 years and longer. It is designed to take advantage of the higher average returns that historically have been offered by small- and large-company stocks over longer time periods when short-term volatility is of little importance, while at the same time reducing a portfolio's overall volatility as the goals, and the need for the money, approach.

The Matrix[sm] also includes investments in international equities for the benefits of capital appreciation and diversification. Although interna-

TABLE 12–1   Cost of Achieving a $1 Million Nest Egg (Over 20 Years*)

Asset Class	Lump Sum	Annual Contributions
US Small-Company Stocks	$ 64,715	$ 8,852
US Large-Company Stocks	80,010	10,317
US Corporate Bonds	296,896	24,876
US Government Bonds	318,949	26,008
US Treasury Bills	365,585	28,276

*Based on average annual returns: 1950–1998.

Note: Past performance is no indication of future results.

Source: Calculated by J. & W. Seligman & Co. Inc. using data presented in *Stocks, Bonds, Bills and Inflation® 1999 Yearbook*, © 1999 Ibbotson Associates, Inc. Based on copyrighted works by Ibbotson and Sinquefield. All rights reserved. Used with permission.

tional equity markets have lagged the U.S. market in recent years, the sign-posts on economic policy are pointing toward lower tax rates, stable prices, and free trade in Europe and Japan. At the same time, currency stability and more stable prices are being restored to developing economies.

International equity markets are therefore likely to provide competitive returns and diversification in the years ahead. Therefore, allocating a portion of your portfolio to international equities is an important component of the overall strategy. Investing a relatively small portion of your portfolio in emerging markets through a well-diversified portfolio is also recommended, especially for time horizons of ten years and longer.

Benchmark Portfolios Here is how the Time Horizon Matrix[sm] works. We begin with four benchmark Horizon Model Portfolios. Each Portfolio is risk-adjusted for a specific time horizon.

The Horizon 30 Model Portfolio, for example, is designed to maximize the opportunity for capital appreciation that is likely in the years ahead (Figure 12–7). It is an all-equity portfolio with significant allocations to small- and mid-cap stocks, both domestically and internationally.

FIGURE 12–7 Horizon 30 Model Portfolio (Maximum Capital Accumulation)

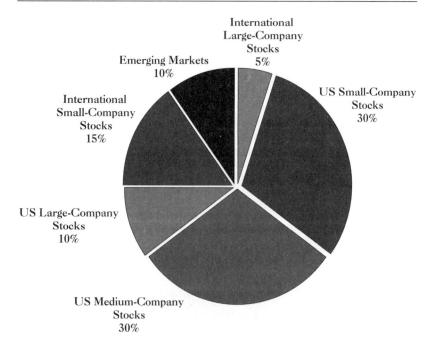

It also has a 10 percent allocation to emerging markets. This recommendation is a perfect example of how time horizons change risk. An investment in emerging markets should be considered highly speculative in the short term. Some of these stock markets fell 50 percent and more during the Asian currency crisis. Because of their volatility in the short-term, an investment in emerging markets would be inappropriate as anything other than a speculative investment for time frames of less than five years. However, from a strategic point of view, an investment in emerging markets represents a secular bet on the spread of freedom and a return to price stability in the developing world. If this part of our outlook proves correct, you can expect well-above-average returns in the emerging markets in the years ahead.

An all-equity allocation is also recommended for a goal that is 20 years away (Figure 12–8). Both the historical data and the outlook for reaching Dow 100,000 by 2020 make a compelling case for this portfolio, which is slightly more diversified, but still focused on capital appreciation. In this portfolio, the allocations to U.S. and international small- and mid-sized company stocks have been reduced in favor of U.S. and international large-company stocks.

FIGURE 12–8 Horizon 20 Model Portfolio (Diversified Capital Accumulation)

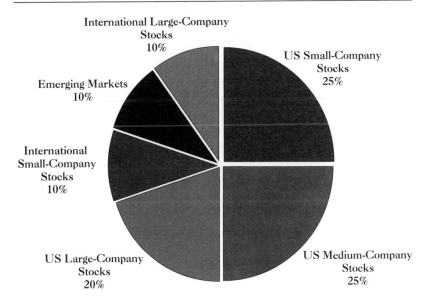

Over ten-year horizons, the relative risk of small- and large-cap stocks, and stocks and bonds has begun to change, and so has the asset allocation (Figure 12–9). The allocation to small company stocks, in particular, has been reduced in favor of large- and mid-size company stocks. Investments in emerging markets also has been reduced to a modest 5 percent of the overall portfolio. Finally, a 20-percent allocation to fixed-income investments provides some current income and provides a modest damper on yearly fluctuations in value. Overall, this portfolio has about the same year-to-year volatility as the S&P 500 with somewhat higher historic returns.

Finally, the Harvester Portfolio is designed for capital preservation and current income (Figure 12–10). It was designed for an individual or institution that will be relying on a pool of financial assets to generate current income and the growth of capital and income over time. Now, equities constitute only 60 percent of the overall portfolio, with 40 percent invested in a combination of corporate and government bonds or cash. Twenty-five percent of the equity allocation, or 15 percent of the total portfolio, is invested in international large-company stocks. Exposure to U.S. and international small-cap stocks and emerging markets have been eliminated, while the allocation to mid-cap stocks has been trimmed to

FIGURE 12–9 Horizon 10 Model Portfolio (Capital Growth and Income)

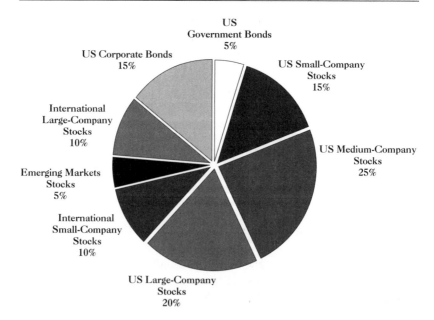

US Government Bonds 5%

US Corporate Bonds 15%

US Small-Company Stocks 15%

International Large-Company Stocks 10%

US Medium-Company Stocks 25%

Emerging Markets Stocks 5%

International Small-Company Stocks 10%

US Large-Company Stocks 20%

FIGURE 12–10   Harvester Portfolio (Capital Preservation and Income)

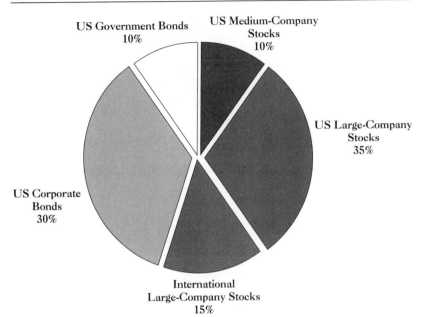

10 percent. One of the key design parameters of the Harvester Portfolio was to have no negative investment results for five-year periods going back to 1950. That is something that no single asset class other than Treasury bills can claim. We will have more to say about the design and use of the Harvester Portfolio in the next chapter.

These four Horizon Model Portfolios offer the opportunity to manage risk over time. Over one-year periods, they all have significant downside risk—the only prudent investment for periods of one year or less is cash. For five-year periods, however, we realized the key design objective for the Harvester Portfolio. It produces a positive total return for each five-year period going back to 1950. Over horizons of 10 and 20 years, we observe the same ladder effect where all returns are positive, and, on a worse-case basis, the longer-term Horizon Portfolios outperform the shorter-term Horizon Portfolios (Figure 12–11). Of course, this past performance is no guarantee of future results, but it is an indicator of relative risk over time.

We expanded these four benchmark portfolios to an entire Matrix that reaches from Harvesting all the way out to 30 years (Table 12–2). Now take out that piece of paper that you used to write down your goals and

FIGURE 12–11 Different Time Horizons–Different Risks Horizon Model Portfolios [High/Low Average Annual Returns (1950–1998)]

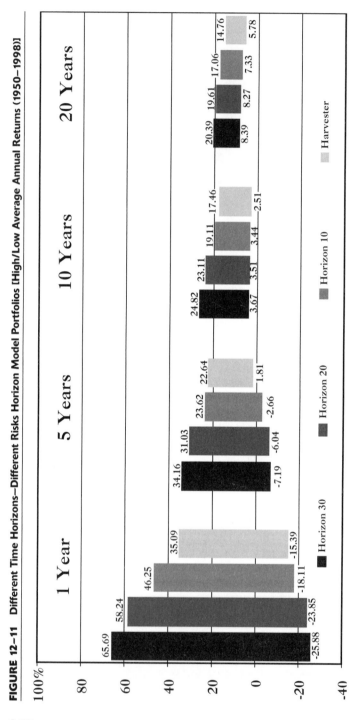

Note: Past performance is no indication of future results.
Source: Calculated by J. & W. Seligman & Co. Inc. using data presented in *Stocks, Bonds, Bills and Inflation®* *1999 Yearbook,* © 1999 Ibbotson Associates, Inc. Based on copyrighted works by Ibbotson and Sinquefield. All rights reserved. Used with permission.

the amount of time you have to reach each one, and use the Time Horizon Matrix^{sm} to help you choose a prudent starting point or asset allocation for each of your respective goals. For a goal 15 years from a Harvesting Portfolio, for example, look under Horizon 15, or for an 8-year goal, use the asset allocation under Horizon 8.

If your investment goal is something like paying for a college education, you may want to reach the Harvester allocation three to five years before you will actually need the money. From that point, you can gradually increase your fixed income and cash investments to further reduce the risk of a fall in the value of your portfolio just before you need the money.

Managing Risk over Time   Now that you have established an initial asset allocation for each of your goals, we can use the Time Horizon Matrix^{sm} to manage risk over time. Here is how it works.

As each year goes by, you probably get one year closer to your goal. As time frames change, so does the relative risk of the various asset classes, such as stocks and bonds. Rather than rebalance your portfolio each year to a static allocation, such as provided by the Horizon 20 Model Portfolio, you can modestly change your allocation each year to take into account that you are now one year closer to your goal. For example, if today your financial goal is 15 years away, in a year it would be 14 years away. At that time, you can modestly shift your asset allocation to Horizon 14. This process, which is called "migration," can be followed all the way down to the Harvester Portfolio.

By taking a strategic approach toward reaching your goals, you are more likely to stay invested during periods of short-term volatility, thereby increasing your chances of reaching your long-term goals. Moreover, Seligman Time Horizon Matrix^{sm} differs from most asset allocation strategies in the following important ways:

1. Instead of trying to avoid volatility, the Time Horizon Matrix^{sm} is designed to manage it.

2. Instead of allocating your investments based on some notion of whether or not you are a "conservative "or an "aggressive" investor, the Matrix^{sm} focuses on the prudent allocation of assets, given the amount of time you have to reach each of your specific goals.

3. Instead of focusing on the ever present risk of the value of your portfolio going down over the short term, this strategic approach is designed to reduce the risk of not meeting your investment goals.

TABLE 12–2 Seligman Time Horizon Matrix℠

Asset Class/Horizon	30	29	28	27	26	25	24	23	22	21	20
Domestic Equity											
Small-Cap	30.0%	29.5%	29.0%	28.5%	28.0%	27.5%	27.0%	26.5%	26.0%	25.50%	25.0%
Mid-Cap	30.0%	29.5%	29.0%	28.5%	28.0%	27.5%	27.0%	26.5%	26.0%	25.50%	25.0%
Large-Cap	10.0%	11.0%	12.0%	13.0%	14.0%	15.0%	16.0%	17.0%	18.0%	19.0%	20.0%
International Equity											
Small-Cap	15.0%	14.5%	14.0%	13.5%	13.0%	12.5%	12.0%	11.5%	11.0%	10.5%	10.0%
Emerging Markets	10.0%	10.0%	10.0%	10.0%	10.0%	10.0%	10.0%	10.0%	10.0%	10.0%	10.0%
Large-Caps	5.0%	5.5%	6.0%	6.5%	7.0%	7.5%	8.0%	8.5%	9.0%	9.5%	10.0%
Fixed Income											
Corporate Bonds	0.0%	0.0%	0.0%	0.0%	0.0%	0.0%	0.0%	0.0%	0.0%	0.0%	0.0%
Government Bonds	0.0%	0.0%	0.0%	0.0%	0.0%	0.0%	0.0%	0.0%	0.0%	0.0%	0.0%
Total	100.0%	100.0%	100.0%	100.0%	100.0%	100.0%	100.0%	100.0%	100.0%	100.0%	100.0%

Asset Class/Horizon	20	19	18	17	16	15	14	13	12	11	10
Domestic Equity											
Small-Cap	25.0%	24.0%	23.0%	22.0%	21.0%	20.0%	19.0%	18.0%	17.0%	16.0%	15.0%
Mid-Cap	25.0%	25.0%	25.0%	25.0%	25.0%	25.0%	25.0%	25.0%	25.0%	25.0%	25%
Large-Cap	20.0%	20.0%	20.0%	20.0%	20.0%	20.0%	20.0%	20.0%	20.0%	20.0%	20%
International Equity											
Small-Cap	10.0%	9.5%	9.0%	8.5%	8.0%	7.5%	7.0%	6.5%	6.0%	5.5%	5%
Emerging Markets	10.0%	9.5%	9.0%	8.5%	8.0%	7.5%	7.0%	6.5%	6.0%	5.5%	5%
Large-Caps	10.0%	10.0%	10.0%	10.0%	10.0%	10.0%	10.0%	10.0%	10.0%	10.0%	10%
Fixed Income											
Corporate Bonds	0.0%	1.5%	3.0%	4.5%	6.0%	7.5%	9.0%	10.5%	12.0%	13.5%	15%
Government Bonds	0.0%	0.5%	1.0%	1.5%	2.0%	2.5%	3.0%	3.5%	4.0%	4.5%	5%
Total	100.0%	100.0%	100.0%	100.0%	100.0%	100.0%	100.0%	100.0%	100.0%	100.0%	100.0%

Asset Class/Horizon	10	9	8	7	6	5	4	3	2	1	Harvester
Domestic Equity											
Small-Cap	15.0%	13.5%	12.0%	10.5%	9.0%	7.5%	6.0%	4.5%	3.0%	1.5%	0.0%
Mid-Cap	25.0%	23.5%	22.0%	20.5%	19.0%	17.5%	16.0%	14.5%	13.0%	11.5%	10.0%
Large-Cap	20.0%	21.5%	23.0%	24.5%	26.0%	27.5%	29.0%	30.5%	32.0%	33.5%	35.0%
International Equity											
Small-Cap	5.0%	4.5%	4.0%	3.5%	3.0%	2.5%	2.0%	1.5%	1.0%	0.5%	0.0%
Emerging Markets	5.0%	4.5%	4.0%	3.5%	3.0%	2.5%	2.0%	1.5%	1.0%	0.5%	0.0%
Large-Caps	10.0%	10.5%	11.0%	11.5%	12.0%	12.5%	13.0%	13.5%	14.0%	14.5%	15.0%
Fixed Income											
Corporate Bonds	15.0%	16.5%	18.0%	19.5%	21.0%	22.5%	24.0%	25.5%	27.0%	28.5%	30.0%
Government Bonds	5.0%	5.5%	6.0%	6.5%	7.0%	7.5%	8.0%	8.5%	9.0%	9.5%	10.0%
Total	100.0%	100.0%	100.0%	100.0%	100.0%	100%	100%	100%	100%	100%	100%

By asking different questions, and providing different answers, using a strategic approach like the Matrix^sm can produce very different results. To give you an idea of how different, we looked at all of the hypothetical results going back to 1950 for a 30-year investment strategy that began with the all-equity allocation of Horizon 30 and migrated down to the Harvester Portfolio of 60-percent equities and 40-percent fixed income. (See Appendix.) Rather than take the last 30 years, which would have produced well-above-average returns, we examined every 30-year period going back to 1950 and took the median, or most typical, result. We also took the median 30-year return for inflation, Treasury bills, and the S&P 500 and applied it to a lump-sum investment of $10,000.

Here is what we found.

- To keep up with inflation, at the end of 30 years, the $10,000 lump-sum investment would have had to grow to $42,001.

- A $10,000 investment in Treasury bills would have grown to $56,788 after 30 years.

- Using the median result for the S&P 500, the initial investment would have grown to $201,560.

- Using the strategy of the Seligman Time Horizon Matrix^sm, starting with a $10,000 investment in Horizon 30 and migrating each year down to the Harvester Portfolio, your $10,000 would have grown to $423,543 after 30 years (Figure 12–12).

In using Seligman Time Horizon Matrix^sm remember that it is a process created to help you design a strategy that makes sense to you, given your financial goals, the time to reach those goals, and your specific financial situation. You may wish to follow the Matrix^sm with precision, or to use it as a guideline for your actual strategy. For example, along the way, you may wish to overweight small- or large-company stocks relative to the Matrix^sm, or to emphasize investing in international versus domestic stocks. We will be looking at some of these considerations in the current environment in the final chapter.

In any case, by using the Matrix^sm as a guide to your investments, you will be able to put in place an investment strategy that is coherent with the time to reach each of your investment goals. That may appear to be a modest accomplishment, but from my experience, I can tell you it is a vital step toward reaching your financial goals.

FIGURE 12–12 Average 30-Year Hypothetical Compounded Returns for $10,000 Lump Sum Investments* (1950–1998)

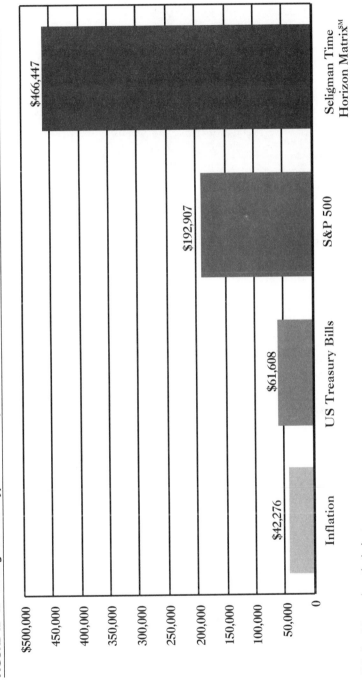

*Median 30-year hypothetical returns

Note: Past performance is no indication of future resluts.

CHAPTER THIRTEEN

THE JOURNEY AHEAD— HARVESTING A LIFETIME OF SAVING

In many ways, building wealth is a relatively easy challenge compared to designing a way to conserve your capital while generating sufficient income to maintain your standard of living in retirement. When you are saving to meet some future goal, you have a degree of flexibility. If market performance lags, you may be able to add additional funds. If one investment does not quite work out as planned, another may work out better than planned.

But when you are relying on your assets to generate income to maintain your standard of living, or to "harvesting" a lifetime of savings, one or two bad investment decisions can have catastrophic implications for your living standards for the rest of your life.

The biggest difference between building wealth and harvesting a lifetime of savings is the importance of time. When you are a wealth builder, time is on your side. Time allows the magic of compounding to work in your favor. Reaching Dow 100,000, by 2020 exemplifies the power of time and compounding returns. But when you are harvesting, the biggest concern typically is the risk of outliving your money. The longer the time you will need to rely on your assets as a source of income, the greater this risk.

A second difference is market volatility. For wealth builders, who are following a long-term strategy such as the Matrix^{sm}, the ups and downs of the markets are of little consequence. They all average out. The key is to have a long-term strategy that keeps you in the market during the difficult times so your capital will be there to catch every one of the most important 30 days during the next 10 years. One of the most valuable aspects of following the Matrix^sm is that it increases the chances that you will maintain a disciplined approach to investing and thereby overcome the emotions that would have you sell at the bottom out of short-term uncertainties, or fall into the habit of chasing last year's winners.

If you are relying on a pool of financial assets to generate income during the year, short-term volatility adds risk. Because you are drawing money from your account, the ups and downs of markets don't necessarily all average out. Selling in down markets depletes capital. When the market rebounds, there are fewer assets left to participate in the upswing.

Finally, current income is of little importance to wealth builders. Since they are accumulating assets, the appropriate focus is on total return. But, as we shall see, reliable current dividend and interest income can be a vital component of an investment strategy for wealth harvesters.

Managing risk for harvesters is far more difficult than it is for wealth builders. The root of the problem is that harvesters have incoherent time frames. Their money may have to last another 20 or 30 years, but they also need to spend some of it each year. There is no simple matrix that can act as a blueprint or road map for harvesters because the issues are more nuanced. As a consequence, for harvesters, the investment process revolves first around recognizing several fallacies and, second, around using several principles for designing a specific overall strategy.

Myths about Risk

If you are a harvester, perhaps the biggest risk you face is being taken in by the highly seductive myth that you can avoid risk. Myths have an element of truth in them, but ultimately mislead, like a mirage on the desert. In an attempt to avoid risk, many individuals invest in certificates of deposit or bonds, but they are just substituting one kind of risk for another.

You may be asking: What could be risky about investing in certificates of deposit, or savings accounts, or money-market funds? After all, my money or principal is well protected by such an investment.

Your principal is protected. However, *the income generated by such investments is at risk.* The last time inflation was as low as it was in 1998, the first half of the 1960s, the yield on 91-day Treasury bills averaged 3 percent. Today, the yield on 91-day Treasury bills is above 4.5 percent. If,

247

as I expect, price stability is maintained, then interest rates could trend down toward these lower levels. Therefore, if you have invested in Treasury bills, your capital may be safe, but your income could drop as much as one-third if short-term interest rates trend down to 3 percent from today's 4.5 percent over the next several years.

One way to get around this risk, known as the reinvestment risk, is to invest in long-term bonds, such as 20- or 30–year government bonds. What is the risk of investing in such fixed-income investments? Well, they fix your income, providing no protection against inflation. The fallacy with *fixed income* investing is that it confuses the certainty of a fixed amount of principal or income with safety. Thinking in strategic terms makes this risk more obvious. For example, even if inflation averages only 1.5 percent a year for the next 20 years, that means that the buying power of the interest income produced by a 20-year bond will fall by about one-third.

A second fallacy is assuming that the past 20 years of equity performance is typical. It is actually the best 20 years since 1950. Getting to 100,000 on the Dow by the year 2020 requires the Dow to compound at an 11.1-percent average annual return for the 21 years starting from a projected 11,000 at the end of 1999. For the past 20 years, however, the Dow has increased at a 12.9-percent annual rate of return. Moreover, the four consecutive years of 20 percent-plus returns posted by the S&P 500 between 1995 and 1998 were unprecedented. Therefore, in developing a strategy for harvesters, we did not want to base it solely on our optimistic view of the next 20 years. Nor did we want to end up with a strategy that was based solely on a worse-case scenario. Instead we sought to produce a prudent strategy that would balance all of the potential risks, and the potential rewards, of investing for long-term growth of capital and income while providing reasonable current income on the road to Dow 100,000. Consequently, we used the entire experience of the period 1950 through 1997 in developing an investment strategy for harvesters.

The "Nest-Egg" Test

Let me put the challenge faced by harvesters into perspective with what I call the "nest-egg" test. The question I pose is this:

How safe is it to withdraw 10 percent of your initial nest egg—say $50,000 out of a $500,000 investment in the S&P 500—every year for 20 years? Using this strategy, in how many of the thirty 20-year periods since 1950 (1950–1969; 1951–1970 . . .) would you have ended up with a nest egg versus a goose egg?

Here are some facts to help you answer this question.

- The S&P 500 has had an average annual rate of return including dividends of 13.5 percent since 1950. So, a 10-percent withdrawal provides an apparent 3.5 percentage-point margin of safety.

- If you had followed this strategy and had invested $500,000 in the S&P 500 at the beginning of 1979 and had withdrawn $4,167 per month ($50,000 per year), the value of your nest egg would have grown to $5.4 million by the end of 1998.

- If you had followed the same strategy beginning in 1970, your nest egg would have been exhausted in just 14 years.

As it turns out, an investor withdrawing $50,000 a year from a $500,000 investment would have ended the 20 years with his initial investment in only eleven of the thirty 20-year periods (Figure 13–1). Why? Because average annual returns do not take into account the year-to-year fluctuations in the market.

FIGURE 13–1 Systematic Withdrawals: A Dangerous Financial Strategy
Results of Systematic 10% Withdrawals Over 20-Year Periods Between 1950–1998 from a $500,000 Investment in the S&P 500*

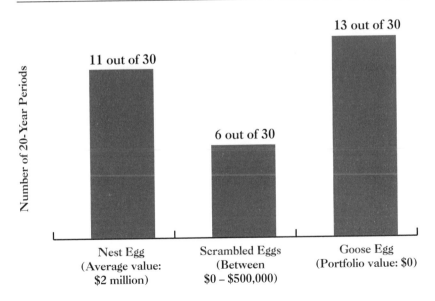

*An investor cannot invest directly in an unmanaged index, such as the S&P 500.

Note: Past performance is no indication of future results.

249

Seligman Harvester[sm]

At Seligman, Steve Hodgdon, the President of Seligman Advisors, and I led the team that developed a risk-management strategy for harvesters called "Seligman Harvester[sm]."[1] By using standard asset-class databases and statistical techniques to perform 15 million simulations, we analyzed more than 1,500 combinations of withdrawal strategies and asset allocations.

Out of that research, we developed the following principles for managing risk when drawing on a pool of assets for 20 or 30 years or even longer. Although the outlook for equity markets over the next 10 to 20 years is positive, a prudent strategy for harvesters should seek to conserve capital in the event of a correction, but at the same time give individuals the opportunity to enjoy a higher living standard if, as I expect, markets rise at above-average rates.

To achieve those goals, the first thing that we discovered is that *how you withdraw your money can be as important as how much you take and how the money is invested.* For harvesters, step one in designing an appropriate withdrawal strategy is to distinguish between "needs" and "wants."

- Think of "needs" as commitments such as paying the rent, providing for health care, paying taxes, and, of course, the money you have to have to meet the expenses of day-to-day living including food, sundries, and the like.

- "Wants" are everything else, everything you have saved for and deserve, including vacations, new cars, and gifts to the children— any expense that you can postpone or, if necessary, do without (Figure 13–2).

- Since needs cannot be compromised, they should be met to the extent possible with *fixed-dollar* withdrawals. But, fixed-dollar withdrawals add risk. They require you to sell more shares in down markets. *Fixed-dollar withdrawals should be kept as low as possible.*

- As a general rule, fixed-dollar withdrawals that are increased each year for inflation should not exceed 6 percent of your initial investment.

- Wants can be met with *fixed-percentage* withdrawals. Using a fixed-percentage withdrawal helps you manage risk because it automatically adjusts the amount of money you take to market conditions. If the market is down, you withdraw less money, conserving your capital, so when the market rebounds, you have enough invested to

250

FIGURE 13–2 Distinguishing "Needs" vs. "Wants"

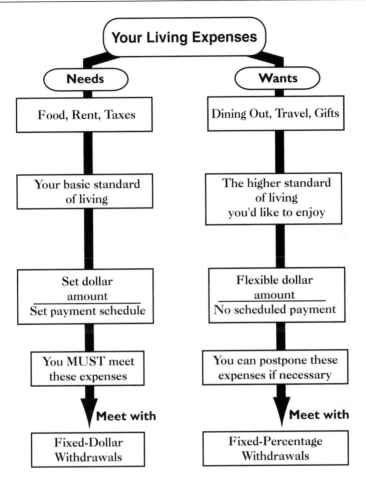

rebound as well. And, as the market goes higher, the amount of money you withdraw can rise with the value of your portfolio, automatically giving you the opportunity to participate in the Great Prosperity that lies ahead.

- As a general rule, for each one percentage-point reduction in your fixed-dollar withdrawal below 6 percent, you can add a 2-percent withdrawal, which varies with the market value of your portfolio. For example, reaching an 8-percent initial withdrawal could be accomplished by combining a 4-percent fixed-dollar and a 4-percent fixed-percent withdrawal.

Allocating Your Investments

The last part of our research was to develop rules of thumb for allocating investments among various asset classes, such as stocks, bonds, and cash. The performance of each asset class is important. But in developing a strategy for investing over the next 10 to 20 years, how the various investments behave as part of an overall portfolio over different time periods is the key to managing risk and reward. While there is no single solution that is appropriate for all individuals in different circumstances, the following rules of thumb can be used as a starting point in designing an allocation that best suits your specific overall financial situation.

1. Allocate ten percent of your portfolio to short-term government bonds or cash. Cash investments, such as money-market funds or Treasury bills, provide for the certainty of principal and also for some modest protection against inflation. The foremost contribution of such short-term investments is to provide a cushion against the unexpected. If inflation remains low, interest rates are likely to decline, reducing the current income from these investments. Interest income from government bonds would also fall as they mature and the money is reinvested. However, if inflation should head higher, interest rates are likely to rise as well, increasing the income generated from investments in short-term money-market instruments. Similarly, as any investments in short-term government bonds matured, bonds yielding higher interest rates could be purchased.

2. Meet at least half of your fixed-dollar needs with reliable interest- and-dividend income. In a world of no inflation, you would want to meet all of your fixed-dollar needs with the certain income of bonds. However, in a world with even modest year-to-year increases in the price of everything you purchase, such a strategy risks a slow, steady decline in living standards because it does not leave enough capital to invest in growth. High-yield-bond mutual funds and dividend-paying stocks are important investments for reaching this goal.

3. Allocate at least half of your investments to equities. Such an allocation might seem risky. Equities can and do introduce short-term volatility to any portfolio. Even the road to Dow 100,000 will no doubt include short-term corrections and uncertainties in equity markets. But remember, the whole purpose of taking a strategic approach to investing is to allow us to see beyond the short term to time frames of five years and longer. Investors in large-cap stocks have seen that, since 1950, the S&P 500—on a *worst-case* basis over five years or longer—has not performed much differently from bonds.

As a harvester, you not only need current income for today, but growth of income for tomorrow as well. An investment in a portfolio of dividend-paying, large-cap stocks, or in a growth-and-dividend mutual fund, has the potential of providing not only dividend income now, but growth of income and capital over time. Even during the Great Inflation of the 1970s, for example, the dividend income of the S&P 500 increased nearly in line with the rise in the consumer-price index. During the past 10 years, that dividend income has increased even faster than the rise in the CPI (Figure 13–3).

4. Diversify a portion of your equity portfolio into international, large-company stocks. Investments in emerging markets, or even in specific countries or regions of the world, should be limited to the speculative portion of your portfolio because these markets can add significant downside volatility to a portfolio. However, an allocation to the equities of large companies that operate in the developed world of Europe, Australia, and the Far East (EAFE) offers opportunities for growth of capital and for diversification of risk without the kind of volatility experienced by smaller companies or in smaller countries.

In recent years, the S&P 500 has performed far better than the EAFE international large-cap index. However, global competition is transmitting the benefits of the Great Prosperity to Europe and Japan as well. Creation of the euro, the growing pressure for tax reductions in Europe, and a shift toward equity investing by Europeans suggest that these markets may be poised to begin to catch up with recent U.S. equity-market performance. Similarly, recent policy changes in Japan point to an end to that country's deflationary monetary policy and tax-rate reductions as well. In addition, by not having at least some international-equity exposure, you are making a one-sided bet that U.S. officials never again make a policy error. International large-cap stocks have reduced risk through diversification in the past, and they are likely to again in the future (Figure 13–4). On both counts, an allocation of between 10 percent and 15 percent of your overall portfolio to international large-cap stocks should be considered.

FIGURE 13-3 Equity Investment Can Increase Your Income Stream and Grow Your Capital (S&P 500 vs. Inflation 1970–1998*)

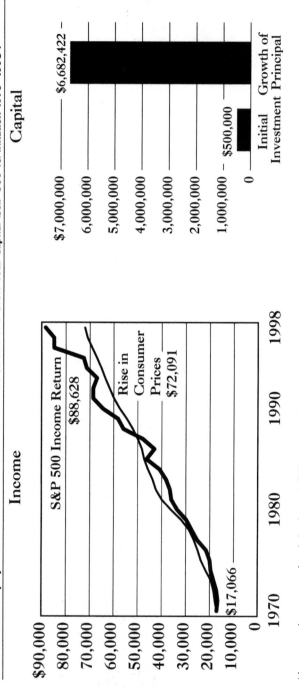

*Assumes reinvestment of capital gains and dividends taken in cash.

Note: An investor cannot invest directly in an unmanaged index, such as the S&P 500.

Past performance is no indication of future results.

Source: Ibbotson Associates

FIGURE 13–4 International Large-Cap Stocks Have Reduced Risk Through Diversification (International Large-Cap Stock Performance vs. U.S. Large-Cap Stocks 1970–1998*)

	Underperform	Outperform		Underperform	Outperform
1970	✓		1984		✓
1971		✓	1985		✓
1972		✓	1986		✓
1973		✓	1987		✓
1974		✓	1988		✓
1975	✓		1989	✓	
1976	✓		1990	✓	
1977		✓	1991	✓	
1978		✓	1992	✓	
1979	✓		1993		✓
1980	✓		1994		✓
1981		✓	1995	✓	
1982	✓		1996	✓	
1983		✓	1997	✓	
			1998	✓	

*For periods ended 12/31.
Note: Foreign stock performance is measured by the Morgan Stanley Capital Index Europe Australasia Far East (MSCI EAFE) of non-U.S. industrial country stocks. U.S. stock performance is measured by the unmanaged S&P 500 Index.
Note: An investor cannot invest directly in an unmanaged index. Past performance is no indication of future results.

The above rules of thumb are just that, starting points from which you can begin to design a strategy that is coherent with your specific financial needs and situations. After consulting on hundreds of cases with financial advisors, I can tell you that a "one size fits all" approach to harvesters is seldom appropriate. Each time I have had the privilege of meeting an individual or couple either approaching or in retirement, I have been struck by both the power of the principles that we have developed as part of the Harvester strategy, and the need to use them to customize a solution that makes sense given the specific situation of each individual client.

These principles are equally applicable to the management of endowments and other investable assets supporting foundations, churches,

255

community hospitals, and the like. Whether it's an individual or institution that is looking to a pool of assets to generate income over time, the Harvester strategy can be used as a starting point in the design of their investment policy.

We turn now to our final chapter, in which we will discuss some of the "how to's" in implementing your investment strategies on the road to Dow 100,000 and, where appropriate, in selecting a financial advisor.

NOTES

1. Patent pending on business methodologies and apparatus for implementing the Seligman Harvester℠ Risk Management System. Seligman Harvester℠ is a proprietary service mark of Seligman Advisors, Inc.

CHAPTER FOURTEEN

IMPLEMENTING YOUR INVESTMENT STRATEGY

The final step in investing in the Great Prosperity is to participate in the journey to Dow 100,000 by actually choosing the stocks, bonds, and mutual funds to implement your strategy. This can be an exciting process that you engage in or manage yourself. Or, you may find it advantageous to implement your investment strategy with the assistance of a financial adviser. In either case, you can use the Time Horizon Matrix^sm or Harvester as the basis of your strategic plan, and then customize it to your own unique financial situation.

Both the Time Horizon Matrix^sm and Harvester strategies are based on the year-by-year returns of various indexes or asset classes. Although these are extremely helpful in designing a strategy, the fact is no one can actually invest directly in these indexes. In addition, the index returns do not include management, brokerage, or other fees associated with investing in stocks, bonds, or mutual funds.

Still, there are several benefits to having strategies formulated around asset classes such as large, mid-size, and small-company stocks.

First, it puts you in charge. It shifts the conversation away from "Which stock or mutual fund is likely to outperform over the next week or year?"—a question no one can promise to answer correctly—to "Where is my money invested relative to a plan that can help me reach my financial goals?" This question can be answered by you and therefore can show you what investments are appropriate for your unique plan.

Second, an asset-class-based strategy gives you the ability to combine investments in individual securities and mutual funds into a single, coherent strategy. To the extent you own large-company stocks such as Microsoft or General Electric or Exxon, you can count the value of those investments against your target large-cap allocation. Similarly, if you own individual government, corporate, or municipal bonds, they can be counted against your fixed-income allocation. For most asset classes, however, including international large- and small-cap equities, domestic small- and mid-cap stocks, emerging markets, and high-yield bonds, you should consider investing in a professionally managed account, such as a mutual fund.

Third, by using a generic asset-class approach, Time Horizon Matrix^{sm} *and Harvester give you the ability to integrate your present investments into one of these strategies.* You don't have to sell everything and start over to get to implementation. Rather, you can review your current investments and assign each to its respective asset class. Group your holdings of individual securities in terms of domestic and international equities, and large-company, mid-size company, and small-company stocks. Generally, large-company stocks have a market capitalization (the total market value of the company[1]) of more than $10 billion. Mid-size companies have a market value of between $1 billion and $10 billion. And small-company stocks are considered those with a market cap of $1 billion or less.

You can take the same steps and apply them to the mutual funds you own. If you own global funds, you will need to consult with your manager or financial adviser to learn the typical, or "market-neutral," allocation between domestic and international equity investments. Similarly, if you own a balanced fund that invests in stocks and bonds, you need to know the typical allocation between equities and fixed-income investments.

This may sound like a lot of work. However, it should take only a few phone calls. If you are feeling a little intimidated by this first step, it may be because you are beginning to see the difference between implementing a long-term strategy and buying whatever mutual fund or stock seemed "hot" or "good" at the time. Like everything else that is new, this strategy may take some getting used to. Or perhaps your nervousness is because this exercise has revealed what a mess your investments are in. In that case, cheer up! Remember, you can only move up from where you are today. Completing the classification of your investments is the essential first step in getting ready for the journey toward Dow 100,000, implementing your investment strategy and achieving your investment goals.

In doing this work, remember the goal is to bring order to your portfolio and to provide a strategy for your investments. Day-to-day changes in market conditions, alone, will alter the relative weightings among your investments, so just get a sense of where your money is invested and how it may differ from where you would like it to be, either in terms of the Matrix^{sm} or the Harvester.

Implementing the Matrix^{sm} and Harvester^{sm}

To help get you started, let me show you how to implement one of the most popular benchmark portfolios using the Seligman group of funds. (The entire Matrix^{sm} using the Seligman funds can be found in the Appendix.) Of course, you can use individual stocks or other mutual funds in building your strategy, and we will provide guidelines for selecting mutual funds in the next section.

The Horizon 10 Model Portfolio calls for a mix of 80-percent equities and 20-percent fixed income. Within the domestic-equity portion, 20 percent is allocated to large-cap stocks, 25 percent to mid-cap stocks, and 15 percent to small-cap stocks. The international equity allocation totals 20 percent of the entire portfolio (or 25 percent of the total equity allocation). In addition, the international-equity investments have been divided into 10-percent large-cap, 5-percent small-cap, and 5-percent emerging markets stocks. Finally, the fixed-income allocation consists of a 15-percent investment in corporate bonds and a 5-percent allocation to government bonds or cash (Table 14–1).

Domestic Equity Allocation

We approach this "model" portfolio as a *template* for building a recommended portfolio of our funds for a 10-year goal. As you will see, in some cases, the actual allocations will be somewhat different from the model asset allocations. You can find a summary of our implementation in Table 14–1, which may prove helpful in following some of the steps listed below.

Our implementation reflects in part our strategic allocation to overweight the technology sector investing 10 percent of the portfolio into Seligman's Communication and Information Fund. The C&I Fund was

259

TABLE 14–1 Implementing Horizon 10 (Model Portfolio)

Equities

Domestic		International	
Large-Cap Allocation	20%	Large-Cap Allocation	10%
Large-Cap Value Fund	9%	International Fund	10%
Growth Fund	9%		
Communications and Information Fund	2.5%	Small-Cap Allocation	5%
		Global Smaller Companies Fund	4.8%
Mid-Cap Allocation	25%		
Capital Fund	20%	Emerging Markets Allocation	5%
Communications and Information Fund	5%	Emerging Markets Fund	5%
Small-Cap Allocation	15%		
Small-Cap Value Fund	6%		
Frontier Fund	3%		
Global Smaller Companies Fund	3.2%		
Communications and Information Fund	2.5%		

Fixed-Income

Corporate Bonds	15%
High-Yield Bond Fund	15%
Government Bonds/ Cash Allocation	5%
Government Fund/Cash Management Fund	5%

created in 1983, making it one of the oldest and best known technology funds.

Integrating the C&I Fund into the strategy requires some explanation because the fund invests across the full spectrum of small, mid-sized, and large-cap companies in the technology sector. Moreover, its weighting to any specific asset class can change over time. Finally, the fund can be highly volatile over periods of a year and longer, making its investment characteristic more akin to small- rather than the more stable large-company asset class. As you will see, based on these considerations, we assigned 25 percent of this weight (2.5%) to large-company stocks, half (5%) to mid-cap stocks, and 25 percent (2.5%) to small-cap stocks.

Let's begin with the domestic equity allocation of 20 percent to large-company stocks. As part of our overall strategy, we equal weight the "growth" and "value" styles of investing by putting 9 percent of the portfolio into both the Growth Fund and the Large Cap Value Fund. Growth managers focus on growth stocks that typically have above-average earnings growth and that sell at higher price earnings ratios than the overall market. Growth portfolios tend to be overweight in the faster growing sectors of the market, including technology and health care, and underweight in the slower growing sectors of the market, including cyclical companies such as machinery manufacturers and banks. By contrast, the value style focuses on companies with lower price-to-earnings ratios and frequently also emphasizes dividend yields as well. As a consequence, "value" portfolios tend to be underweight in the technology and health care sectors, and overweight in financial and energy stocks.

Both styles come in and out of favor, tending to outperform and then underperform the broader index. But over the entire investment cycle, both growth and value managers have the opportunity to add value by producing above-average investment results. By equal weighting these styles, we gain the advantage of specialization and, at the same time, diversify away risk. We also make possible the fine tuning that some investors like to pursue in terms of overweighting one style or the other during various market cycles.

The final 2.0-percent allocation to domestic large-cap equities is met by the 2.5 percent of the C&I investment that is allocated to large-cap stocks.

Achieving the 25-percent allocation to mid-cap stocks is met by putting 20 percent of the portfolio into the Capital Fund, and counting 5 percent of our investment in the C&I Fund toward mid-cap stocks.

In meeting our small-cap allocation, we again seek to equal weight both the growth and value styles of investing. The 15-percent allocation to domestic small-cap stocks is also made somewhat complex by the fact that we will be using the Global Smaller Companies Fund to achieve a portion of the domestic allocation to small-cap growth and all of the allocation below to international small-company stocks.

So, let's take it a step at a time. We start with a 3-percent allocation to the Frontier Fund, a small-cap growth fund. Next, we invest 6 percent in the Small-Cap Value Fund. We add 3.2 percent from our 8-percent investment in Global Smaller Companies Fund to our small-cap growth allocation. (The "market" neutral weighting in this fund is 40 percent domestic, 60 percent international.) We complete our overall commitment to small-caps with the 2.5 percent allocated from our investment in the C&I Fund.

International Equities

The international equity implementation is pretty straightforward. The 10-percent allocation to large-company stocks is met with a 10-percent

261

investment in the International Fund. The 5-percent allocation to small-company stocks is met with the 4.8-percent international component of our investment in the Global Smaller Companies Fund. And the 5-percent allocation toward emerging markets is met with the Emerging Markets Fund.

Fixed-Income Allocation

Implementation of the fixed-income allocation also illustrates how you can use the Matrix^{sm} as a guide or template for investing your money in various mutual funds or individual securities. We use the High Yield Bond Fund to meet the 15-percent allocation to corporate bonds, even though the research was based on the returns provided by high-grade corporate bonds. Individual high-yield bonds carry a greater risk of default than do investment-grade bonds. If you owned a bond that went into default, that would mean the interest payments would be suspended and the value of the bond would fall, perhaps to zero. However, a professionally managed portfolio of high-yield bonds reduces that risk through diversification and good management. At the same time, it provides a higher yield than more conservative corporate and government bonds.

Finally, we allocate 5 percent of the portfolio into the government-bond fund, which invests in a diversified portfolio of government and agency bonds. Although these bonds carry a lower interest rate, the risk of default is minimal. Of course, the net-asset value of the fund does vary based on changes in interest rates.

As you utilize the Matrix^{sm} in implementing your own portfolio, you may choose to use a corporate-bond fund or individual corporate or government bonds. You may also wish to count your stable cash holdings against the 5-percent allocation to government bonds. And finally, depending on your specific tax situation, you may wish to invest in individual municipal bonds, or in a municipal-bond fund that concentrates its holdings in tax-free securities issued by the state and local governments of your state.

Seligman's implementation of the Matrix^{sm} is admittedly sophisticated and, therefore, somewhat complex. As a result, we have provided the entire implementation using the Seligman Group of Funds in the Appendix as a guideline for your use. In designing your own implementation, don't get bogged down in the details and lose sight of the overall goal, which is to put in place and then to actually implement a long-term strategy-and-investment process that will assist you in seeking your financial goals on the road to Dow 100,000. The patient implementation of such a plan is usually far more effective in building or managing your wealth over a lifetime than jumping from fund to fund or trying to time markets.

The benchmark Harvester℠ Portfolio is provided as the end-point of the Time Horizon Matrix℠. The Seligman solution to implementing this model portfolio can also be found in the Appendix. You can use the Harvester℠ model portfolio as the starting point for designing your own asset allocation if you are now harvesting a flow of income from a pool of financial assets. Remember that designing your withdrawal strategy is as important as your asset allocation in implementing a Harvester℠ strategy. The rules of thumb for how to withdraw money can be found in Chapter 13, pages 250 and 251.

Selecting Mutual Funds

The Matrix℠ or Harvester℠ strategies can be implemented using a variety of mutual funds and individual securities. You may choose to invest in an index fund that, for example, charges a low fee and seeks to replicate the overall performance of an index, such as the S&P 500. Such an investment would count toward your large-cap allocation.

S&P 500 index funds have become very popular in recent years, in part because they have produced total returns that have been better than those produced by 80 percent of active investment managers. Only time will tell if that relative performance will continue. One of the main reasons these index funds have done so well is because their holdings are concentrated in the 25 largest companies that are at the top of the S&P 500. Since the performance of this index is weighted by the market capitalization of each company, more than 38 percent of these funds are invested in just these 25 stocks. As it turns out, these 25 stocks have produced significantly higher returns than the overall market. For example, the 25 largest stocks in the S&P 500, which includes Coke, Microsoft, Intel, Merck, and General Electric, were up 63 percent in 1998. But the other 475 stocks were up only 12 percent. Thus, most active managers did not do so well because their portfolios are more diversified and hence less concentrated in those 25 "mega-cap" stocks.

This kind of disparity is highly unusual. Inevitably, I would expect the rest of the market to begin to "catch up" with the mega-cap stocks. As they do, active managers are likely to once again produce above-average returns.

Selecting Mutual Funds or Investment Managers

1. In selecting a mutual fund or investment manager, avoid the temptation of chasing last year's winners. Such a strategy feels good, but more often than not will reduce the money you earn on your investment. The fact is, you cannot buy last year's results. I know this is obvious, but it is what many investors seem to be trying to achieve when they switch from a fund that is underperforming the market to one that recently has outperformed the market. Too often, this strategy causes you to sell low and buy high—and costs you real money.

Studies have shown that many of the funds that Morningstar gives its highest, five-star rating each year have three stars or less the following year. Another study by SEI Investments shows that nearly half of the investment managers who were in the top quartile of performance for the five-year period ending 1970 were among the bottom half of managers the following five years.[2] The standard disclaimer: "Past performance is no guarantee of future results" is absolutely true, especially when looking at results over short periods of time.

2. Select an investment manager based on his or her long-term investment results. By that I mean results that span at least three if not five years and that are compared to each fund's respective asset class or investment discipline. Many investors simply use Morningstar's rankings to choose their mutual-fund managers. However, just using Morningstar can create a significant distortion in your asset allocation. At the end of January 1999, for example, there were 239 mutual funds that had five stars. However, 224 of these, or 94 percent, were large-cap funds. By contrast, there were no more than six five-star funds in each of the mid- and small-cap categories.

Does this mean that there are virtually no "five-star" mid- and small-cap managers? I don't think so. Instead, the Morningstar rankings, like so much of the recent market data, simply reflect the fact that the largest, and therefore most heavily weighted, stocks have done exceptionally well relative to all other stocks.

The overweighting given to small- and mid-cap stocks in the Matrix^{sm}, especially for time horizons of 10 years and longer, has meant that these model portfolios have underperformed the S&P 500 in recent years. But you must remember that the promise of the Matrix℠ is not that it will outperform in each and every year. I do not know of any strategy that can fulfill that promise. Instead, the promise of the Matrix℠ is to provide a disciplined investment process that will keep you from falling prey to the temptation to chase last year's winners. Following the Matrix℠ will enable you to invest in various asset classes not only when they are at their peak relative performances and getting five stars, but also when they are out of favor and represent potential great value. That is the best way I know of to participate fully on the road to Dow 100,000.

3. **Select mutual funds that are committed to investing in specific asset classes.** Otherwise, your carefully constructed diversification can be overridden by portfolio managers that are chasing stars instead of managing within their discipline. The result could be increased risk through lack of diversification and below-average performance because such managers are, in the end, engaged in a kind of market timing.

Many portfolio managers are under pressure to outperform the S&P 500 index every year, whether or not their market capitalization or style is in or out of favor. As a consequence, they will "change their stripes," if you will, in an effort to keep up with the latest investment fad. This may sound alluring. In a perfect world and with the benefit of hindsight, why wouldn't you want to invest your money with a manager who is always "in favor." The reason is that few, if any, managers can successfully adapt their investment processes to different asset classes and styles. That is why the sponsors of some of the largest pension plans and other institutional portfolios insist that the managers they hire stay "true to their asset class." My advice: Do what the professionals do and invest in mutual funds that stay true to their asset class and style of investing.

Selecting a Financial Adviser

The final step in setting out on the road to Dow 100,000 is to select a financial adviser who can help you take advantage of the extraordinary investment opportunities that lie ahead. Most people, either directly or indirectly, seek advice before investing. Some talk to their neighbors or friends. Others read investment magazines and other periodicals. E-traders—the epitome of the "do-it-yourself" investor—spend time in on-line chat rooms getting advice. The best portfolio managers have well-established networks of individuals and colleagues whom they talk to in reaching their investments decisions. Having an adviser who can assist you in designing and implementing an investment strategy can be an essential step in realizing your financial goals.

Choose your adviser carefully. Your financial well-being is too important to put in the hands of an amateur investment adviser, which most of us are. Would you trust your investments to someone who works only in the evenings and on weekends, whose outside commitments preempt his or her management of your assets at any time? If this description fits you and you have been attempting to do it yourself, it is probably time to find an adviser who can provide the advice and counsel that your future financial well-being deserves.

You may be thinking: But what about the fees that I would have to pay? Shouldn't I just stick with no-load funds?

My answer goes under the old warning against being penny wise and pound foolish. The price you are likely to pay for *not* having the benefit of professional advice, which may result in making mistakes or not executing your strategy, can easily exceed the fees charged by most professional financial advisers. A study by Dalbar, for example, showed that for the eleven years ending in 1995 individuals who worked with financial advisers achieved higher returns with load funds than those who pursued a do-it-yourself strategy with no-load funds.[3]

In addition, like anything else, to invest properly takes time and commitment. Unless you plan to make investing an avocation, not only are you likely to do a poor job, but you are also going to be spending time that would be better spent pursuing your career or some well-earned leisure activity.

A financial adviser can be critical to the successful implementation of a strategy. For all of my experience, from time to time I feel the impulse to abandon my strategy and chase the winners of the past year. However, I have learned through experience that these are usually the exact moments when that sector or style that I yearn to invest in has peaked. As a result, I have set aside a small amount of money with which to "speculate" on some specific investment ideas, but all of my "serious" money has been invested based on the Time Horizon Matrix[sm].

Choosing a financial adviser is a deeply personal decision. At a minimum, you will be giving this individual significant influence over the manner in which you invest and manage your financial affairs. In selecting a professional adviser, here are several questions to keep in mind.

1. Does the financial adviser have an investment process that can balance risk, reward, and time in the management of your financial affairs?

2. What promise is the financial adviser making to you? Is he or she promising short-term "performance," or a long-term strategic approach to helping you invest your money to seek your financial goals? Seligman Time Horizon Matrix^{sm} and Seligman Harvester^{sm} can provide you and your financial adviser the context for the design and implementation of such a plan.

3. What will the adviser *not* do? When you work with a financial adviser, it is important to understand not only what he or she is willing to do, but also, what he or she may not be willing to do. How often will you receive status updates and complete reviews of your portfolio? How many face-to-face meetings will your adviser expect a year? Does that match what you are expecting? You should be open and frank with a potential adviser about your expectations. Many advisers will be interviewing you at the same time you are interviewing them. They, too, want the opportunity to build a relationship over time. And, the really good ones will not accept a client, no matter how large the account, if the prospect's expectations are inconsistent with the commitments that the adviser is willing to make.

4. Can you trust the individual to deliver on his or her promise? To assess the adviser's trustworthiness, you must consider both his or her sincerity or desire to fulfill the promise made to you. In addition, you must consider the adviser's competence at doing what he or she says he or she will do. Don't be bashful. Ask for references and, without breaking any confidences, a case study or two.

5. Understand the amount the financial adviser will charge you and the manner in which it is collected. Sometimes it is in the form of a one-time charge at the time of an investment. Such charges would include brokerage fees on the purchase of an individual security, or the so-called "load" on the purchase of a mutual fund. Other times, the financial adviser will charge you an on-going fee that is a small percentage of the assets that he or she is managing

for you. Typically, these fees range from 1 percent to 2.5 percent of the assets in your portfolio, depending on the level of service and the amount of money that you are investing. Many mutual funds, for example, pay the financial adviser 1 percent of the assets under management. Such fees are deducted on a pro-rata basis from your account. Keep in mind, the investment returns that are reported to you are net of these fees and, therefore, reflect the cost of the advice that you are receiving.

Do your research before selecting your adviser. But, then, be prepared to make at least a three-year commitment to that adviser and your plan. The goal is to find an adviser with whom you can have a mutually beneficial exchange. The adviser receives fees for his or her advice. And, you benefit from that advice by increasing your ability to achieve your financial goals over time. If you don't do your research and fail to ask these questions, you are at risk of entering into what you no doubt want to avoid: a one-sided exchange in which the adviser gets paid a fee, but you do not benefit from his or her advice.

Too many individuals try to pick a financial adviser in the same way they would test drive a car. "I'll give it a quick spin, and if I don't like it, I'll just try another one." The problem with this approach is that you end up giving a succession of advisers a short period of time, say three months, to "show what they can do." In the process, you may never really get a plan in place or give it a chance to work. By default, you are actually pursuing a short-term approach to investing that can increase the fees you pay at the same time it reduces the chances of you achieving your financial goals.

Finally, in working with your financial adviser, I suggest the following steps:

1. *Review your plan annually.* Consider this an annual checkup for your financial well-being as important as seeing your doctor for your physical well-being. Things change. We have more children, inherit some money, get a promotion, win the lottery, or perhaps have a sudden health problem or change of jobs and careers. Whatever plan you are pursuing, it should reflect your current financial and personal situation as well as your long-term goals.
2. *Stick to your plan.* The biggest danger is to be knocked off your plan because of short-term moves in the financial markets and the

attendant emotions they trigger. No plan can work in every quarter, or in every year. But a well-thought-out strategy can work over the long term, and that is the most vital result you can obtain. Every time you are tempted to abandon your plan, take out this book, turn to page 226, and look at Figure 12-1, "Penalty for Missing the Market."

3. *When there is a correction in the market, review what is happening in the world.* If the historical forces that are producing the Great Prosperity are still at work, then one of the riskiest things you can do is sell your good investments out of fear or out of hope that you will be able to buy them back at a lower price. Corrections are almost sure to take place in the years ahead. But remember, short-term market reversals are called corrections for a reason: They bring forth corrective policies. As long as your assessment shows that we are on the road to 100,000 on the Dow, maintain your investments and stick to your strategy.

If, however, one of the risks to the Great Prosperity is unfolding, meet with your financial adviser to reassess your strategy. Review this checklist:

- Does the signpost for taxes point to higher, stable, or lower tax rates?
- Does the signpost for monetary policy point to continued price stability or to monetary instability in the form of deflation or inflation?
- Does the signpost regarding trade point to freer or more restricted international trade in the years ahead?
- Review the five historical forces. Are they still dominating the direction of policy? If so, is the negative development likely to be stopped, if not reversed?

If two or more of the signposts are pointing in a negative direction, the Great Prosperity could be at risk of coming to an end. At that point, it could be essential to design a new investment strategy that would be coherent with the revised outlook.

Let me conclude this chapter with one final admonition. *Avoid the temptation to talk to your adviser only in terms of money, or in terms of short-term performance.* After speaking with thousands of financial advisers, I am convinced that it is a mistake to think of our portfolios only in terms of their monetary value or their most recent performance.

I say this because I have yet to meet anyone who truly cares about money.

269

That might sound strange. But consider this: You can always tell what people care about by looking at the pictures on their walls, desks, or credenzas. I have not yet been in a financial adviser's office, or in an individual's home, where pictures of money hang on the walls.

Look at the pictures in your home or office. I am sure they depict what you care about—your spouse or children, your parents. I also see pictures of places people have been, including golf courses or vacation resorts, places that hold fond memories. Trophies and mementos that acknowledge the achievements in our lives also are prominent.

Don't misunderstand. Of course money is important. But it is important because it is essential to meeting the commitments that we have to those we care most deeply about. Money, after all, is just the means of entering into exchanges with other human beings to achieve our goals and ambitions.

When you are speaking to your adviser, talk about those ambitions and dreams, the commitments that are most important for you. And then, working with your adviser, use investments in stocks and bonds and cash and any other financial instrument in a manner that is consistent with realizing those goals and fulfilling those commitments. When you do that, you will be able to find a way to enrich your entire life. You will also have the opportunity to create a certain level of serenity that is absolutely essential to answering the question, "fact or fiction?" and that will allow you to execute an investment strategy through the ups as well as the downs that lie between today and 100,000 on the Dow.

NOTES

1. You can calculate the total market value by multiplying the number of shares outstanding by its current market price.

2. "SEI Investment Philosophy," SEI Investments, p. 3.

3. "Dalbar Special Report: Quantitative Analysis of Investor Behavior Study," Dalbar Inc., June 1996.

EPILOGUE

During the past five years, I have twice updated the presentation that is at the heart of this book. At the end of 1997, with the Dow approaching 8000, I began to ask: Are we headed to 15,000 on the Dow? Then, in the spring of 1998, when I sat down to write this book, I realized that we were at the beginning of a Great Prosperity and that a reasonable case could be made for reaching Dow 30,000 by the end of the next decade.

By the time I had finished writing this book, the Dow had already crossed the 11,000 mark, and my conviction that the Great Prosperity could last at least 20 years caused me to take a step back and ask an even bigger question than I had dared to ask before: Where could the Dow be in the year 2020, after 22 years of a Great Prosperity?

The answer surprised even me, to say nothing of my editor. For good reason. Dow 100,000 at first blush seems impossible, almost fanciful. But so did 10,000 on the Dow back in 1982, when the Great Inflation ended, and a new era of Disinflation began.

The pattern of events that have occurred since the end of 1994 are at the foundation of my increased conviction in the power of the historical forces that are operating to produce lower tax rates, stable prices, and freer trade. In just these five years, Federal budget deficits have given way to trillion-dollar surpluses—surpluses so vast that if you had predicted them, you and your forecast would have been disregarded out of hand.

Reductions in tax rates have not been as broad based as I had anticipated at the Federal level, but the growing number of states that are passing broad-based tax-rate reductions remains impressive.

Price stability has been restored, with the Consumer Price Index rising less than 2 percent for only the second time since the 1960s. The only other time was 1985, and that was caused by the sudden collapse of energy prices. The currency crisis of 1998 has discredited the notion that devaluations improve a country's competitiveness and has started the search for a global monetary system that can provide people all over the world what in the United States we have only recently achieved, a reliable currency and a stable price environment.

The United States has pulled back from the vision of a free-trade area that would encompass the entire Western Hemisphere. Yet, it has also negotiated a global free-trade pact in technology and telecommunications equipment. The use of the Internet as a commercial thoroughfare has soared, as have the prices of companies that are the leaders in providing E-commerce.

All the while, the risks to the outlook have faded. War is still a wild card. The United States and NATO have stumbled into a potential quagmire with a bombing campaign against Yugoslavia. At the time of this writing, NATO and Russian peacekeeping forces were entering Kosovo. Throughout the conflict, it was clear that no country sought a wider war in Europe.

On a more positive note, as we go to press, the Chinese have made significant concessions demonstrating their commitment to join the World Trade Organization. Successful completion of these negotiations would bring China's trade policies under the rule of international law. Moreover, it would all but eliminate one of the 5 key risks to Dow 100,000. At the same time, better-than-expected economic growth has improved the financial foundation of both the Social Security and Medicare programs.

This pattern of events has not gone unnoticed by the stock market, as it has raced ahead at a pace well above the 11.1 percent a year needed to reach Dow 100,000 by 2020. Yet, poor performance of small-company stocks and the relative underperformance of mid-sized companies suggest that there are no shortage of investment opportunities as we look toward the new millennium.

The pattern of events has also been noticed by other observers, some of whom are now projecting even higher goals for the Dow. One study argues that investments in the U.S. stock market today have little more risk than a government bond. Adjusting for this lower-risk premium leads them to argue that the stock market should sell at 100 times earnings.[1] At such a valuation, the Dow Industrials would be at 36,000 today and could reach 100,000 by 2010.

Another, by Yale finance professor Roger Ibbotson, projects the Dow will advance at an average rate of 11.6 percent a year and reach 120,000 by the year 2025. (Because he starts from a lower base year he projects the Dow will cross 100,000 in early 2024.)

Dow 100,000 as a Guide

However, never forget that the future is not known, that it cannot be predicted. In the years ahead, use this book as a guide and map of the Great Prosperity and the road to Dow 100,000. Continue to monitor the patterns of economic-policy developments and the advances in technology so that you can either confirm that the road ahead remains clear, that Dow 100,000 will become fact, or be among the first to understand if there has been a fundamental change in the outlook.

Use the Seligman Time Horizon Matrix[sm] and Seligman Harvester[sm] as starting points in the design of an investment strategy that makes sense to you, that is coherent not only with the future that lies ahead, but also with your own specific financial situation and ability to take on risk. Seek out good financial advice in completing the design and then implementing your strategy in the years ahead. Then, stick to your strategy. Buy and hold good mutual funds and, where appropiate, individual stocks and bonds.

Finally, I invite you to reach out beyond your financial concerns and to embrace the wonderful time in which we live. Just as this remarkable moment in history was not preordained, neither is the future predetermined. Rather, it rests in some measure, to some extent, in each of our hands.

There are a few individuals whom historians will record as the actors on the stage of today and who will be credited with creating the future that lies ahead. We already know some of their names: Bill Gates, chairman of Microsoft; Gordon Moore, founder of Intel Corporation; Steve Jobs and Stephan Wozniak, cofounders of Apple Computer; Sam Walton, founder of Wal-Mart; Presidents Ronald Reagan, George Bush, and Bill Clinton.

But, to think of the future only in those terms creates the risk that we will fail to see that each of us, through our own actions, also contributes to the shape of the future that lies ahead. For most of us, the reality we produce will extend no further than our families, our place of work, and our community. Yet, even here we can and do take great pride in leaving the world a little better for our children and grandchildren.

Our most important contributions to the future probably cannot be quantified, nor will they be measured. Much of our say in the shape of the future will be the result of a thousand different decisions we make and actions we take as individuals participating in a community of human beings. For example, the votes we cast in every local, state, and Federal election *do* determine the outcome, even though it is impossible to identify precisely which individual vote determined victory. Moreover, whether the candidate we favor wins or loses, our vote influences the direction of policy, and, hence, the shape of the future of our society. The politicians we support, the policies we advocate, or through our inaction, fail to oppose, can trump all of our other efforts to provide for our families and produce a better world for our children and ourselves.

We also shape the future by pursuing our dreams and ambitions in the world. The Great Prosperity will not be created by government or bureaucrats, though they play a crucial role in setting the economic policies that make a Great Prosperity possible. Governments cannot create prosperity by spending money that they collect from the general populace. In this act, government is merely an agent acting on behalf of the populace.

Prosperity is always produced by men and women who create new ways to transform the scarce resources of the globe into goods and services that increase our capacity to take care of our concerns and increase our possibilities however we define them as human beings. Medical researchers discover new drugs that fight disease and increase our ability to survive heart attacks or strokes. Technologists find new ways to combine their ingenuity with sand, in the form of silicon wafers and fiber-optic cables, to give us computers and cell phones and communications systems that are leveraging our imaginations into concrete products and services even as they increase geometrically our ability to enter into mutually beneficial exchanges with other people. The financial-services industry creates new mutual funds and other investment vehicles that increase our ability to take care of our financial concerns while transforming our investments into the capital businesses needed to expand the productive capacity and create the employment opportunities that are at the heart of rising living standards. Businesses find ways to harness technology to conserve precious capital while delivering superior goods and services to their customers at lower costs. Entrepreneurs produce innovations that obsolete the old and create a new world. And everywhere, competition elevates satisfying consumers over the greedy pursuit of self-interest as the goal of economic activity.

Finally, we shape the future by the manner in which we lead our lives. Our day-to-day actions at work are what show those who work for us what we deem important. It is in our everyday actions, in the institutions we support, and in the conversations we have around the dining-room table that we teach our children what we value in life. They will see how we take responsibility for our actions and our lives. Both our subordinates and our children will inherit the future we are creating, and will create a new future out of, in part, what we have taught them.

When we are immersed in a prosperity that we could not imagine, we are at risk of forgetting the source of our good fortune, the hard work and inventiveness of ourselves and our fellow human beings. Those who would use the coercive power of government instead of the discipline of private charity to take care of those less fortunate flirt with undermining that which has produced the Great Prosperity in the first place. And those who prosper and do not provide for private charity similarly risk forfeiting their future to the coercive forces of government. But these are the rightful struggles of a free people in a democratic and free society. It is thus our obligation as members of that society to participate fully in its political as well as its economic processes.

In all of this, I invite you to not only be an active participant in the manner in which you invest your money, but also to be an active participant in the creation of the future that lies ahead. Taking the future for granted, or forgetting that each of us through our actions and inactions are creating that future, is one of the biggest risks to any era of prosperity. As good as prosperity is, history shows that unless the foundation of that prosperity is understood, nurtured, and defended, seemingly well-intentioned actions inevitably bring the good times to an untimely end.

This book is not a prophecy of the future. Rather, it is a map of sorts that has the potential to help us chart the road that lies ahead. My first ambition in writing this book was to contribute to your financial success in positioning your portfolios, investments, businesses, and careers for the Great Prosperity by providing a strategic framework for analyzing and thinking about the future. In addition, it is my hope that you will use what you have learned from this book to inform your conversations, judgments, and debates regarding the direction of economic policy in the United States and elsewhere in the world. In that event, this book will have made its own, perhaps immeasurable, contribution to achieving the Great Prosperity and the milestone of reaching Dow 100,000 by the year 2020.

NOTES

1. James K. Glassman and Kevin A. Hassett, "Stock Prices Are Still Far Too Low," *The Wall Street Journal*, March 17, 1998, p. A26.

APPENDIX

Description of Asset Classes

The hypothetical examples were created based upon the unmanaged indices' historical returns with the weights appropriate to each Horizon Model Portfolio. Where indices representing the various asset classes were not available, estimates were made as follows: **US Small-Company Stocks:** 1979–1998: Russell 2000 Index; 1950–1978; NYSE Fifth Quintile Returns, **US Medium-Company Stocks:** 1979–1998: Russell Midcap Index; 1950–1978; Estimated as the midpoint between the total return for the Ibbotson Small Stock Index and the Standard & Poor's 500 Composite Stock Price Index, **US Large-Company Stocks:** Standard & Poor's 500 Composite Stock Index (S&P 500), **International Small-Company Stocks:** 1990–1998: Salomon Smith Barney EMI World X-US; 1986–1989: NatWest Securities Ltd. (NWSL) global ex. U.S. Smaller Companies Index; 1970–1985: Estimated as the difference between the MSCI EAFE Index and the S&P 500, added to the Ibbotson Small Stock Index; 1950–1969: Estimated as the Ibbotson Small Stock Index, **Emerging Markets:** 1989–1998: IFC Investables Composite; 1985–1988: IFC Global Emerging Composite; 1970–1984: Estimated as the difference between the MSCI EAFE Index and the S&P 500, added to the Ibbotson Small Stock Index; 1950–1969: Estimated as the Ibbotson Small Stock Index, **International Large-Company Stocks:** 1970–1998: Morgan Stanley Capital International (MSCI) Europe Australasia and Far East (EAFE) Index; 1950–1969: Estimated as the Standard & Poor's 500 Composite Stock Price Index, **US Corporate Bonds:** Salomon Brothers Long-Term High Grade Corporate Bond Index, **US Government Bonds:** 1950–1998: Ibbotson "One Bond" Portfolio. To the greatest extent possible, each year, a one-bond portfolio with a term of approximately 20 years and a reasonably current coupon, and whose returns did not reflect potential tax benefits, impaired negotiability, or special redemption or call privileges, was used, **Inflation:** 1978–1998: Consumer Price Index for All Urban Consumers; 1950–1977: Consumer Price Index.

277

Appendix

The Seligman Solution for Seligman Time Horizon Matrix^{sm}

Fund/Horizon	30	29	28	27	26	25	24	23	22	21	20	19	18	17
Seligman Frontier Fund	3.0%	3.0%	3.0%	3.0%	3.0%	3.0%	3.0%	3.0%	3.0%	3.0%	3.0%	3.0%	3.0%	3.0%
Seligman Small-Cap Value Fund	13.0%	12.9%	12.8%	12.7%	12.6%	12.5%	12.4%	12.3%	12.2%	12.1%	12.0%	11.4%	10.8%	10.2%
Seligman Communications and Information Fund	16.0%	15.4%	14.8%	14.2%	13.6%	13.0%	12.4%	11.8%	11.2%	10.6%	10.0%	10.0%	10.0%	10.0%
Seligman Capital Fund	22.0%	21.8%	21.6%	21.4%	21.2%	21.0%	20.8%	20.6%	20.4%	20.2%	20.0%	20.0%	20.0%	20.0%
Seligman Growth Fund	3.0%	3.6%	4.2%	4.8%	5.4%	6.0%	6.6%	7.2%	7.8%	8.4%	9.0%	9.0%	9.0%	9.0%
Seligman Large-Cap Value Fund	3.0%	3.6%	4.2%	4.8%	5.4%	6.0%	6.6%	7.2%	7.8%	8.4%	9.0%	9.0%	9.0%	9.0%
Seligman Common Stock Fund	0.0%	0.0%	0.0%	0.0%	0.0%	0.0%	0.0%	0.0%	0.0%	0.0%	0.0%	0.0%	0.0%	0.0%
Seligman Henderson Emerging Markets Growth Fund	10.0%	10.0%	10.0%	10.0%	10.0%	10.0%	10.0%	10.0%	10.0%	10.0%	10.0%	9.5%	9.0%	8.5%
Seligman Henderson Global Smaller Companies Fund	25.0%	24.2%	23.4%	22.6%	21.8%	21.0%	20.2%	19.4%	18.6%	17.8%	17.0%	16.1%	15.2%	14.3%
Seligman Henderson Global Growth Opportunities Fund	0.0%	0.0%	0.0%	0.0%	0.0%	0.0%	0.0%	0.0%	0.0%	0.0%	0.0%	0.0%	0.0%	0.0%
Seligman Henderson International Fund	5.0%	5.5%	6.0%	6.5%	7.0%	7.5%	8.0%	8.5%	9.0%	9.5%	10.0%	9.5%	9.0%	8.5%
Seligman High-Yield Bond Fund	0.0%	0.0%	0.0%	0.0%	0.0%	0.0%	0.0%	0.0%	0.0%	0.0%	0.0%	1.5%	3.0%	4.5%
Seligman U.S. Government Securities Fund	0.0%	0.0%	0.0%	0.0%	0.0%	0.0%	0.0%	0.0%	0.0%	0.0%	0.0%	0.5%	1.0%	1.5%
Total	100.0%	100.0%	100.0%	100.0%	100.0%	100.0%	100.0%	100.0%	100.0%	100.0%	100.0%	100.0%	100.0%	100.0%

	16	15	14	13	12	11	10	9	8	7	6	5	4	3	2	1	Harvester
Seligman Frontier Fund	3.0%	3.0%	3.0%	3.0%	3.0%	3.0%	3.0%	2.7%	2.4%	2.1%	1.8%	1.5%	1.2%	0.9%	0.6%	0.3%	0.0%
Seligman Small-Cap Value Fund	9.6%	9.0%	8.4%	7.8%	7.2%	6.6%	6.0%	5.4%	4.8%	4.2%	3.6%	3.0%	2.4%	1.8%	1.2%	0.6%	0.0%
Seligman Communications and Information Fund	10.0%	10.0%	10.0%	10.0%	10.0%	10.0%	10.0%	9.0%	8.0%	7.0%	6.0%	5.0%	4.0%	3.0%	2.0%	1.0%	0.0%
Seligman Capital Fund	20.0%	20.0%	20.0%	20.0%	20.0%	20.0%	20.0%	19.0%	18.0%	17.0%	16.0%	15.0%	14.0%	13.0%	12.0%	11.0%	10.0%
Seligman Growth Fund	9.0%	9.0%	9.0%	9.0%	9.0%	9.0%	9.0%	9.0%	9.0%	9.0%	9.0%	9.0%	9.0%	9.0%	9.0%	9.0%	9.0%
Seligman Large-Cap Value Fund	9.0%	9.0%	9.0%	9.0%	9.0%	9.0%	9.0%	9.0%	9.0%	9.0%	9.0%	9.0%	9.0%	9.0%	9.0%	9.0%	9.0%
Seligman Common Stock Fund	0.0%	0.0%	0.0%	0.0%	0.0%	0.0%	0.0%	1.5%	3.0%	4.5%	6.0%	7.5%	9.0%	10.5%	12.0%	13.5%	15.0%
Seligman Henderson Emerging Markets Growth Fund	8.0%	7.5%	7.0%	6.5%	6.0%	5.5%	5.0%	4.5%	4.0%	3.5%	3.0%	2.5%	2.0%	1.5%	1.0%	0.5%	0.0%
Seligman Henderson Global Smaller Companies Fund	13.4%	12.5%	11.6%	10.7%	9.8%	8.9%	8.0%	7.2%	6.4%	5.6%	4.8%	4.0%	3.2%	2.4%	1.6%	0.8%	0.0%
Seligman Henderson Global Growth Opportunities Fund	0.0%	0.0%	0.0%	0.0%	0.0%	0.0%	0.0%	0.5%	1.0%	1.5%	2.0%	2.5%	3.0%	3.5%	4.0%	4.5%	5.0%
Seligman Henderson International Fund	10.0%	10.0%	10.0%	10.0%	10.0%	10.0%	10.0%	10.2%	10.4%	10.6%	10.8%	11.0%	11.2%	11.4%	11.6%	11.8%	12.0%
Seligman High-Yield Bond Fund	6.0%	7.5%	9.0%	10.5%	12.0%	13.5%	15.0%	16.5%	18.0%	19.5%	21.0%	22.5%	24.0%	25.5%	27.0%	28.5%	30.0%
Seligman U.S. Government Securities Fund	2.0%	2.5%	3.0%	3.5%	4.0%	4.5%	5.0%	5.5%	6.0%	6.5%	7.0%	7.5%	8.0%	8.5%	9.0%	9.5%	10.0%
Total	100.0%	100.0%	100.0%	100.0%	100.0%	100.0%	100.0%	100.0%	100.0%	100.0%	100.0%	100.0%	100.0%	100.0%	100.0%	100.0%	100.0%

BIBLIOGRAPHY

Adams, Charles. *For Good and Evil, The Impact of Taxes on the Course of Civilization.* London, New York, Lanham: Madison Books, 1993.

Adams, James Ring. *Secrets of the Tax Revolt.* San Diego, New York and London: Harcourt Brace Jovanovich, Publishers, 1984.

Bartley, Robert L. *The Seven Fat Years: And How to Do It Again.* New York: The Free Press, 1992.

Bell, Jeffry. *Populism and Elitism.* Washington, DC: Regency Gateway, 1992.

Bethell, Tom. *The Noblest Triumph, Property and Prosperity Through the Ages.* New York: St. Martin's Press, 1998.

Blaug, Mark. *Economic Theory in Retrospect, Fourth Edition.* Cambridge: Cambridge University Press, 1985.

Braudel, Fernand. *The Structures of Everyday Life, Civilization & Capitalism, 15th–18th Century, Volume I.* Translation from the French revised by Sian Reynolds. New York: Harper & Row, 1981.

————. *The Wheels of Commerce, Civilization & Capitalism, 15th–18th Century, Volume 2.* Translation from the French by Sian Reynolds. New York: Harper & Row, 1982.

————. *The Perspective of the World, Civilization & Capitalism, 15th–18th Century, Volume 3.* Translation from the French by Sian Reynolds. New York: Harper & Row, 1984.

Canto, Victor A., Charles W. Kadlec and Arthur B. Laffer, editors. *The Financial Analyst's Guide to Fiscal Policy.* New York: Praeger, 1986.

—————, editors. *The Financial Analyst's Guide to Monetary Policy*. New York: Praeger, 1986.

Chandler, Alfred D. Jr. *The Visible Hand, The Managerial Revolution in American Business*. Cambridge and London: The Belknap Press of Harvard University Press, 1977.

The Constitution of the United States.

Cox, W. Michael and Richard Alm. *Myths of Rich & Poor*. New York: Basic Books, 1999.

Davis, Bob and David Wessel. *Prosperity: The Coming 20-Year Boom and What It Means to You*. New York: Random House, 1999.

Dent, Harry S., Jr. *The Great Boom Ahead*. New York: Hyperion, 1993.

—————. *The Roaring 2000s: Building the Wealth and Lifestyle You Desire in the Greatest Boom in History*. New York: Simon & Schuster, 1998.

Durant, Will. *Caesar and Christ, The Story of Civilization III*. New York: Simon & Schuster, 1944.

Economic Report of the President. Transmitted to Congress, February 1998, together with the Annual Report of the Council of Economic Advisers. Washington, DC: U.S. Government Printing Office.

—————. Transmitted to Congress, February 1999, together with the Annual Report of the Council of Economic Advisers. Washington, DC: U.S. Government Printing Office.

Emerging Stock Markets Factbook 1997. Washington, DC: International Finance Corporation, 1996.

Friedman, Milton and Rose. *Free to Choose, A Personal Statement*. San Diego: A Harvest Book, Harcourt Brace & Company, 1980.

Friedman, Milton and Anna Jacobson Schwartz. *A Monetary History of the United States, 1867-1960*. Princeton, NJ: Princeton University Press, 1963.

Fukuyama, Francis. *The End of History and The Last Man*. New York: The Free Press, 1992.

Gilder, George. *Microcosm, The Quantum Revolution in Economics and Technology*. New York: Simon & Schuster, 1989.

—————. *The Spirit of Enterprise*. New York: Simon & Schuster, 1984.

—————. *Wealth and Poverty*. New York: Basic Books, Inc., 1981.

Hall, Robert E. and Alvin Rabushka. *The Flat Tax, Second Edition*. Stanford, CA: Hoover Institution Press, 1995.

Hayek, F. A. *The Road to Serfdom*. Chicago: The University of Chicago Press, 1944.

—————. *The Fatal Conceit, The Errors of Socialism*. Chicago: The University of Chicago Press, 1988.

Homer, Sidney. *A History of Interest Rates: Second Edition*. New Brunswick, NJ: Rutgers University Press, 1977.

Irwin, Douglas A. *Against the Tide: An Intellectual History of Free Trade*. Princeton, NJ: Princeton University Press, 1996.

Johnson, Bryan T., Kim R. Holmes and Melanie Kirkpatrick. *1998 Index of Economic Freedom.* Washington, DC: Heritage Foundation, 1998.

——. *1999 Index of Economic Freedom.* Washington, DC: Heritage Foundation, 1999.

Kudlow, Lawrence A. *American Abundance: The New Economic and Moral Prosperity.* New York: Forbes, 1997.

Laffer, Arthur B. and Marc A. Miles. *International Economics in an Integrated World.* Glenview, IL: Scott, Foresman and Company, 1982.

Lane, Rose Wilder. *The Discovery of Freedom, Man's Struggle Against Authority.* San Franciso: Fox & Wilkes, 1943.

Manchester, William. *A World Lit Only by Fire, The Medieval Mind and the Renaissance.* Boston: Little, Brown And Company, 1992.

Maturana, Humberto R. and Francisco J. Varela. *The Tree of Knowledge: The Biological Roots of Human Understanding.* Boston and London: New Science Library-Shambhala, 1987.

Matusow, Allen J. *Nixon's Economy: Booms, Busts, Dollars, & Votes.* Lawrence: University Press of Kansas, 1998.

Meiselman, David I. and Arthur B. Laffer, editors. *The Phenomenon of Worldwide Inflation.* Washington DC: American Enterprise Institute for Public Policy Research, 1975.

Moynihan, Michael. *The Coming American Renaissance: How to Benefit From America's Economic Resurgence.* New York: Simon & Schuster, 1996.

Nixon, Richard. *The Memoirs of Richard Nixon.* New York: Grossett & Dunlap, 1978.

Novak, Michael. *Business as a Calling, Work and the Examined Life.* New York: The Free Press, 1996.

Ohmae, Kenichi. *The Borderless World: Power and Strategy in the Interlinked Economy.* New York: Harper Business, 1990.

Ohno, Taiichi. *Toyota Production System: Beyond Large-Scale Production.* Cambridge, Massachusetts: English translation Productivity Press, 1988.

Pechman, Joseph A. *Federal Tax Policy: Fifth Edition.* Washington DC: Studies of Government Finance—The Brookings Institution, 1987.

Rothchild, John. *The Bear Book: Survive and Profit in Ferocious Markets.* New York: John Wiley & Sons, Inc., 1998.

Schilling, A. Gary. *Deflation: Why It's Coming, Whether It's Good or Bad, and How It Will Affect Your Investments, Business, and Personal Affairs.* Short Hills, NJ: Lakeview Publishing Company, 1998.

Shelton, Judy. *Money Meltdown.* New York: The Free Press, 1994.

Siegel, Jeremy J. *Stocks for the Long Run: A Guide to Selecting Markets for Long-Term Growth.* Burr Ridge, IL: Irwin Professional Publishing, 1994.

Smith, Adam. *The Wealth of Nations, The Cannan Edition.* New York: The Modern Library, 1937.

Sowell, Thomas. *Conquest and Cultures: An International History.* New York: Basic Books, 1998.

Spicer, Michael. *The Challenge From the East & The Rebirth of the West.* New York: St. Martin's Press, 1996.

Sterling, William and Stephen Waite. *Boomernomics: The Future of Your Money in the Upcoming Generational Warfare.* New York: Ballantine Publishing Group, 1998.

Stocks, Bonds, Bills & Inflation 1999 Yearbook. Chicago, Illinois: Ibbotson Associates, 1999.

Wanniski, Jude. *The Way the World Works.* New York: Simon & Schuster, 1978.

Winograd, Terry and Fernando Flores. *Understanding Computers and Cognition, A New Foundation for Design.* Norwood, NJ: Ablex Publishing Corporation, 1986.

Wood, Christopher. *The Bubble Economy: Japan's Extraordinary Speculative Boom of the '80s and the Dramatic Bust of the '90s.* New York: The Atlantic Monthly Press, 1992.

Womack, James P., Daniel T. Jones and Daniel Roos. *The Machine That Changed The World: Based on The Massachusetts Institute of Technology 5-Million-Dollar 5-Year Study on the Future of The Automobile.* New York: Macmillan Publishing, 1990.

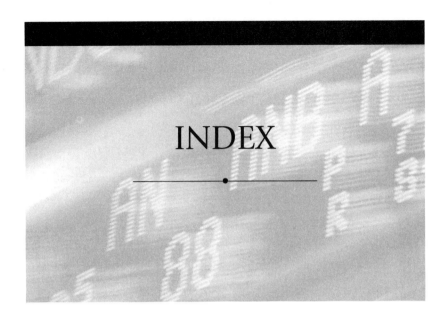

INDEX

285